CERTAIN DIFFICULTIES

FELT BY ANGLICANS

IN CATHOLIC TEACHING

CONSIDERED:

*In a Letter addressed to the Rev. E. B. Pusey, D.D.,
on occasion of his Eirenicon of 1864;*

*And in a Letter addressed to the Duke of Norfolk, on
occasion of Mr. Gladstone's Expostulation of 1874.*

BY

JOHN HENRY CARDINAL NEWMAN

NEW EDITION.

VOL. II.

LONGMANS, GREEN, AND CO.

LONDON, NEW YORK, AND BOMBAY

1896

A LETTER ADDRESSED TO THE REV. E. B. PUSEY, D.D.,

ON OCCASION OF HIS EIRENICON.

CONTENTS.

A LETTER,

&c.

------- ❋ -------

NO one who desires the union of Christendom after
its many and long-standing divisions, can have
any other feeling than joy, my dear Pusey, at finding
from your recent Volume, that you see your way to
make definite proposals to us for effecting that great
object, and are able to lay down the basis and conditions on which you could co-operate in advancing it.
It is not necessary that we should concur in the details
of your scheme, or in the principles which it involves,
in order to welcome the important fact, that, with your
personal knowledge of the Anglican body, and your
experience of its composition and tendencies, you consider the time to be come when you and your friends
may, without imprudence, turn your minds to the contemplation of such an enterprise. Even were you an
individual member of that Church, a watchman upon a
high tower in a metropolis of religious opinion, we
should naturally listen with interest to what you had to
report of the state of the sky and the progress of the

B

night, what stars were mounting up or what clouds gathering,—what were the prospects of the three great parties which Anglicanism contains within it, and what was just now the action upon them respectively of the politics and science of the time. You do not go into these matters; but the step you have taken is evidently the measure and the issue of the view which you have formed of them all.

However, you are not a mere individual: from early youth you have devoted yourself to the Established Church, and, after between forty and fifty years of unremitting labour in its service, your roots and your branches stretch out through every portion of its large territory. You, more than any one else alive, have been the present and untiring agent by whom a great work has been effected in it: and, far more than is usual, you have received in your lifetime, as well as merited, the confidence of your brethren. You cannot speak merely for yourself; your antecedents, your existing influence, are a pledge to us, that what you may determine will be the determination of a multitude. Numbers, too, for whom you cannot properly be said to speak, will be moved by your authority or your arguments; and, numbers, again, who are of a school more recent than your own, and who are only not your followers because they have outstripped you in their free speeches and demonstrative acts in our behalf, will, for the occasion, accept you as their spokesman. There is no one anywhere,—among ourselves, in your own body, or, I suppose, in the Greek Church,—who can affect so large a circle of men, so virtuous, so able,

so learned, so zealous, as come, more or less, under
your influence; and I cannot pay them a greater compliment than to tell them they ought all to be Catholics,
nor do them a more affectionate service than to pray
that they may one day become such. Nor can I address
myself to an act more pleasing, as I trust, to the Divine
Lord of the Church, or more loyal and dutiful to His
Vicar on earth, than to attempt, however feebly, to
promote so great a consummation.

I know the joy it would give those conscientious men,
of whom I am speaking, to be one with ourselves. I
know how their hearts spring up with a spontaneous
transport at the very thought of union; and what
yearning is theirs after that great privilege, which they
have not, communion with the see of Peter, and its
present, past, and future. I conjecture it by what I
used to feel myself, while yet in the Anglican Church.
I recollect well what an outcast I seemed to myself,
when I took down from the shelves of my library the
volumes of St. Athanasius or St. Basil. and set myself
to study them; and how, on the contrary, when at
length I was brought into Catholic communion, I
kissed them with delight, with a feeling that in them I
had more than all that I had lost; and, as though I were
directly addressing the glorious saints, who bequeathed
them to the Church, how I said to the inanimate pages,
" You are now mine, and I am now yours, beyond any
mistake." Such, I conceive, would be the joy of the
persons I speak of, if they could wake up one morning,
and find themselves rightfully possessed of Catholic
traditions and hopes, without violence to their own

sense of duty; and, certainly, I am the last man to say that such violence is in any case lawful, that the claims of conscience are not paramount, or that any one may overleap what he deliberately holds to be God's command, in order to make his path easier for him or his heart lighter.

I am the last man to quarrel with them for this jealous deference to the voice of their conscience, whatever be the judgment that others may form of them in consequence, for this reason, because their present circumstances have once, as you know, been my own. You recollect well what hard things were said against us twenty-five years ago, which we knew in our hearts we did not deserve. Accordingly, I am now in the position of the fugitive Queen in the well-known passage; who, "non ignara mali" herself, had learned to sympathize with those who were the inheritors of her past wanderings. There were Priests, good men, whose zeal outstripped their know-ledge, and who in consequence spoke confidently, when it would have been wiser in them to have suspended their adverse judgment of those whom, in no long time, they had to welcome as brethren in communion. We at that time were in worse plight than your friends are now, for our opponents put their very hardest thoughts of us into print. One of them wrote thus in a Letter addressed to one of the Catholic Bishops :—

"That this Oxford crisis is a real progress to Catholicism, I have all along considered a perfect delusion. . I look upon Mr. Newman, Dr. Pusey, and their associates, as wily and crafty, though unskilful guides. The embrace of Mr. Newman is the kiss that would betray us. . But,—what is the most striking feature in the rancorous malignity of these men,—their calumnies are often lavished upon us, when we should be led to think that the subject-matter of their treatises closed every avenue against their vituperation. The three last volumes [of the Tracts] have opened my eyes to the craftiness and the cunning, as well as the malice, of the members of the Oxford Convention. . If the Puseyites are to be the new Apostles of Great Britain, my hopes for my country are lowering and gloomy. . I would never have consented to enter the lists against this strange confraternity . . if I did not feel that my own Prelate was opposed to the guile and treachery of these men. . I impeach Dr. Pusey and his friends of a deadly hatred of our religion. . What, my lord, would the Holy See think of the works of these Puseyites? . . ."

Another priest, himself a convert, wrote:—

" As we approach towards Catholicity, our love and respect increases, and our violence dies away; but the bulk of these men become more rabid as they become like Rome,—a plain proof of their designs. . I do not believe that they are any nearer the portals of the Catholic Church than the most prejudiced Methodist and Evangelical preacher. . Such, Rev. Sir, is an outline of my views on the Oxford movement."

I do not say that such a view of us was unnatural; and, for myself, I readily confess, that I had at one time used about the Church such language, that I had no claim on Catholics for any mercy. But, after all, and in fact, they were wrong in their anticipations,—nor did their brother Catholics agree with them at the time. Especially Dr. Wiseman (Co-adjutor Bishop as he was then) took a larger and more generous view of us, nor did the Holy See interfere against us, though the writer of one of these passages invoked its judgment. The event showed that the more cautious line of conduct was the more prudent ; and one of the Bishops, who had taken part against us, with a supererogation of charity, sent me on his deathbed an expression of his sorrow for having in past years mistrusted me. A faulty conscience, faithfully obeyed, through God's mercy, had in the long-run brought me right.

Fully, then, do I recognize the rights of conscience in this matter. I find no fault with your stating, as clearly and completely as you can, the difficulties which stand in the way of your joining us. I cannot wonder that you begin with stipulating conditions of union, though I do not concur in them myself, and think that in the event you yourself would be content to let them drop. Such representations as yours are necessary to open the subject in debate; they ascertain how the land lies, and serve to clear the ground. Thus I begin :—but after allowing as much as this, I am obliged in honesty to add what I fear, my dear Pusey, will pain you. Yet I am confident, my very dear friend, that at least you will not be angry with me if I say, what I must say if I say anything at all, viz., that there is much, both in the matter and in the manner of your Volume, calculated to wound those who love you well, but love truth more. So it is; with the best motives and kindest intentions,—" Cædimur, et totidem plagis con-

sumimus hostem." We give you a sharp cut, and you
return it. You complain of our being "dry, hard and
unsympathizing;" and we answer that you are unfair
and irritating. But we at least have not professed to
be composing an Irenicon, when we were treating you
as foes. There was one of old time who wreathed his
sword in myrtle; excuse me—you discharge your olive-
branch as if from a catapult.

Do not think I am not serious; if I spoke as seriously as I feel, I should seem to speak harshly. Who
will venture to assert, that the hundred pages which you
have devoted to the subject of the Blessed Virgin give
other than a one-sided view of our teaching about her,
little suited to win us? This may be a salutary casti-
gation of us, if any of us have fairly provoked it; but
it is not making the best of matters; it is not smooth-
ing the way for an understanding or a compromise.
Your representation of what we hold, leads a writer in
the most moderate and liberal Anglican newspaper of
the day, the *Guardian*, to turn away from us, shocked
and dismayed. "It is language," says your reviewer,
" which, after having often heard it, we still can only
hear with horror. We had rather not quote any of it,
or of the comments upon it." What could an Exeter Hall
orator, what could a Scotch commentator on the Apocalypse, do more for his own side of the controversy in the
picture he drew of us? You may be sure that charges
which create horror on one side, will be repelled by indignation on the other; and these are not the most
favourable dispositions of mind for a peace conference.
I had been accustomed to suppose, that you, who in

times past were ever less declamatory in controversy
than myself, now that years had gone on, and circumstances changed, had come to look on our old warfare
against Rome as cruel and inexpedient.   Indeed, I
know that it was a chief objection urged only last year
against the scheme then in agitation of introducing the
Oratory into Oxford, that such an undertaking on my
part would be a signal for the rekindling of that fierce
style of polemics which is now long out of date.   I had
fancied you shared in that opinion; but now, as if to
show how imperative you deem the renewal of that old
violence, you actually bring to life one of my own strong
sayings in 1841, which had long been in the grave,
that " the Roman Church comes as near to idolatry as
can be supposed in a Church, of which it is said, ' The
idols He shall utterly abolish.' "—P. 111.

§ 2.—*Remarks on various statements introduced into the Eirenicon.*

I KNOW, indeed, and feel deeply, that your frequent references, in your Volume, to what I have lately or formerly written, are caused by your strong desire to be still one with me as far as you can, and by that true af- fection, which takes pleasure in dwelling on such sayings of mine as you can still accept with the full approbation of your judgment. I trust I am not ungrateful or irre- sponsive to you in this respect; but other considerations have an imperative claim to be taken into account. Pleasant as it is to agree with you, I am bound to explain myself in cases in which I have changed my mind, or have given a wrong impression of my meaning, or have been wrongly reported; and, while I trust that I have higher than mere personal motives for addressing you in print, yet it will serve to introduce my main subject, and give me an opportunity for remarks which bear upon it indirectly, if I dwell for a page or two on such matters contained in your Volume as concern myself.

1. The mistake which I have principally in view is the belief which is widely spread, that I have publicly spoken of the Anglican Church as "the great *bulwark* against infidelity in this land." In a pamphlet of yours a year old, you spoke of "a very earnest body of Roman Catholics," who "rejoice in all the workings

of God the Holy Ghost in the Church of England (whatever they think of her), and are saddened by what weakens her who is, in God's hands, the great *bulwark* against infidelity in this land." The concluding words you were thought to quote from my *Apologia.* In consequence, Dr. Manning, now our Archbishop, replied to you, asserting, as you say, "the contradictory of that statement." In that counter-assertion, he was at the time generally considered (rightly or wrongly as it may be), though writing to you, to be really glancing at my *Apologia,* and correcting it, without introducing my name, where he thought it needed correction. Further, in the Volume, which you have now published, you recur to the phrase; and you speak of its author in terms which, did I not know your partial kindness for me, would hinder me from identifying him with myself. You say, " The saying was not mine, but that of one of the deepest thinkers and observers in the Roman Communion," p. 7. A friend has suggested to me that perhaps you mean De Maistre; and, from an anonymous letter which I have received from Dublin, I find it is certain that the very words in question were once used by Archbishop Murray; however, you speak of the author of them as if now alive. At length, a reviewer of your Volume in the " Weekly Register," distinctly attributes them to me by name, and gives me the first opportunity I have had of disowning them; and this I now do. What, at some time or other, I may have said in conversation or in private letter, of course I cannot tell; but I have never, I am sure, used the word "bulwark" of the

Anglican Church deliberately, or speaking of it in its religious aspect, nor, as I think, at all.[1] What I said in my *Apologia* was this :—that that Church was " a serviceable *breakwater* against errors more fundamental than its own." A bulwark is an integral part of the thing it defends; whereas the word "breakwater" implies such a protection of the Catholic truth, as is, in its nature, accidental and *de facto,*—and again, such a protection as does not utterly exclude error, but detracts from its volume and force. "Serviceable," too, implies a something external to the thing served. Again, in saying that the Anglican Church is a defence against " errors more fundamental than its own." I imply that it has errors, and those fundamental.

2. There is another passage of your book, at p. 337, which it may be right to observe upon. You have made a collection of passages from the Fathers, as witnesses in behalf of your doctrine that the whole Christian faith is contained in Scripture, as if, in your sense of the words, Catholics contradicted you here. And you refer to my Notes on St. Athanasius as contributing passages to your list ; but, after all, neither do you, nor do I in my Notes, affirm any doctrine which Rome denies. Those Notes also make frequent reference to a traditional teaching, which (be the faith ever so certainly contained in Scripture), still is necessary as a Regula Fidei, for showing us that it is contained there ; vid. pp. 283. 341 [2] ; and this tradition,

[1] In the former of these volumes, p. 1, speaking of " Institutions " (i.e. " the Church and Universities of the nation "), I call them " the only *political* bulwarks " remaining of the " dogmatic principle."

[2] Oxford Edition.

I know, you uphold as fully as I do in the Notes in question. In consequence, you allow that there is a two-fold rule, Scripture and Tradition; and this is all that Catholics say. How, then, do Anglicans differ from Rome here? I believe the difference is merely one of words; and I shall be doing, so far, the work of an Irenicon, if I make clear what this verbal difference is. Catholics and Anglicans (I do not say Protestants), attach different meanings to the word "proof," in the controversy as to whether the whole faith is, or is not, contained in Scripture. We mean that not every article of faith is so contained there, that it may thence be logically proved, *independently* of the teaching and authority of the Tradition ; but Anglicans mean that every article of faith is so contained there, that it may thence be proved, *provided* there be added the illustrations and compensations supplied by the Tradition. And it is in this latter sense that the Fathers also speak in the passages which you quote from them. I am sure at least that St. Athanasius frequently adduces passages in proof of points in controversy, which no one would see to be proofs, unless Apostolical Tradition were taken into account, first as suggesting, then as authoritatively ruling their meaning. Thus *you* do not say, that the whole revelation is in Scripture in such sense that pure unaided logic can draw it from the sacred text; nor do *we* say, that it is not in Scripture, in an improper sense, in the sense that the *Tradition* of the Church is able to recognize and determine it there. You do not profess to dispense with Tradition ; nor do we forbid the idea of probable, secondary, symbolical, connotative, senses of Scripture, over and above those which properly belong to the wording and context. I hope you will agree with me in this.

3. Nor is it only in isolated passages that you give me a place in your Volume. A considerable portion of it is written with a reference to two publications of mine, one of which you name and defend, the other you implicitly protest against; Tract 90, and the Essay on Doctrinal Development. As to Tract 90, you have from the first, as all the world knows, boldly stood up for it, in spite of the obloquy which it brought upon you, and have done me a great service. You are now republishing it with my cordial concurrence; but I take this opportunity of noticing, lest there should be any mistake on the part of the public, that you do so with a different object from that which I had when I wrote it. Its original purpose was simply that of justifying myself and others in subscribing to the Thirty-nine Articles, while professing many tenets which had popularly been considered distinctive of the Roman faith. I considered that my interpretation of the Articles, as I gave it in that Tract, would stand, provided the parties imposing them allowed it; otherwise, I thought it could not stand; and, when in the event the Bishops and public opinion did not allow it, I gave up my Living, as having no right to retain it. My feeling about the interpretation is expressed in a passage in "Loss and Gain," which runs thus :—

" 'Is it,' asked Reding, 'a received view?' 'No view is received,' said the other; 'the Articles them-

selves are received, but there is no authoritative interpretation of them at all.' 'Well,' said Reding, 'is it a
tolerated view?' 'It certainly has been strongly
opposed,' answered Bateman; 'but it has never been
condemned.' 'That is no answer,' said Charles.
'Does any one Bishop hold it? Did any one Bishop ever
hold it? Has it ever been *formally* admitted as tenable
by any one Bishop? Is it a view got up to meet existing
difficulties, or has it an historical existence?' Bateman
could give only one answer to these questions, as they
were successively put to him. 'I thought so,' said
Charles; 'the view is specious certainly. I don't see
why it might not have answered, had it been tolerably
sanctioned; but you have no sanction to show me. As
it stands, it is a mere theory struck out by individuals.
Our Church *might* have adopted this mode of interpreting the Articles; but, from what you tell me, it
certainly has not done so.'"—Ch. 15.

However, the Tract did not carry its object and conditions on its face, and necessarily lay open to interpretations very far from the true one. Dr. Wiseman (as
he then was), in particular, with the keen apprehension
which was his characteristic, at once saw in it a basis of
accommodation between Anglicanism and Rome. He
suggested broadly that the decrees of the Council of
Trent should be made the rule of interpretation for the
Thirty-nine Articles, a proceeding, of which Sancta
Clara, I think, had set the example; and as you have
observed, published a letter to Lord Shrewsbury on the
subject, of which the following are extracts:—

"We Catholics must necessarily deplore [England's]

separation as a deep moral evil,—as a state of schism, of which nothing can justify the continuance. Many members of the Anglican Church view it in the same light as to the first point—its sad evil, though they excuse their individual position in it as an unavoidable misfortune. . . . We may depend upon a willing, an able, and most zealous co-operation with any effort which we may take, towards bringing her into her rightful position, into Catholic unity with the Holy See and the Churches of its obedience,—in other words, with the Church Catholic. Is this a visionary idea? Is it merely the expression of a strong desire? I know that many will so judge it; and, perhaps, were I to consult my own quiet, I would not venture to express it. But I will, in simplicity of heart, cling to hopefulness, cheered, as I feel it, by so many promising appearances . . . .

"A natural question here presents itself;—what facilities appear in the present state of things for bringing about so happy a consummation, as the reunion of England to the Catholic Church, beyond what have before existed, and particularly under Archbishops Laud or Wake. It strikes me, many. First, &c. . A still more promising circumstance I think your Lordship will with me consider the *plan* which the eventful Tract No. 90 has pursued, and in which Mr. Ward, Mr. Oakeley, and even Dr. Pusey have agreed. I allude to the method of *bringing their doctrines into accordance with ours by explanation.* A foreign priest has pointed out to us a valuable document for our consideration, — 'Bossuet's Reply to the Pope,'—when consulted on the

best method of reconciling the followers of the Augsburg
Confession with the Holy See. The learned Bishop
observes, that Providence had allowed so much Catholic
truth to be preserved in that Confession, that full advantage should be taken of the circumstance; that no re-
tractations should be demanded, but an explanation of
the Confession in accordance with Catholic doctrines.
Now, for such a method as this, the way is in part prepared by the demonstration that such interpretation
may be given of the most difficult Articles, as will strip
them of all contradiction to the decrees of the Tridentine
Synod. The same method may be pursued on other
points; and much pain may thus be spared to individuals,
and much difficulty to the Church."—Pp. 11, 35, 38.

This use of my Tract, so different from my own, but
sanctioned by the great name of our Cardinal, you are
now reviving; and I gather from your doing so, that your
Bishops and the opinion of the public are likely now, or
in prospect, to admit what twenty-five years ago they
refused. On this point, much as it rejoices me to know
your anticipation, of course I cannot have an opinion.

4. So much for Tract 90. On the other hand, as to
my hypothesis of Doctrinal Development, I am sorry
to find you do not look upon it with friendly eyes;
though how, without its aid, you can maintain the doctrines of the Holy Trinity and Incarnation, and others
which you hold, I cannot understand. You consider my
principle may be the means, in time to come, of introducing into our Creed, as portions of the necessary
Catholic faith, the Infallibility of the Pope, and various
opinions, pious or profane, as it may be, about our

Blessed Lady. I hope to remove your anxiety as to the character of these consequences, before I bring my observations to an end ;[3] at present I notice it as my apology for interfering in a controversy which at first sight is no business of mine.

5. I have another reason for writing; and that is, unless it is rude in me to say so, because you seem to think writing does not become me, as being a convert. I do not like silently to acquiesce in such a judgment. You say at p. 98 :—

" Nothing can be more unpractical than for an individual to throw himself into the Roman Church, because he could accept the *letter* of the Council of Trent. Those who were born Roman Catholics, have a liberty, which, in the nature of things, a person could not have, who left another system, to embrace that of Rome. I cannot imagine how any faith could stand the shock of leaving one system, criticizing *it*, and cast himself into another system, criticizing *it*. For myself, I have always felt that had (which God of His mercy avert hereafter also) the English Church, by accepting heresy, driven me out of it, I could have gone in no other way than that of closing my eyes, and accepting whatever was put before me. But a liberty which individuals could not use, and explanations, which so long as they remain individual, must be unauthoritative, might be formally made by the Church of Rome to the Church of England as the basis of re-union."

---

[3] Father Ryder of the Oratory removed the necessity of my fulfilling this intention as far as Infallibility is concerned, by his able pamphlets in answer to Mr. Ward.

And again, p. 210 :—

"It seems to me to be a psychological impossibility for one who has already exchanged one system for another to make those distinctions.   One who, by his own act, places himself under authority, cannot make conditions about his submission.   But definite explanations of our Articles have, before now, been at least tentatively offered to us on the Roman and Greek side, as sufficient to restore communion ; and the Roman explanations too were, in most cases, mere supplements to our Articles, on points upon which **our** Church had not spoken."

Now passages such as these seem almost a challenge to me to speak ; and to keep silence would be to assent to the justice of them.   At the cost, then, of speaking about myself, of which I feel there has been too much of late, I observe upon them as follows :—Of course, as you say, a convert comes to learn, and not to pick and choose.   He comes in simplicity and confidence, and it does not occur to him to weigh and measure every proceeding, every practice which he meets with among those whom he has joined.   He comes to Catholicism as to a living system, with a living teaching, and not to a mere collection of decrees and canons, which by themselves are of course but the framework, not the body and substance of the Church.   And this is a truth which concerns, which binds, those also who never knew any other religion, not only the convert. By the Catholic system, I mean that rule of life, and those practices of devotion, for which we shall look in vain in the Creed of Pope Pius.   The convert comes, not only to believe the Church, but also to trust and obey her priests, and to conform himself in charity to her people. It would never do for him to resolve that he never would say a Hail Mary, never avail himself of an indulgence, never kiss a crucifix, never accept the Lent dispensations, never mention a venial sin in confession. All this would not only be unreal, but would be dangerous, too, as arguing a wrong state of mind, which could not look to receive the divine blessing. Moreover, he comes to the ceremonial, and the moral theology, and the ecclesiastical regulations, which he finds on the spot where his lot is cast. And again, as regards matters of politics, of education, of general expedience, of taste, he does not criticize or controvert. And thus surrendering himself to the influences of his new religion, and not risking the loss of revealed truth altogether by attempting by a private rule to discriminate every moment its substance from its accidents, he is gradually so indoctrinated in Catholicism, as at length to have a right to speak as well as to hear. Also in course of time a new generation rises round him; and there is no reason why he should not know as much, and decide questions with as true an instinct, as those who perhaps number fewer years of life than he numbers Easter communions. He has mastered the fact and the nature of the differences of theologian from theologian, school from school, nation from nation, era from era. He knows that there is much of what may be called fashion in opinions and practices, according to the circumstances of time and place, according to current politics, the character of the Pope of the day, or the chief Prelates of a particular country;—and that fashions change. His experience tells him, that sometimes what is denounced in one place as a great offence, or preached up as a first principle, has in another nation been immemorially regarded in just a contrary sense, or has made no sensation at all, one way or the other, when brought before public opinion; and that loud talkers are apt to carry all before them in the Church, as elsewhere, while quiet and conscientious persons commonly have to give way. He perceives that, in matters which happen to be in debate, ecclesiastical authority watches the state of opinion and the direction and course of controversy, and decides accordingly; so that in certain cases to keep back his own judgment on a point, is to be disloyal to his superiors.

So far generally; now in particular as to myself. After twenty years of Catholic life, I feel no delicacy in giving my opinion on any point when there is a call for me,—and the only reason why I have not done so sooner or more often than I have, is that there has been no call. I have now reluctantly come to the conclusion that your Volume *is* a call. Certainly, in many instances in which theologian differs from theologian and country from country, I have a definite judgment of my own; I can say so without offence to any one, for the very reason that from the nature of the case it is impossible to agree with all of them. I prefer English habits of belief and devotion to foreign, from the same causes, and by the same right, which justifies foreigners in preferring their own. In following those of my people, I show less singularity, and create less disturbance than if I made a flourish with what is novel and exotic. And in this line of conduct I am but availing myself of the teaching which I fell in with on becoming a Catholic; and it is a pleasure to me to think that what I hold now, and would transmit after me if I could, is only what I received then. The utmost delicacy was observed on all hands in giving me advice: only one warning remains on my mind, and it came from Dr. Griffiths, the late Vicar-Apostolic of the London district. He warned me against books of devotion of the Italian school, which were just at that time coming into England; and when I asked him what books he recommended as safe guides, he bade me get the works of Bishop Hay. By this I did not understand that he was jealous of all Italian books, or made himself responsible for all that Dr. Hay happens to have said; but I took him to caution me against a character and tone of religion, excellent in its place, not suited for England.

When I went to Rome, though it may seem strange to you to say it, even there I learned nothing inconsistent with this judgment. Local influences do not form the atmosphere of its institutions and colleges, which are Catholic in teaching as well as in name. I recollect one saying among others of my Confessor, a Jesuit Father, one of the holiest, most prudent men I ever knew. He said that we could not love the Blessed Virgin too much, if we loved our Lord a great deal more. When I returned to England, the first expression of theological opinion which came in my way, was *apropos* of the series of translated Saints' Lives which the late Dr. Faber originated. That expression proceeded from a wise prelate, who was properly anxious as to the line which might be taken by the Oxford converts, then for the first time coming into work. According as I recollect his opinion, he was apprehensive of the effect of Italian compositions, as unsuited to this country, and suggested that the Lives should be original works, drawn up by ourselves and our friends from Italian sources. If at that time I was betrayed into any acts which were of a more extreme character than I should approve now, the responsibility of course is my own ; but the impulse came, not from old Catholics or superiors, but from men whom I loved and trusted, who were younger than myself. But to whatever extent I might be carried away, and I cannot recollect any tangible instances, my mind in no long time fell back to what seems to me a safer and more practical course.

Though I am a convert, then, I think I have a right to speak out ; and that the more because other converts have spoken for a long time, while I have not spoken ; and with still more reason may I speak without offence in the case of your present criticisms of us, considering that, in the charges you bring, the only two English writers you quote in evidence, are both of them converts, younger in age than myself. I put aside the Archbishop of course, because of his office. These two authors are worthy of all consideration, at once from their character and from their ability. In their respective lines they are perhaps without equals at this particular time ; and they deserve the influence they possess. One is still in the vigour of his powers ; the other has departed amid the tears of hundreds. It is pleasant to praise them for their real excellences; but why do you rest on them as authorities? You say of the one that he was "a popular writer;" but is there not sufficient reason for this in the fact of his remarkable gifts, of his poetical fancy, his engaging frankness, his playful wit, his affectionateness, his sensitive piety, without supposing that the wide diffusion of his works is caused by a general sympathy with his particular sentiments about the Blessed Virgin? And as to our other friend, do not his energy, acuteness, and theological reading, displayed on the vantage ground of the historic "Dublin Review," fully account for the sensation he has produced, without supposing that any great number of our body go his lengths in their view of the Pope's infallibility? Our silence as regards their writings is very intelligible: it is not agreeable to protest, in the sight of the world, against the writings of men in our own Communion whom we love and respect. But the plain fact is this,— they came to the Church, and have thereby saved their souls; but they are in no sense spokesmen for English Catholics, and they must not stand in the place of those who have a real title to such an office. The chief authors of the passing generation, some of them still alive, others gone to their reward, are Cardinal Wiseman, Dr. Ullathorne, Dr. Lingard, Mr. Tierney, Dr. Oliver, Dr. Rock, Dr. Waterworth, Dr. Husenbeth, and Mr. Flanagan; which of these ecclesiastics has said anything extreme about the prerogatives of the Blessed Virgin or the infallibility of the Pope?

I cannot, then, without remonstrance, allow you to

identify the doctrine of our Oxford friends in question,
on the two subjects I have mentioned, with the present
spirit or the prospective creed of Catholics; or to assume,
as you do, that, because they are thorough-going and
relentless in their statements, therefore they are the
harbingers of a new age, when to show a deference to
Antiquity will be thought little else than a mistake. For
myself, hopeless as you consider it, I am not ashamed
still to take my stand upon the Fathers, and do not
mean to budge. The history of their times is not yet
an old almanac to me. Of course I maintain the value
and authority of the " Schola," as one of the *loci theologici;* nevertheless I sympathize with Petavius in preferring to the " contentious and subtle theology" of the
middle age, that " more elegant and fruitful teaching
which is moulded after the image of erudite Antiquity."
The Fathers made me a Catholic, and I am not going
to kick down the ladder by which I ascended into the
Church. It is a ladder quite as serviceable for that
purpose now, as it was twenty years ago. Though I
hold, as you know, a process of development in Apostolic truth as time goes on, such development does not
supersede the Fathers, but explains and completes
them. And, in particular, as regards our teaching
concerning the Blessed Virgin, with the Fathers I am
content;—and to the subject of that teaching I mean
to address myself at once. I do so, because you say, as
I myself have said in former years, that " That vast
system as to the Blessed Virgin . . to all of us has
been the special *crux* of the Roman system."—P. 101.
Here, let me say, as on other points, the Fathers are

enough for me. I do not wish to say more than they suggest to me, and will not say less. You, I know, will profess the same; and thus we can join issue on a clear and broad principle, and may hope to come to some intelligible result. We are to have a Treatise on the subject of our Lady soon from the pen of the Most Reverend Prelate; but that cannot interfere with such a mere argument from the Fathers as that to which I shall confine myself here. Nor indeed, as regards that argument itself, do I profess to be offering you any new matter, any facts which have not been used by others,—by great divines, as Petavius,—by living writers, nay, by myself on other occasions. I write afresh nevertheless, and that for three reasons; first, because I wish to contribute to the accurate statement and the full exposition of the argument in question; next, because I may gain a more patient hearing than has sometimes been granted to better men than myself; lastly, because there just now seems a call on me, under my circumstances, to avow plainly what I do and what I do not hold about the Blessed Virgin, that others may know, did they come to stand where I stand, what they would, and what they would not, be bound to hold concerning her.

§ 3.—*The Belief of Catholics concerning the blessed Virgin,
as distinct from their Devotion to her.*

I begin by making a distinction which will go far to
remove good part of the difficulty of my undertaking,
as it presents itself to ordinary inquirers,—the distinction between faith and devotion. I fully grant that *devotion* towards the blessed Virgin has increased among
Catholics with the progress of centuries; I do not allow
that the *doctrine* concerning her has undergone a growth,
for I believe that it has been in substance one and the
same from the beginning.

By "faith" I mean the Creed and assent to the
Creed; by "devotion" I mean such religious honours
as belong to the objects of our faith, and the payment
of those honours. Faith and devotion are as distinct in
fact, as they are in idea. We cannot, indeed, be devout
without faith, but we may believe without feeling devotion. Of this phenomenon every one has experience
both in himself and in others; and we bear witness to it
as often as we speak of realizing a truth or not realizing
it. It may be illustrated, with more or less exactness,
by matters which come before us in the world. For
instance, a great author, or public man, may be acknowledged as such for a course of years; yet there may be
an increase, an ebb and flow, and a fashion, in his popu-

larity. And if he takes a lasting place in the minds of his countrymen, he may gradually grow into it, or suddenly be raised to it. The idea of Shakespeare as a great poet, has existed from a very early date in public opinion; and there were at least individuals then who understood him as well, and honoured him as much, as the English people can honour him now; yet, I think, there is a national devotion to him in this day such as never has been before. This has happened, because, as education spreads in the country, there are more men able to enter into his poetical genius, and, among these, more capacity again for deeply and critically understanding him; and yet, from the first, he has exerted a great insensible influence over the nation, as is seen in the circumstance that his phrases and sentences, more than can be numbered, have become almost proverbs among us. And so again in philosophy, and in the arts and sciences, great truths and principles have sometimes been known and acknowledged for a course of years; but, whether from feebleness of intellectual power in the recipients, or external circumstances of an accidental kind, they have not been turned to account. Thus the Chinese are said to have known of the properties of the magnet from time immemorial, and to have used it for land expeditions, yet not on the sea. Again, the ancients knew of the principle that water finds its own level, but seem to have made little application of their knowledge. And Aristotle was familiar with the principle of induction; yet it was left for Bacon to develope it into an experimental philosophy. Illustrations such as these, though not altogether apposite, serve to convey that distinction be-

tween faith and devotion on which I am insisting. It
is like the distinction between objective and subjective
truth. The sun in the spring-time will have to shine
many days before he is able to melt the frost, open the
soil, and bring out the leaves; yet he shines out from
the first notwithstanding, though he makes his power
felt but gradually. It is one and the same sun, though
his influence day by day becomes greater; and so in the
Catholic Church it is the one Virgin Mother, one and
the same from first to last, and Catholics may have ever
acknowledged her; and yet, in spite of that acknow-
ledgment, their devotion to her may be scanty in one
time and place, and overflowing in another.

This distinction is forcibly brought home to a convert,
as a peculiarity of the Catholic religion, on his first introduction to its worship. The faith is everywhere one
and the same, but a large liberty is accorded to private
judgment and inclination as regards matters of devotion.
Any large church, with its collections and groups of
people, will illustrate this. The fabric itself is dedicated
to Almighty God, and that, under the invocation of the
Blessed Virgin, or some particular Saint; or again, of
some mystery belonging to the Divine Name or the Incarnation, or of some mystery associated with the Blessed
Virgin. Perhaps there are seven altars or more in it,
and these again have their several Saints. Then there
is the Feast proper to this or that day; and during the
celebration of Mass, of all the worshippers who crowd
around the Priest, each has his own particular devotions,
with which he follows the rite. No one interferes with
his neighbour; agreeing, as it were, to differ, they pur-

sue independently a common end, and by paths, distinct but converging, present themselves before God. Then there are confraternities attached to the church,—of the Sacred Heart, or of the Precious Blood ; associations of prayer for a good death, or for the repose of departed souls, or for the conversion of the heathen ; devotions connected with the brown, blue, or red scapular ; not to speak of the great ordinary Ritual observed through the four seasons, or of the constant Presence of the Blessed Sacrament, or of its ever-recurring rite of Benediction, and its extraordinary forty hours' Exposition. Or, again, look through such manuals of prayers as the *Raccolta,* and you at once will see both the number and the variety of devotions, which are open to individual Catholics to choose from, according to their religious taste and prospect of personal edification.

Now these diversified modes of honouring God did not come to us in a day, or only from the Apostles ; they are the accumulations of centuries ; and, as in the course of years some of them spring up, so others decline and die. Some are local, in memory of some particular Saint, who happens to be the Evangelist, or Patron, or pride of the nation, or who lies entombed in the church or in the city where it is found ; and these devotions, necessarily, cannot have an earlier date than the Saint's day of death or interment there. The first of these sacred observances, long before such national memories, were the devotions paid to the Apostles, then those which were paid to the Martyrs ; yet there were Saints nearer to our Lord than either Martyrs or Apostles ; but, as if these sacred persons were immersed and lost in the effulgence

of His glory, and because they did not manifest themselves, when in the body, in external works separate
from Him, it happened that for a long while they were
less dwelt upon. However, in process of time, the
Apostles, and then the Martyrs, exerted less influence
than before over the popular mind, and the local Saints,
new creations of God's power, took their place, or again,
the Saints of some religious order here or there established. Then, as comparatively quiet times succeeded,
the religious meditations of holy men and their secret
intercourse with heaven gradually exerted an influence
out of doors, and permeated the Christian populace, by
the instrumentality of preaching and by the ceremonial
of the Church. Hence at length those luminous stars
rose in the ecclesiastical heavens, which were of more
august dignity than any which had preceded them, and
were late in rising, for the very reason that they were so
specially glorious. Those names, I say, which at first
sight might have been expected to enter soon into the
devotions of the faithful, with better reason might have
been looked for at a later date, and actually were late in
their coming. St. Joseph furnishes the most striking
instance of this remark ; here is the clearest of instances
of the distinction between doctrine and devotion. Who,
from his prerogatives and the testimony on which they
come to us, had a greater claim to receive an early recognition among the faithful than he ? A Saint of
Scripture, the foster-father of our Lord, he was an
object of the universal and absolute faith of the
Christian world from the first, yet the devotion to him
is comparatively of late date. When once it began,

men seemed surprised that it had not been thought of before ; and now, they hold him next to the Blessed Virgin in their religious affection and veneration.

As regards the Blessed Virgin then, I shall postpone the question of devotion for a while, and inquire first into the doctrine of the undivided Church (to use your controversial phrase), on the subject of her prerogatives.

1.

What is the great rudimental teaching of Antiquity from its earliest date concerning her ? By "rudimental teaching," I mean the *primâ facie* view of her person and office, the broad outline laid down of her, the aspect under which she comes to us, in the writings of the Fathers. She is the Second Eve.[4] Now let us consider what this implies. Eve had a definite, essential position in the First Covenant. The fate of the human race lay with Adam ; he it was who represented us. It was in Adam that we fell ; though Eve had fallen, still, if Adam had stood, we should not have lost those supernatural privileges which were bestowed upon him as our first father. Yet though Eve was not the head of the race, still, even as regards the race, she had a place of her own ; for Adam, to whom was divinely committed the naming of all things, named her "the Mother of all the living," a name surely expressive, not of a fact only, but of a dignity ; but further, as she thus had her own general relation to the human race, so again had she her own special

[4] Vide Essay on Development of Doctrine, 1845, p. 384, &c.

place, as regards its trial and its fall in Adam. In those primeval events, Eve had an integral share. "The woman, being seduced, was in the transgression." She listened to the Evil Angel; she offered the fruit to her husband, and he ate of it. She co-operated, not as an irresponsible instrument, but intimately and personally in the sin : she brought it about. As the history stands, she was a *sine-qua-non*, a positive, active, cause of it. And she had her share in its punishment; in the sentence pronounced on her, she was recognized as a real agent in the temptation and its issue, and she suffered accordingly. In that awful transaction there were three parties concerned,—the serpent, the woman, and the man; and at the time of their sentence, an event was announced for a distant future, in which the three same parties were to meet again, the serpent, the woman, and the man; but it was to be a second Adam and a second Eve, and the new Eve was to be the mother of the new Adam. "I will put enmity between thee and the woman, and between thy seed and her seed." The Seed of the woman is the Word Incarnate, and the Woman, whose seed or son He is, is His mother Mary. This interpretation, and the parallelism it involves, seem to me undeniable; but at all events (and this is my point) the parallelism is the doctrine of the Fathers, from the earliest times; and, this being established, we are able, by the position and office of Eve in our fall, to determine the position and office of Mary in our restoration.

I shall adduce passages from their writings, noting their respective countries and dates; and the dates shall extend from their births or conversions to their deaths, since what they propound is at once the doctrine which they had received from the generation before them, and the doctrine which was accepted and recognized as true by the generation to whom they transmitted it.

First, then, St. Justin Martyr (A.D. 120—165), St. Irenæus (120—200), and Tertullian (160—240). Of these Tertullian represents Africa and Rome; St. Justin represents Palestine; and St. Irenæus Asia Minor and Gaul;—or rather he represents St. John the Evangelist, for he had been taught by the Martyr St. Polycarp, who was the intimate associate of St. John, as also of other Apostles.

1. St. Justin:[5]—

"We know that He, before all creatures, proceeded from the Father by His power and will, . . . and by means of the Virgin became man, that by what way the disobedience arising from the serpent had its beginning, by that way also it might have an undoing. For Eve, being a Virgin and undefiled, conceiving the word that was from the serpent, brought forth disobedience and death; but the Virgin Mary, taking faith and joy, when the Angel told her the good tidings, that the Spirit of the Lord should come upon her and the power of the Highest overshadow her, and therefore the Holy One that was born of her was Son of God, answered, 'Be it to me according to thy word.'"
—*Tryph.* 100.

[5] I have attempted to translate literally without caring to write English. The original passages are in Note I. infr.

D

2. Tertullian :—

"God recovered His image and likeness, which the
devil had seized, by a rival operation. For into Eve, as
yet a virgin, had crept the word which was the framer
of death. Equally into a virgin was to be introduced
the Word of God which was the builder-up of life; that,
what by that sex had gone into perdition by the same
sex might be brought back to salvation. Eve had
believed the serpent; Mary believed Gabriel; the fault
which the one committed by believing, the other by
believing has blotted out."—*De Carn. Christ.* 17.

3. St. Irenæus :—

"With a fitness, Mary the Virgin is found obedient,
saying, 'Behold Thy handmaid, O Lord; be it to me
according to Thy word.' But Eve was disobedient; for
she obeyed not, while she was yet a virgin. As she,
having indeed Adam for a husband, but as yet being
a virgin . . . becoming disobedient, became the cause
of death both to herself and to the whole human race, so
also Mary, having the predestined man, and being yet a
Virgin, being obedient, became both to herself and to
the whole human race the cause of salvation . . . And
on account of this the Lord said, that the first should be
last and the last first. And the Prophet signifies the
same, saying, 'Instead of fathers you have children.'
For, whereas the Lord, when born, was the first-begotten
of the dead, and received into His bosom the primitive
fathers, He regenerated them into the life of God, He
Himself becoming the beginning of the living, since
Adam became the beginning of the dying. Therefore
also Luke, commencing the line of generations from

the Lord, referred it back to Adam, signifying that He regenerated the old fathers, not they Him, into the Gospel of life. And so the knot of Eve's disobedience received its unloosing through the obedience of Mary; for what Eve, a virgin, bound by incredulity, that Mary, a virgin, unloosed by faith."—*Adv. Hær.* iii. 22. 34.

And again,—

"As Eve by the speech of an Angel was seduced, so as to flee God, transgressing His word, so also Mary received the good tidings by means of the Angel's speech, so as to bear God within her, being obedient to His word. And, though the one had disobeyed God, yet the other was drawn to obey God; that of the virgin Eve the Virgin Mary might become the advocate. And, as by a virgin the human race had been bound to death, by a virgin it is saved,[6] the balance being preserved, a virgin's disobedience by a Virgin's obedience."—*Ibid.* v. 19.

Now, what is especially noticeable in these three writers, is, that they do not speak of the Blessed Virgin merely as the physical instrument of our Lord's taking flesh, but as an intelligent, responsible cause of it; her faith and obedience being accessories to the Incarnation, and gaining it as her reward. As Eve failed in these virtues, and thereby brought on the fall of the race in Adam, so Mary by means of the same had a part in its

[6] Salvatur; some MSS. read Solvatur, "[that] it might be loosed;" and so Augustine contr. Jul. i. n. 5. This variety of reading does not affect the general sense of the passage. Moreover, the word "salvation" occurs in the former of these two passages.

restoration.   You surely imply, pp. 151—156, that the
Blessed Virgin was only a physical instrument of our
redemption ; " what has been said of her by the Fathers
as the chosen *vessel* of the Incarnation, was applied *personally* to her," (that is, by Catholics,) p. 151, and again
" the Fathers speak of the Blessed Virgin as the *instrument* of our salvation, *in that* she gave birth to the
Redeemer," pp. 155, 156; whereas St. Augustine, in
well-known passages, speaks of her as more exalted by
her sanctity than by her relationship to our Lord.[7]   However, not to go beyond the doctrine of the Three Fathers,
they unanimously declare that she was *not* a mere instrument in the Incarnation, such as David, or Judah, may
be considered; they declare she co-operated in our salvation not merely by the descent of the Holy Ghost upon
her body, but by specific holy acts, the effect of the Holy
Ghost within her soul ; that, as Eve forfeited privileges
by sin, so Mary earned privileges by the fruits of grace;
that, as Eve was disobedient and unbelieving, so Mary
was obedient and believing ; that, as Eve was a cause of
ruin to all, Mary was a cause of salvation to all ; that
as Eve made room for Adam's fall, so Mary made room
for our Lord's reparation of it ; and thus, whereas the
free gift was not as the offence, but much greater, it
follows that, as Eve co-operated in effecting a great evil,
Mary co-operated in effecting a much greater good.

And, besides the run of the argument, which reminds
the reader of St. Paul's antithetical sentences in tracing
the analogy between Adam's work and our Lord's work,

[7] Opp. t. 3, p. 2, col. 369, t. 6, col. 342.

it is well to observe the particular words under which the Blessed Virgin's office is described. Tertullian says that Mary "blotted out" Eve's fault, and "brought back the female sex," or "the human race, to salvation;" and St. Irenæus says that "by obedience she wa sthe cause or occasion" (whatever was the original Greek word) "of salvation to herself and the whole human race;" that by her the human race is saved; that by her Eve's complication is disentangled; and that she is Eve's Advocate, or friend in need. It is supposed by critics, Protestant as well as Catholic, that the Greek word for Advocate in the original was Paraclete; it should be borne in mind, then, when we are accused of giving our Lady the titles and offices of her Son, that St. Irenæus bestows on her the special Name and Office proper to the Holy Ghost.

So much as to the nature of this triple testimony; now as to the worth of it. For a moment put aside St. Irenæus, and put together St. Justin in the East with Tertullian in the West. I think I may assume that the doctrine of these two Fathers about the Blessed Virgin, was the received doctrine of their own respective times and places; for writers after all are but witnesses of facts and beliefs, and as such they are treated by all parties in controversial discussion. Moreover, the coincidence of doctrine which they exhibit, and again, the antithetical completeness of it, show that they themselves did not originate it. The next question is, Who did? for from one definite organ or source, place or person, it must have come. Then we must inquire, what length of time would it take for such a doctrine to have

extended, and to be received, in the second century over
so wide an area; that is, to be received before the year
200 in Palestine, Africa, and Rome. Can we refer the
common source of these local traditions to a date much
later than that of the Apostles, since St. John died
within twenty years of St. Justin's conversion and sixty
of Tertullian's birth? Make what allowance you will
for whatever possible exceptions can be taken to this
representation; and then, after doing so, add to the
concordant testimony of these two Fathers the evidence
of St. Irenæus, which is so close upon that of the School
of St. John himself in Asia Minor. "A three-fold
cord," as the wise man says, "is not quickly broken."
Only suppose there were so early and so broad a testimony, to the effect that our Lord was a mere man, the
son of Joseph; should we be able to insist upon the
faith of the Holy Trinity as necessary to salvation? Or
supposing three such witnesses could be brought to
the fact that a consistory of elders governed the local
churches, or that each local congregation was an independent Church, or that the Christian community was
without priests, could Anglicans maintain their doctrine that the rule of Episcopal succession is necessary
to constitute a Church? And then recollect that the
Anglican Church especially appeals to the ante-Nicene
centuries, and taunts us with having superseded their
testimony.

Having then adduced these Three Fathers of the
second century, I have at least got so far as this: viz.,
that no one, who acknowledges the force of early testimony in determining Christian truth, can wonder, no

one can complain, can object, that we Catholics should hold a very high doctrine concerning the Blessed Virgin, unless indeed stronger statements can be brought for a contrary conception of her, either of as early, or at least of a later date. But, as far as I know, no statements can be brought from the ante-Nicene literature, to invalidate the testimony of the Three Fathers concerning her; and little can be brought against it from the fourth century, while in that fourth century the current of testimony in her behalf is as strong as in the second; and, as to the fifth, it is far stronger than in any former time, both in its fulness and its authority. That such is the concordant verdict of "the undivided Church" will to some extent be seen as I proceed.

4. St. Cyril of Jerusalem (315—386) speaks for Palestine :—

"Since through Eve, a Virgin, came death, it behoved, that through a Virgin, or rather from a Virgin, should life appear; that, as the Serpent had deceived the one, so to the other Gabriel might bring good things."—*Cat.* xii. 15.

5. St. Ephrem Syrus (he died 378) is a witness for the Syrians proper and the neighbouring Orientals, in contrast to the Græco-Syrians. A native of Nisibis on the farther side of the Euphrates, he knew no language but Syriac.

"Through Eve, the beautiful and desirable glory of men was extinguished; but it has revived through Mary."—*Opp. Syr.* ii. p. 318.

Again :—

"In the beginning, by the sin of our first parents,

death passed upon all men; to-day, through Mary we
are translated from death unto life.   In the beginning,
the serpent filled the ears of Eve, and the poison spread
thence over the whole body; to-day, Mary from her
ears received the champion of eternal happiness : what,
therefore, was an instrument of death, was an instrument of life also."—iii. p. 607.

I have already referred to St. Paul's contrast between
Adam and our Lord in his Epistle to the Romans, as
also in his first Epistle to the Corinthians.   Some
writers venture to say that there is no doctrinal truth,
but a mere rhetorical display, in those passages.   It is
quite as easy to say so, as to attempt so to dispose of
this received comparison, in the writings of the Fathers,
between Eve and Mary.

6. St. Epiphanius (320—400) speaks for Egypt,
Palestine, and Cyprus :—

"She it is, who is signified by Eve, enigmatically
receiving the appellation of the Mother of the living.
. . . . It was a wonder, that after the transgression she
had this great epithet.   And, according to what is
material, from that Eve all the race of men on earth
is generated.   But thus in truth from Mary the Life
itself was born in the world, that Mary might bear
living things, and become the Mother of living things.
Therefore, enigmatically, Mary is called the Mother of
living things. . . . . Also, there is another thing to
consider as to these women, and wonderful,—as to Eve
and Mary.   Eve became a cause of death to man . .
and Mary a cause of life ; . that life might be instead of
death, life excluding death which came from the woman,

viz., He who through the woman has become our life."
—*Hær.* 78. 18.

7. By the time of St. Jerome (331—420), the contrast between Eve and Mary had almost passed into a proverb. He says (*Ep.* xxii. 21, *ad Eustoch.*), "Death by Eve, life by Mary." Nor let it be supposed that he, any more than the preceding Fathers, considered the Blessed Virgin a mere physical instrument of giving birth to our Lord, who is the Life. So far from it, in the Epistle from which I have quoted, he is only adding another virtue to that crown which gained for Mary her divine Maternity. They have spoken of faith, joy, and obedience; St. Jerome adds, what they had only suggested, virginity. After the manner of the Fathers in his own day, he is setting forth the Blessed Mary to the high-born Roman Lady, whom he is addressing, as the model of the virginal life; and his argument in its behalf is, that it is higher than the marriage-state, not in itself, viewed in any mere natural respect, but as being the free act of self-consecration to God, and from the personal religious purpose which it involves.

"Higher wage," he says, "is due to that which is not a compulsion, but an offering; for, were virginity commanded, marriage would seem to be put out of the question; and it would be most cruel to force men against nature, and to extort from them an angel's life."—20.

I do not know whose testimony is more important than St. Jerome's, the friend of Pope Damasus at Rome, the pupil of St. Gregory Nazianzen at Constantinople, and of Didymus in Alexandria, a native of Dalmatia,

yet an inhabitant, at different times of his life, of Gaul,
Syria, and Palestine.

8. St. Jerome speaks for the whole world, except
Africa; and for Africa in the fourth century, if we must
limit so world-wide an authority to place, witnesses
St. Augustine (354—430). He repeats the words as
if a proverb, "By a woman death, by a woman life"
(*Opp. t.* v. *Serm.* 232); elsewhere he enlarges on the idea
conveyed in it. In one place he quotes St. Irenæus's
words, as cited above (*adv. Julian* i. n. 5.). In another
he speaks as follows:—

"It is a great sacrament that, whereas through
woman death became our portion, so life was born to us
by woman; that, in the case of both sexes, male and
female, the baffled devil should be tormented, when on
the overthrow of both sexes he was rejoicing; whose
punishment had been small, if both sexes had been
liberated in us, without our being liberated through
both."—*Opp. t.* vi. *De Agon. Christ.* c. 24.

9. St. Peter Chrysologus (400—450), Bishop of
Ravenna, and one of the chief authorities in the 4th
General Council:—

"Blessed art thou among women; for among women,
on whose womb Eve, who was cursed, brought punishment, Mary, being blest, rejoices, is honoured, and is
looked up to. And woman now is truly made through
grace the Mother of the living, who had been by nature
the mother of the dying. . . . Heaven feels awe of God,
Angels tremble at Him, the creature sustains Him
not, nature sufficeth not; and yet one maiden so takes,
receives, entertains Him, as a guest within her breast,

that, for the very hire of her home, and as the price of her womb, she asks, she obtains peace for the earth, glory for the heavens, salvation for the lost, life for the dead, a heavenly parentage for the earthly, the union of God Himself with human flesh."—*Serm.* 140.

It is difficult to express more explicitly, though in oratorical language, that the Blessed Virgin had a real meritorious co-operation, a share which had a "hire" and a "price," in the reversal of the fall.

10. St. Fulgentius, Bishop of Ruspe in Africa (468—533). The Homily which contains the following passage, is placed by Ceillier (t. xvi. p. 127), among his genuine works :—

" In the wife of the first man, the wickedness of the devil depraved her seduced mind; in the mother of the Second Man, the grace of God preserved both her mind inviolate and her flesh. On her mind it conferred the most firm faith; from her flesh it took away lust altogether. Since then man was in a miserable way condemned for sin, therefore without sin was in a marvellous way born the God-man."—*Serm.* 2, p. 124. *De Dupl. Nativ.*

Accordingly, in the Sermon which follows (if it is his), he continues thus, illustrating her office of universal Mother, as ascribed to her by St. Epiphanius :—

" Come ye virgins to a Virgin, come ye who conceive to her who conceived, ye who bear to one who bore, mothers to a mother, ye that suckle to one who suckled, young girls to the young girl. It is for this reason that the Virgin Mary has taken on her in our Lord Jesus Christ all these divisions of nature, that to all women who have recourse to her, she may be a succour, and so restore the whole race of women who come to her, being the new Eve, by keeping virginity, as the new Adam the Lord Jesus Christ, recovers the whole race of men."

Such is the rudimental view, as I have called it, which the Fathers have given us of Mary, as the Second Eve, the Mother of the living: I have cited ten authors. I could cite more, were it necessary: except the two last, they write gravely and without any rhetoric. I allow that the two last write in a different style, since the extracts I have made are from their sermons; but I do not see that the colouring conceals the outline. And after all, men use oratory on great subjects, not on small;—nor would they, and other Fathers whom I might quote, have lavished their high language upon the Blessed Virgin, such as they gave to no one else, unless they knew well that no one else had such claims, as she had, on their love and veneration.

And now, I proceed to dwell for a while upon two inferences, which it is obvious to draw from the rudimental doctrine itself; the first relates to the sanctity of the Blessed Virgin, the second to her dignity.

1. Her sanctity. She holds, as the Fathers teach us, that office in our restoration which Eve held in our fall:—now, in the first place, what were Eve's endowments to enable her to enter upon her trial? She could not have stood against the wiles of the devil, though she was innocent and sinless, without the grant of a large grace. And this she had;—a heavenly gift, which was over and above and additional to that nature of hers, which she received from Adam, a gift

which had been given to Adam also before her, at the very time (as it is commonly held) of his original formation. This is Anglican doctrine, as well as Catholic; it is the doctrine of Bishop Bull. He has written a dissertation on the point. He speaks of the doctrine which "many of the Schoolmen affirm, that Adam was created in grace, that is, received a principle of grace and divine life from his very creation, or in the moment of the infusion of his soul; of which," he says, "for my own part I have little doubt." Again, he says, "It is abundantly manifest from the many testimonies alleged, that the ancient doctors of the Church did, with a general consent, acknowledge, that our first parents in the state of integrity, had in them something more than nature, that is, were endowed with the divine principle of the Spirit, in order to a supernatural felicity."

Now, taking this for granted, because I know that you and those who agree with you maintain it as well as we do, I ask you, have you any intention to deny that Mary was as fully endowed as Eve? is it any violent inference, that she, who was to co-operate in the redemption of the world, at least was not less endowed with power from on high, than she who, given as a help-mate to her husband, did in the event but co-operate with him for its ruin? If Eve was raised above human nature by that indwelling moral gift which we call grace, is it rash to say that Mary had even a greater grace? And this consideration gives significance to the Angel's salutation of her as "full of grace,"—an interpretation of the original word which is undoubtedly the

right one, as soon as we resist the common Protestant
assumption that grace is a mere external approbation or
acceptance, answering to the word "favour," whereas it
is, as the Fathers teach, a real inward condition or
superadded quality of soul.   And if Eve had this supernatural inward gift given her from the first moment of
her personal existence, is it possible to deny that Mary
too had this gift from the very first moment of her
personal existence?   I do not know how to resist
this inference:—well, this is simply and literally the
doctrine of the Immaculate Conception.   I say the
doctrine of the Immaculate Conception is in its substance this, and nothing more or less than this (putting
aside the question of degrees of grace) ; and it really
does seem to me bound up in the doctrine of the
Fathers, that Mary is the second Eve.

It is indeed to me a most strange phenomenon that so
many learned and devout men stumble at this doctrine;
and I can only account for it by supposing that in matter
of fact they do not know what we mean by the Immaculate Conception ; and your Volume (may I say it?)
bears out my suspicion.   It is a great consolation to
have reason for thinking so,—reason for believing that in
some sort the persons in question are in the position of
those great Saints in former times, who are said to have
hesitated about the doctrine, when they would not have
hesitated at all, if the word "Conception" had been
clearly explained in that sense in which now it is universally received.   I do not see how any one who holds with
Bull the Catholic doctrine of the supernatural endowments of our first parents, has fair reason for doubting

our doctrine about the Blessed Virgin. It has no reference whatever to her parents, but simply to her own
person; it does but affirm that, together with the nature
which she inherited from her parents, that is, her own
nature, she had a superadded fulness of grace, and that
from the first moment of her existence. Suppose Eve
had stood the trial, and not lost her first grace; and
suppose she had eventually had children, those children
from the first moment of their existence would, through
divine bounty, have received the same privilege that she
had ever had; that is, as she was taken from Adam's
side, in a garment, so to say, of grace, so they in turn
would have received what may be called an immaculate
conception. They would have then been conceived in
grace, as in fact they are conceived in sin. What is
there difficult in this doctrine? What is there unnatural? Mary may be called, as it were, a daughter
of Eve unfallen. You believe with us that St. John
Baptist had grace given to him three months before his
birth, at the time that the Blessed Virgin visited his
mother. He accordingly was *not* immaculately conceived, because he was alive before grace came to him;
but our Lady's case only differs from his in this respect,
that to her the grace of God came, not three months
merely before her birth, but from the first moment of
her being, as it had been given to Eve.

But it may be said, How does this enable us to say
that she was conceived without *original sin*? If Anglicans knew what we mean by original sin, they would
not ask the question. Our doctrine of original sin is
not the same as the Protestant doctrine. "Original

s'n," with us, cannot be called sin, in the mere ordinary
sense of the word "sin;" it is a term denoting Adam's
sin as transferred to us, or the state to which Adam's
sin reduces his children; but by Protestants it seems to
be understood as sin, in much the same sense as actual
sin. We, with the Fathers, think of it as something
negative, Protestants as something positive. Protestants hold that it is a disease, a radical change of
nature, an active poison internally corrupting the soul,
infecting its primary elements, and disorganizing it;
and they fancy that we ascribe a different nature from
ours to the Blessed Virgin, different from that of her
parents, and from that of fallen Adam. We hold
nothing of the kind; we consider that in Adam she
died, as others; that she was included, together with
the whole race, in Adam's sentence; that she incurred
his debt, as we do; but that, for the sake of Him who
was to redeem her and us upon the Cross, to her the
debt was remitted by anticipation, on her the sentence
was not carried out, except indeed as regards her natural
death, for she died when her time came, as others.[8] All
this we teach, but we deny that she had original sin;
for by original sin we mean, as I have already said,
something negative, viz., this only, the *deprivation* of
that supernatural unmerited grace which Adam and
Eve had on their first formation,—deprivation and the
consequences of deprivation. Mary could not merit,
any more than they, the restoration of that grace; but
it was restored to her by God's free bounty, from the

[8] Vid. Note II. infr.

very first moment of her existence, and thereby, in fact, she never came under the original curse, which consisted in the loss of it. And she had this special privilege, in order to fit her to become the Mother of her and our Redeemer, to fit her mentally, spiritually for it ; so that, by the aid of the first grace, she might so grow in grace, that, when the Angel came and her Lord was at hand, she might be " full of grace," prepared as far as a creature could be prepared, to receive Him into her bosom.

1 have drawn the doctrine of the Immaculate Conception, as an immediate inference, from the primitive doctrine that Mary is the second Eve. The argument seems to me conclusive : and, if it has not been universally taken as such, this has come to pass, because there has not been a clear understanding among Catholics, what exactly was meant by the "Immaculate Conception." To many it seemed to imply that the Blessed Virgin did not die in Adam, that she did not come under the penalty of the fall, that she was not redeemed, that she was conceived in some way inconsistent with the verse in the *Miserere* Psalm. If controversy had in earlier days so cleared the subject as to make it plain to all, that the doctrine meant nothing else than that in fact in her case the general sentence on mankind was not carried out, and that, by means of the indwelling in her of divine grace from the first moment of her being (and this is all the decree of 1854 has declared), I cannot believe that the doctrine would have ever been opposed ; for an instinctive sentiment has led Christians jealously to put the Blessed Mary

E

aside when sin comes into discussion. This is expressed
in the well-known words of St. Augustine, All have
sinned "except the Holy Virgin Mary, concerning
whom, for the honour of the Lord, I wish no question
to be raised at all, when we are treating of sins" (*de
Nat. et Grat.* 42); words which, whatever was St.
Augustine's actual occasion of using them (to which
you refer, p. 176), certainly, in the spirit which they
breathe, are well adapted to convey the notion, that,
though her parents had no privilege beyond other
parents, she had not personally any part in sin whatever.
It is true that several great Fathers of the fourth century
do imply or assert that on one or two occasions she
did sin venially or showed infirmity. This is the only
real objection which I know of; and as I do not wish
to pass it over lightly, I propose to consider it at the
end of this Letter.[9]

2. Now, secondly, her dignity. Here let us suppose
that our first parents had overcome in their trial; and
had gained for their descendants for ever the full possession, as if by right, of the privileges which were promised to their obedience,—grace here and glory hereafter. Is it possible that those descendants, pious and
happy from age to age in their temporal homes, would
have forgotten their benefactors? Would they not have
followed them in thought into the heavens, and grate-
fully commemorated them on earth? The history of
the temptation, the craft of the serpent, their steadfast-

[9] Vid. Note III. infr.

ness in obedience,—the loyal vigilance, the sensitive
purity of Eve,—the great issue, salvation wrought out
for all generations,—would have been never from their
minds, ever welcome to their ears. This would have
taken place from the necessity of our nature. Every
nation has its mythical hymns and epics about its first
fathers and its heroes. The great deeds of Charlemagne,
Alfred, Cœur de Lion, Louis the ninth, Wallace, Joan
of Arc, do not die; and though their persons are gone
from us, we make much of their names. Milton's
Adam, after his fall, understands the force of this law,
and shrinks from the prospect of its operation.

> " Who of all ages to succeed, but, feeling
> The evil on him brought by me, will curse
> My head ? Ill fare our ancestor impure,
> For this we may thank Adam."

If this anticipation of the first man has not been fulfilled in the event, it is owing to the exigencies of our
penal life, our state of perpetual change, and the ignorance
and unbelief incurred by the fall; also because, fallen as
we are, still from the hopefulness of our nature, we feel
more pride in our national great men, than dejection at
our national misfortunes. Much more then in the great
kingdom and people of God ;—the Saints are ever in our
sight, and not as mere ineffectual ghosts or dim memories, but as if present bodily in their past selves. It is said
of them, " Their works do follow them ; " what they were
here, such are they in heaven and in the Church. As
we call them by their earthly names, so we contemplate
them in their earthly characters and histories. Their acts,
calings, and relations below, are types and anticipations

E 2

of their present mission above. Even in the case of
our Lord Himself, whose native home is the eternal
heavens, it is said of Him in His state of glory. that
He is "a Priest for ever ; " and when He comes again,
He will be recognized by those who pierced Him, as
being the very same that He was on earth. The only
question is, whether the Blessed Virgin had a part, a
real part, in the economy of grace, whether, when she
was on earth, she secured by her deeds any claim on
our memories ; for, if she did, it is impossible we should
put her away from us, merely because she is gone hence,
and should not look at her still according to the measure of her earthly history, with gratitude and expectation.   If, as St. Irenæus says, she acted the part of an
Advocate, a friend in need, even in her mortal life, if as
St. Jerome and St. Ambrose say, she was on earth the
great pattern of Virgins, if she had a meritorious share
in bringing about our redemption, if her maternity was
gained by her faith and obedience, if her Divine Son
was subject to her, and if she stood by the Cross with a
mother's heart and drank in to the full those sufferings
which it was her portion to gaze upon, it is impossible
that we should not associate these characteristics of her
life on earth with her present state of blessedness ; and
this surely she anticipated, when she said in her hymn
that all " generations should call her blessed."

I am aware that, in thus speaking, I am following a
line of thought which is rather a meditation than an
argument in controversy, and I shall not carry it further ;
but still, before turning to other topics, it is to the
point to inquire, whether the popular astonishment, ex-

cited by our belief in the blessed Virgin's present dignity, does not arise from the circumstance that the bulk of men, engaged in matters of this world, have never calmly considered her historical position in the gospels, so as rightly to realize (if I may use the word a second time) what that position imports. I do not claim for the generality of Catholics any greater powers of reflection upon the objects of their faith, than Protestants commonly have; but, putting the run of Catholics aside, there is a sufficient number of religious men among us who, instead of expending their devotional energies (as so many serious Protestants do) on abstract doctrines, such as justification by faith only, or the sufficiency of Holy Scripture, employ themselves in the contemplation of Scripture facts, and bring out before their minds in a tangible form the doctrines involved in them, and give such a substance and colour to the sacred history, as to influence their brethren; and their brethren, though superficial themselves, are drawn by their Catholic instinct to accept conclusions which they could not indeed themselves have elicited, but which, when elicited, they feel to be true. However, it would be out of place to pursue this course of reasoning here; and instead of doing so, I shall take what perhaps you may think a very bold step,—I shall find the doctrine of our Lady's present exaltation in Scripture.

I mean to find it in the vision of the Woman and Child in the twelfth chapter of the Apocalypse :[1]—now here two objections will be made to me at once; first

[1] Vid. Essay on Doctr. Development, p. 384, and Bishop Ullathorne's work on the Immaculate Conception, p. 77.

that such an interpretation is but poorly supported by
the Fathers, and secondly that in ascribing such a
picture of the Madonna (as it may be called) to the
Apostolic age, I am committing an anachronism.

As to the former of these objections, I answer as
follows :—Christians have never gone to Scripture for
proof of their doctrines, till there was actual need, from
the pressure of controversy ;—if in those times the
Blessed Virgin's dignity was unchallenged on all hands,
as a matter of doctrine, Scripture, as far as its argumentative matter was concerned, was likely to remain a
sealed book to them. Thus, to take an instance in
point ; the Catholic party in the Anglican Church (say,
the Nonjurors), unable by their theory of religion
simply to take their stand on Tradition, and distressed
for proof of their doctrines, had their eyes sharpened to
scrutinize and to understand in many places the letter of
Holy Scripture, which to others brought no instruction.
And the peculiarity of their interpretations is this,—
that these have in themselves great logical cogency, yet
are but faintly supported by patristical commentators.
Such is the use of the word $\pi o\iota\epsilon\hat{\iota}\nu$ or *facere* in our Lord's
institution of the Holy Eucharist, which, by a reference
to the Old Testament, is found to be a word of sacrifice.
Such again is $\lambda\epsilon\iota\tau o\upsilon\rho\gamma o\acute{\upsilon}\nu\tau\omega\nu$ in the passage in the Acts
"As they *ministered* to the Lord and fasted," which
again is a sacerdotal term. And such the passage in
Rom. xv. 16, in which several terms are used which
have an allusion to the sacrificial Eucharistic rite. Such
too is St. Paul's repeated message to the *household* of
Onesiphorus, with no mention of Onesiphorus himself, but

in one place with the addition of a prayer that "he might find mercy of the Lord " in the day of judgment, which, taking into account its wording and the known usage of the first centuries, we can hardly deny is a prayer for his soul. Other texts there are, which ought to find a place in ancient controversies, and the omission of which by the Fathers affords matter for more surprise; those for instance, which, according to Middleton's rule, are real proofs of our Lord's divinity, and yet are passed over by Catholic disputants; for these bear upon a then existing controversy of the first moment, and of the most urgent exigency.

As to the second objection which I have supposed, so far from allowing it, I consider that it is built upon a mere imaginary fact, and that the truth of the matter lies in the very contrary direction. The Virgin and Child is *not* a mere modern idea; on the contrary, it is represented again and again, as every visitor to Rome is aware, in the paintings of the Catacombs. Mary is there drawn with the Divine Infant in her lap, she with hands extended in prayer, He with His hand in the attitude of blessing. No representation can more forcibly convey the doctrine of the high dignity of the Mother, and, I will add, of her influence with her Son. Why should the memory of His time of subjection be so dear to Christians, and so carefully preserved? The only question to be determined, is the precise date of these remarkable monuments of the first age of Christianity. That they belong to the centuries of what Anglicans call the "undivided Church" is certain; but lately investigations have been pursued, which place some of them at an earlier date than any one anticipated as pos-

sible. I am not in a position to quote largely from the
works of the Cavaliere de Rossi, who has thrown so
much light upon the subject; but I have his "Imagini
Scelte," published in 1863, and they are sufficient for
my purpose. In this work he has given us from the
Catacombs various representations of the Virgin and
Child; the latest of these belong to the early part of
the fourth century, but the earliest he believes to be referable to the very age of the Apostles. He comes to
this conclusion from the style and the skill of its composition, and from the history, locality, and existing in-
scriptions of the subterranean in which it is found.
However he does not go so far as to insist upon so early
a date; yet the utmost concession he makes is to refer
the painting to the era of the first Antonines, that is,
to a date within half a century of the death of St. John.
I consider then, that, as you would use in controversy
with Protestants, and fairly, the traditional doctrine of
the Church in early times, as an explanation of a particular passage of Scripture, or at least as a suggestion, or
as a defence, of the sense which you may wish to put
upon it, quite apart from the question whether your interpretation itself is directly traditional, so it is lawful
for me, though I have not the positive words of the
Fathers on my side, to shelter my own interpretation of
the Apostle's vision in the Apocalypse under the fact of
the extant pictures of Mother and Child in the Roman
Catacombs. Again, there is another principle of Scripture interpretation which we should hold as well as you,
viz., when we speak of a doctrine being contained in
Scripture, we do not necessarily mean that it is contained

there in direct categorical terms, but that there is no
satisfactory way of accounting for the language and expressions of the sacred writers, concerning the subject-
matter in question, except to suppose that they held
concerning it the opinion which we hold,—that they
would not have spoken as they have spoken, *unless* they
held it. For myself I have ever felt the truth of this
principle, as regards the Scripture proof of the Holy
Trinity; I should not have found out that doctrine in
the sacred text without previous traditional teaching;
but, when once it is suggested from without, it com-
mends itself as the one true interpretation, from its ap-
positeness,—because no other view of doctrine, which
can be ascribed to the inspired writers, so happily solves
the obscurities and seeming inconsistencies of their
teaching. And now to apply what I have been saying
to the passage in the Apocalypse.

If there is an Apostle on whom, *à priori*, our eyes
would be fixed, as likely to teach us about the Blessed
Virgin, it is St. John, to whom she was committed by
our Lord on the Cross;—with whom, as tradition goes,
she lived at Ephesus till she was taken away.   This anticipation is confirmed *à posteriori;* for, as I have said
above, one of the earliest and fullest of our informants
concerning her dignity, as being the second Eve, is
Irenæus, who came to Lyons from Asia Minor, and had
been taught by the immediate disciples of St. John.
The Apostle's vision is as follows :—

" A great sign appeared in heaven : A woman clothed
with the Sun, and the Moon under her feet; and on her
head a crown of twelve stars. And being with child,

she cried travailing in birth, and was in pain to be delivered. And there was seen another sign in heaven;
and behold a great red dragon . . . . And the dragon
stood before the woman who was ready to be delivered,
that, when she should be delivered, he might devour her
son.   And she brought forth a man child, who was to
rule all nations with an iron rod; and her son was taken
up to God and to His throne.   And the woman fled into
the wilderness."   Now I do not deny of course, that
under the image of the Woman, the Church is signified;
but what I would maintain is this, that the Holy
Apostle would not have spoken of the Church under
this particular image, *unless* there had existed a blessed
Virgin Mary, who was exalted on high, and the object
of veneration to all the faithful.

No one doubts that the " man-child " spoken of is an
allusion to our Lord: why then is not " the Woman "
an allusion to His Mother? This surely is the obvious
sense of the words; of course they have a further sense
also, which is the scope of the image; doubtless the
Child represents the children of the Church, and doubtless
the Woman represents the Church; this, I grant, is the
real or direct sense, but what is the sense of the symbol
under which that real sense is conveyed? *who* are the
Woman and the Child ? I answer, they are not personifications but Persons.   This is true of the Child, therefore it is true of the Woman.

But again : not only Mother and Child, but a serpent
is introduced into the vision.   Such a meeting of man,
woman, and serpent has not been found in Scripture,
since the beginning of Scripture, and now it is found

in its end. Moreover, in the passage in the Apocalypse as if to supply, before Scripture came to an end, what was wanting in its beginning, we are told, and for the first time, that the serpent in Paradise was the evil spirit. If the dragon of St. John is the same as the serpent of Moses, and the man-child is " the seed of the woman," why is not the woman herself she, whose seed the man-child is? And, if the first woman is not an allegory, why is the second? if the first woman is Eve, why is not the second Mary?

But this is not all. The image of the woman, according to general Scripture usage, is too bold and prominent for a mere personification. Scripture is not fond of allegories. We have indeed frequent figures there, as when the sacred writers speak of the arm or sword of the Lord; and so too when they speak of Jerusalem or Samaria in the feminine; or of the Church as a bride or as a vine; but they are not much given to dressing up abstract ideas or generalizations in personal attributes. This is the classical rather than the Scriptural style. Xenophon places Hercules between Virtue and Vice, represented as women; Æschylus introduces into his drama Force and Violence; Virgil gives personality to public rumour or Fame, and Plautus to Poverty. So on monuments done in the classical style, we see virtues, vices, rivers, renown, death, and the like, turned into human figures of men and women. Certainly I do not deny there are some instances of this method in Scripture, but I say that such poetical compositions are strikingly unlike its usual method. Thus, we at once feel the difference from Scripture, when we

betake ourselves to the Pastor of Hermas, and find the
Church a woman; to St. Methodius, and find Virtue a
woman; and to St. Gregory's poem, and find Virginity
again a woman.   Scripture deals with types rather than
personifications.   Israel stands for the chosen people,
David for Christ. Jerusalem for heaven.   Consider the
remarkable representations, dramatic I may call them, in
Jeremiah, Ezechiel, and Hosea: predictions, threatenings,
and promises, are acted out by those Prophets.   Ezechiel
is commanded to shave his head, and to divide and scatter
his hair; and Ahias tears his garment, and gives ten
out of twelve parts of it to Jeroboam.   So too the structure of the imagery in the Apocalypse is not a mere
allegorical creation, but is founded on the Jewish ritual.
In like manner our Lord's bodily cures are visible types
of the power of His grace upon the soul; and His prophecy of the last day is conveyed under that of the fall
of Jerusalem.   Even His parables are not simply ideal,
but relations of occurrences, which did or might take
place, under which was conveyed a spiritual meaning.
The description of Wisdom in the Proverbs and other
sacred books, has brought out the instinct of commentators in this respect.   They felt that Wisdom could
not be a mere personification, and they determined that
it was our Lord: and the later-written of these books,
by their own more definite language, warranted that
interpretation.   Then, when it was found that the Arians
used it in derogation of our Lord's divinity, still, unable
to tolerate the notion of a mere allegory, commentators
applied the description to the Blessed Virgin.   Coming
back then to the Apocalyptic vision, I ask, If the Woman

ought to be some real person, who can it be whom the
Apostle saw, and intends, and delineates, but that same
Great Mother to whom the chapters in the Proverbs
are accommodated? And let it be observed, moreover,
that in this passage, from the allusion made in it to the
history of the fall, Mary may be said still to be represented under the character of the Second Eve. I make
a farther remark: it is sometimes asked, Why do not
the sacred writers mention our Lady's greatness? I
answer, she was, or may have been alive, when the
Apostles and Evangelists wrote;—there was just one
book of Scripture certainly written after her death, and
that book does (so to say) canonize and crown her.

But if all this be so, if it is really the Blessed Virgin
whom Scripture represents as clothed with the sun,
crowned with the stars of heaven, and with the moon
as her footstool, what height of glory may we not
attribute to her? and what are we to say of those
who, through ignorance, run counter to the voice of
Scripture, to the testimony of the Fathers, to the
traditions of East and West, and speak and act
contemptuously towards her whom her Lord delighteth
to honour?

2.

Now I have said all I mean to say on what I have
called the rudimental teaching of Antiquity about the
Blessed Virgin; but after all I have not insisted on the
highest view of her prerogatives, which the Fathers
have taught us. You, my dear Friend, who know so
well the ancient controversies and Councils, may have

been surprised why I should not have yet spoken of her as the Theotocos;—but I wished to show on how broad a basis her dignity rests, independent of that wonderful title; and again I have been loth to enlarge upon the force of a word, which is rather matter for devotional thought than for polemical dispute. However I might as well not write to you at all, as altogether be silent upon it.

It is then an integral portion of the Faith fixed by Ecumenical Council, a portion of it which you hold as well as I, that the Blessed Virgin is Theotocos, Deipara, or Mother of God; and this word, when thus used, carries with it no admixture of rhetoric, no taint of extravagant affection,—it has nothing else but a well-weighed, grave, dogmatic sense, which corresponds and is adequate to its sound. It intends to express that God is her Son, as truly as any one of us is the son of his own mother. If this be so, what can be said of any creature whatever, which may not be said of her? what can be said too much, so that it does not compromise the attributes of the Creator? He indeed might have created a being more perfect, more admirable, than she is; He might have endued that being, so created, with a richer grant of grace, of power, of blessedness: but in one respect she surpasses all even possible creations, viz., that she is Mother of her Creator. It is this awful title, which both illustrates and connects together the two prerogatives of Mary, on which I have been lately enlarging, her sanctity and her greatness. It is the issue of her sanctity; it is the origin of her greatness. What dignity can be too great

to attribute to her who is as closely bound up, as intimately one, with the Eternal Word, as a mother is
with a son ? What outfit of sanctity, what fulness and
redundance of grace, what exuberance of merits must
have been hers, when once we admit the supposition,
which the Fathers justify, that her Maker really did
regard those merits, and take them into account, when
He condescended "not to abhor the Virgin's womb"?
Is it surprising then that on the one hand she should
be immaculate in her Conception ? or on the other that
she should be honoured with an Assumption, and exalted as a queen with a crown of twelve stars, with the
rulers of day and night to do her service ? Men sometimes wonder that we call her Mother of life, of mercy,
of salvation ; what are all these titles compared to that
one name, Mother of God ?

I shall say no more about this title here. It is
scarcely possible to write of it without diverging into
a style of composition unsuited to a Letter; so I will
but refer to the history and to instances of its use.

The title of *Theotocos*,[2] as ascribed to the Blessed
Mary, begins with ecclesiastical writers of a date hardly
later than that at which we read of her as the second
Eve. It first occurs in the works of Origen (185—254);
but he, witnessing for Egypt and Palestine, witnesses
also that it was in use before his time; for, as Socrates
informs us, he "interpreted how it was to be used,
and discussed the question at length" (*Hist.* vii. 32).
Within two centuries of his time (431), in the General

---

[2] *Vid.* Oxford Translation of St. Athanasius, pp. 420, 440, 447 ; and
Essay on Doct. Development, pp. 407—409.

Council held against Nestorius, it was made part of
the formal dogmatic teaching of the Church. At that
time, Theodoret, who from his party connexions might
have been supposed disinclined to its solemn recognition, owned that " the ancient and more than ancient
heralds of the orthodox faith taught the use of the
term according to the Apostolic tradition." At the
same date John of Antioch, the temporary protector of
Nestorius, whose heresy lay in the rejection of the
term, said, " This title no ecclesiastical teacher has put
aside. Those who have used it are many and eminent;
and those who have not used it, have not attacked those
who did." Alexander again, one of the fiercest partisans of Nestorius, witnesses to the use of the word,
though he considers it dangerous; "That in festive
solemnities," he says, "or in preaching or teaching,
theotocos should be unguardedly said by the orthodox
without explanation is no blame, because such statements were not dogmatic, nor said with evil meaning."
If we look for those Fathers, in the interval between
Origen and the Council, to whom Alexander refers as
using the term, we find among them no less names
than Archelaus of Mesopotamia, Eusebius of Palestine,
Alexander of Egypt, in the third century; in the
fourth, Athanasius, who uses it many times with
emphasis, Cyril of Palestine, Gregory Nyssen and
Gregory Nazianzen of Cappadocia, Antiochus of Syria,
and Ammonius of Thrace :—not to refer to the Emperor Julian, who, having no local or ecclesiastical
domicile, is a witness for the whole of Christendom.
Another and earlier Emperor, Constantine, in his speech

before the assembled Bishops at Nicæa, uses the still
more explicit title of "the Virgin Mother of God;"
which is also used by Ambrose of Milan, and by
Vincent and Cassian in the south of France, and then
by St. Leo.

So much for the term; it would be tedious to produce the passages of authors who, using or not using
the term, convey the idea. "Our God was carried in
the womb of Mary," says Ignatius, who was martyred
A.D. 106. "The Word of God," says Hippolytus, "was
carried in that Virgin frame." "The Maker of all,"
says Amphilochius, "is born of a Virgin." "She did
compass without circumscribing the Sun of justice,—
the Everlasting is born," says Chrysostom. "God
dwelt in the womb," says Proclus. "When thou
hearest that God speaks from the bush," asks Theodotus,
"in the bush seest thou not the Virgin?" Cassian
says, "Mary bore her Author." "The One God only-
begotten," says Hilary, "is introduced into the womb
of a Virgin." "The Everlasting," says Ambrose,
"came into the Virgin." "The closed gate," says
Jerome, "by which alone the Lord God of Israel enters,
is the Virgin Mary." "That man from heaven," says
Capriolus, "is God conceived in the womb." "He is
made in thee," says St. Augustine, "who made thee."

This being the faith of the Fathers about the Blessed
Virgin, we need not wonder that it should in no long
time be transmuted into devotion. No wonder if their
language should become unmeasured, when so great a
term as " Mother of God" had been formally set down

as the safe limit of it. No wonder if it should be stronger and stronger as time went on, since only in a long period could the fulness of its import be exhausted. And in matter of fact, and as might be anticipated, (with the few exceptions which I have noted above, and which I am to treat of below), the current of thought in those early ages did uniformly tend to make much of the Blessed Virgin and to increase her honours, not to circumscribe them. Little jealousy was shown of her in those times; but, when any such niggardness of affection occurred, then one Father or other fell upon the offender, with zeal not to say with fierceness. Thus St. Jerome inveighs against Helvidius; thus St. Epiphanius denounces Apollinaris, St. Cyril Nestorius, and St. Ambrose Bonosus; on the other hand, each successive insult offered to her by individual adversaries did but bring out more fully the intimate sacred affection with which Christendom regarded her. "She was alone, and wrought the world's salvation and conceived the redemption of all," says Ambrose;[3] "she had so great grace, as not only to preserve virginity herself, but to confer it on those whom she visited." "She is the rod out of the stem of Jesse," says St. Jerome, "and the Eastern gate through which the High Priest alone goes in and out, which still is ever shut." "She is the wise woman," says Nilus, who "hath clad believers, from the fleece of the Lamb born of her, with the clothing of incorruption, and delivered them from their spiritual nakedness." "She is the mother of life,

[3] Essay on Doctr. Dev. *ubi supr.*

of beauty, of majesty, the morning star," according to Antiochus. "The mystical new heavens," "the heavens carrying the Divinity," "the fruitful vine," "by whom we are translated from death unto life," according to St. Ephrem. "The manna, which is delicate, bright, sweet, and virgin, which, as though coming from heaven, has poured down on all the people of the Churches a food pleasanter than honey," according to St. Maximus.

Basil of Seleucia says, that "she shines out above all the martyrs as the sun above the stars, and that she mediates between God and men." "Run through all creation in your thought," says Proclus, "and see if there be one equal or superior to the Holy Virgin, Mother of God." "Hail, Mother, clad in light, of the light which sets not," says Theodotus, or some one else at Ephesus; "hail, all undefiled mother of holiness; hail, most pellucid fountain of the life-giving stream." And St. Cyril too at Ephesus, "Hail, Mary, Mother of God, majestic common-treasure of the whole world, the lamp unquenchable, the crown of virginity, the sceptre of orthodoxy, the indissoluble temple, the dwelling of the Illimitable, Mother and Virgin, through whom He in the holy gospels is called blessed who cometh in the name of the Lord, . . through whom the Holy Trinity is sanctified, . . through whom Angels and Archangels rejoice, devils are put to flight, . . and the fallen creature is received up into the heavens, &c., &c.[4]" Such is but a portion of the panegyrical language which St. Cyril used in the third Ecumenical Council.

[4] Opp. t. 6, p. 355.

3.

I must not close my review of the Catholic doctrine concerning the Blessed Virgin, without directly speaking of her intercessory power, though I have incidentally made mention of it already. It is the immediate result of two truths, neither of which you dispute;—first, that "it is good and useful," as the Council of Trent says, "suppliantly to invoke the Saints and to have recourse to their prayers;" and secondly, that the Blessed Mary is singularly dear to her Son and singularly exalted in sanctity and glory. However, at the risk of becoming didactic, I will state somewhat more fully the grounds on which it rests.

To a candid pagan it must have been one of the most remarkable points of Christianity, on its first appearance, that the observance of prayer formed so vital a part of its organization; and that, though its members were scattered all over the world, and its rulers and subjects had so little opportunity of correlative action, yet they, one and all, found the solace of a spiritual intercourse and a real bond of union, in the practice of mutual intercession. Prayer indeed is the very essence of all religion; but in the heathen religions it was either public or personal; it was a state ordinance, or a selfish expedient for the attainment of certain tangible, temporal goods. Very different from this was its exercise among Christians, who were thereby knit together in one body, different, as they were, in races, ranks, and habits, distant from each other in country, and helpless amid hostile populations. Yet it proved sufficient for its purpose. Christians could not correspond ; they could not combine ; but they could pray one for another. Even their public prayers partook of this character of intercession ; for to pray for the welfare of the whole Church was in fact a prayer for all the classes of men and all the individuals of which it was composed. It was in prayer that the Church was founded. For ten days all the Apostles "persevered with one mind in prayer and supplication, with the women, and Mary the Mother of Jesus, and with his brethren." Then again at Pentecost "they were all with one mind in one place ;" and the converts then made are said to have "persevered in prayer." And when, after a while, St. Peter was seized and put in prison with a view to his being put to death, "prayer was made without ceasing" by the Church of God for him ; and, when the Angel released him, he took refuge in a house "where many were gathered together in prayer."

We are so accustomed to these passages as hardly to be able to do justice to their singular significance ; and they are followed up by various passages of the Apostolic Epistles. St. Paul enjoins his brethren to "pray with all prayer and supplication at all times in the Spirit, with all instance and supplication for all saints," to "pray in every place," "to make supplication, prayers, intercessions, giving of thanks, for all men." And in his own person he "ceases not to give thanks for them, commemorating them in his prayers," and "always in all his prayers making supplication for them all with joy."

Now, was this spiritual bond to cease with life ? or

had Christians similar duties to their brethren departed?
From the witness of the early ages of the Church, it appears that they had; and you, and those who agree with
you, would be the last to deny that they were then in
the practice of praying, as for the living, so for those
also who had passed into the intermediate state between
earth and heaven. Did the sacred communion extend
further still, on to the inhabitants of heaven itself?
Here too you agree with us, for you have adopted in
your Volume the words of the Council of Trent which
I have quoted above. But now we are brought to a
higher order of thought.

It would be preposterous to pray for those who are
already in glory; but at least they can pray for us, and
we can ask their prayers, and in the Apocalypse at least
Angels are introduced both sending us their blessing and
offering up our prayers before the Divine Presence. We
read there of an angel who " came and stood before the
altar, having a golden censer;" and " there was given
to him much incense, that he should offer of the prayers
of all saints upon the golden altar which is before the
Throne of God." On this occasion, surely the Angel
performed the part of a great Intercessor or Mediator
above for the children of the Church Militant below.
Again, in the beginning of the same book, the sacred
writer goes so far as to speak of " grace and peace "
coming to us, not only from the Almighty, " but from
the seven Spirits that are before His throne," thus associating the Eternal with the ministers of His mercies;
and this carries us on to the remarkable passage of St.
Justin, one of the earliest Fathers, who, in his Apology,

says, " To Him (God), and His Son who came from Him
and taught us these things, and the host of the other
good Angels who follow and resemble Him, and the
Prophetic Spirit, we pay veneration and homage."
Further, in the Epistle to the Hebrews, St. Paul introduces, not only Angels, but "the spirits of the just"
into the sacred communion : " Ye have come to Mount
Zion, to the heavenly Jerusalem, to myriads of angels,
to God the Judge of all, to the spirits of the just made
perfect, and to Jesus the Mediator of the New Testament." What can be meant by having "come to the
spirits of the just," unless in some way or other, they
do us good, whether by blessing or by aiding us ? that
is, in a word, to speak correctly, by praying for us, for
it is surely by prayer that the creature above is able to
bless and aid the creature below.

Intercession thus being a first principle of the Church's
life, next it is certain again, that the vital force of that
intercession, as an availing power, is, (according to the
will of God), sanctity. This seems to be suggested by
a passage of St. Paul, in which the Supreme Intercessor
is said to be "the Spirit : "—" the Spirit Himself
maketh intercession for us ; He maketh intercession for
the saints according to God." And, indeed, the truth
thus implied, is expressly brought out for us in other
parts of Scripture, in the form both of doctrine and of
example. The words of the man born blind speak the
common-sense of nature :—" if any man be a worshipper
of God, him He heareth." And Apostles confirm them :
—" the prayer of a just man availeth much," and
" whatever we ask, we receive, because we keep his com-

mandments." Then, as for examples, we read of the
Almighty's revealing to Abraham and Moses beforehand,
His purposes of wrath, in order that they by their intercessions might avert its execution. To the friends of
Job it was said, " My servant Job shall pray for you ;
his face I will accept." Elias by his prayer shut and
opened the heavens. Elsewhere we read of " Jeremias,
Moses, and Samuel ;" and of " Noe, Daniel, and Job,"
as being great mediators between God and His people.
One instance is given us, which testifies the continuance
of this high office beyond this life. Lazarus, in the
parable, is seen in Abraham's bosom. It is usual to
pass over this striking passage with the remark that it
is a Jewish mode of speech ; whereas, Jewish belief or
not, it is recognized and sanctioned by our Lord Himself. What do Catholics teach about the Blessed Virgin
more wonderful than this ? If Abraham, not yet ascended on high, had charge of Lazarus, what offence is
it to affirm the like of her, who was not merely as Abraham, " the friend," but was the very " Mother of God " ?

It may be added, that, though, if sanctity was wanting, it availed nothing for influence with our Lord, to
be one of His company, still, as the Gospel shows, He
on various occasions actually did allow those who were
near Him, to be the channels of introducing suppliants
to Him or of gaining miracles from Him, as in the instance of the miracle of the loaves ; and if on one occasion, He seems to repel His Mother, when she told Him
that wine was wanting for the guests at the marriage
feast, it is obvious to remark on it, that, by saying that
she was then separated from Him (" What have I to do

with thee?") *because* His hour was not yet come, He implied, that when that hour was come, such separation would be at an end. Moreover, in fact He did at her intercession work the miracle to which her words pointed.

I consider it impossible then, for those who believe the Church to be one vast body in heaven and on earth, in which every holy creature of God has his place, and of which prayer is the life, when once they recognize the sanctity and dignity of the Blessed Virgin, not to perceive immediately, that her office above is one of perpetual intercession for the faithful militant, and that our very relation to her must be that of clients to a patron, and that, in the eternal enmity which exists between the woman and the serpent, while the serpent's strength lies in being the Tempter, the weapon of the Second Eve and Mother of God is prayer.

As then these ideas of her sanctity and dignity gradually penetrated the mind of Christendom, so did that of her intercessory power follow close upon them and with them. From the earliest times that mediation is symbolized in those representations of her with uplifted hands, which, whether in plaster or in glass, are still extant in Rome, — that Church, as St. Irenæus says, with which "every Church, that is, the faithful from every side, must agree, because of its more powerful principality;" "into which," as Tertullian adds, "the Apostles poured out, together with their blood, their whole doctrine." As far indeed as existing documents are concerned, I know of no instance to my purpose earlier than A.D. 234, but it is a very remarkable one;

and, though it has been often quoted in the controversy, an argument is not weaker for frequent use.

St. Gregory Nyssen,[5] then, a native of Cappadocia in the fourth century, relates that his namesake, Bishop of Neo-Cæsarea in Pontus, surnamed Thaumaturgus, in the century preceding, shortly before he was called to the priesthood, received in a vision a Creed, which is still extant, from the Blessed Mary at the hands of St. John. The account runs thus:—He was deeply pondering theological doctrine, which the heretics of the day depraved. "In such thoughts," says his namesake of Nyssa, "he was passing the night, when one appeared, as if in human form, aged in appearance, saintly in the fashion of his garments, and very venerable both in grace of countenance and general mien. Amazed at the sight, he started from his bed, and asked who it was, and why he came; but, on the other calming the perturbation of his mind with his gentle voice, and saying he had appeared to him by divine command on account of his doubts, in order that the truth of the orthodox faith might be revealed to him, he took courage at the word, and regarded him with a mixture of joy and fright. Then, on his stretching his hand straight forward and pointing with his fingers at something on one side, he followed with his eyes the extended hand, and saw another appearance opposite to the former, in shape of a woman, but more than human. . . . When his eyes could not bear the apparition, he heard them conversing together on the subject of his doubts; and

---

[5] Vid. Essay on Doctr. Dev., p. 386.

thereby not only gained a true knowledge of the faith, but learned their names, as they addressed each other by their respective appellations. And thus he is said to have heard the person in woman's shape bid 'John the Evangelist' disclose to the young man the mystery of godliness; and he answered that he was ready to comply in this matter with the wish of 'the Mother of the Lord,' and enunciated a formulary, well-turned and complete, and so vanished. He, on the other hand, immediately committed to writing that divine teaching of his mystagogue, and henceforth preached in the Church according to that form, and bequeathed to posterity, as an inheritance, that heavenly teaching, by means of which his people are instructed down to this day, being preserved from all heretical evil." He proceeds to rehearse the Creed thus given, "There is One God, Father of a Living Word," &c. Bull, after quoting it in his work on the Nicene Faith, alludes to this history of its origin, and adds, "No one should think it incredible that such a providence should befall a man whose whole life was conspicuous for revelations and miracles, as all ecclesiastical writers who have mentioned him (and who has not?) witness with one voice."

Here our Lady is represented as rescuing a holy soul from intellectual error. This leads me to a further reflection. You seem, in one place of your Volume, to object to the Antiphon, in which it is said of her, "All heresies thou hast destroyed alone." Surely the truth of it is verified in this age, as in former times, and especially by the doctrine concerning her, on which I have been dwelling. She is the great exemplar of prayer in a generation, which emphatically denies the power of prayer *in toto*, which determines that fatal laws govern the universe, that there cannot be any direct communication between earth and heaven, that God cannot visit His own earth, and that man cannot influence His providence. ⁎

§ 4.—*Belief of Catholics concerning the Blessed Virgin,
as coloured by their Devotion to her.*

I CANNOT help hoping that your own reading of the
Fathers will on the whole bear me out in the above
account of their teaching concerning the Blessed Virgin.
Anglicans seem to me simply to overlook the strength of
the argument adducible from the works of those ancient
doctors in our favour; and they open the attack upon
our mediæval and modern writers, careless of leaving a
host of primitive opponents in their rear. I do not
include you among such Anglicans, as you know what
the Fathers assert; but, if so, have you not, my dear
Friend, been unjust to yourself in your recent Volume,
and made far too much of the differences which exist
between Anglicans and us on this particular point? It
is the office of an Irenicon to smoothe difficulties; I
shall be pleased if I succeed in removing some of yours
Let the public judge between us here. Had you happened in your Volume to introduce your notice of our
teaching about the Blessed Virgin, with a notice of the
teaching of the Fathers concerning her, which you
follow, ordinary men would have considered that there
was not much to choose between you and us. Though
you appealed ever so much, in your defence, to the
authority of the " undivided Church," they would have

said that you, who had such high notions of the Blessed
Mary, were one of the last men who had a right to
accuse us of quasi-idolatry.   When they found you
with the Fathers calling her Mother of God, Second
Eve, and Mother of all Living, the Mother of Life, the
Morning Star, the Mystical New Heaven, the Sceptre
of Orthodoxy, the All-undefiled Mother of Holiness,
and the like, they would have deemed it a poor compensation for such language, that you protested against
her being called a Co-redemptress or a Priestess.   And,
if they were violent Protestants, they would not have
read you with the relish and gratitude with which, as
it is, they have perhaps accepted your testimony against
us.   Not that they would have been altogether fair in
their view of you ;—on the contrary I think there is a
real difference between what you protest against, and
what with the Fathers you hold ; but unread men of
the world form a broad practical judgment of the
things which come before them, and they would have
felt in this case that they had the same right to be
shocked at you, as you have to be shocked at us ;—and
further, which is the point to which I am coming, they
would have said, that, granting some of our modern
writers go beyond the Fathers in this matter, still the
line cannot be logically drawn between the teaching
of the Fathers concerning the Blessed Virgin and our
own.   This view of the matter seems to me true and
important ; I do not think the line *can* be satisfactorily drawn, and to this point I shall now direct my
attention.

It is impossible, I say, in a doctrine like this, to draw

the line cleanly between truth and error, right and wrong. This is ever the case in concrete matters, which have life. Life in this world is motion, and involves a continual process of change. Living things grow into their perfection, into their decline, into their death. No rule of art will suffice to stop the operation of this natural law, whether in the material world or in the human mind. We can indeed encounter disorders, when they occur, by external antagonism and remedies; but we cannot eradicate the process itself, out of which they arise. Life has the same right to decay, as it has to wax strong. This is specially the case with great ideas. You may stifle them; or you may refuse them elbow-room; or again, you may torment them with your continual meddling; or you may let them have free course and range, and be content, instead of anticipating their excesses, to expose and restrain those excesses after they have occurred. But you have only this alternative; and for myself, I prefer much wherever it is possible, to be first generous and then just; to grant full liberty of thought, and to call it to account when abused.

If what I have been saying be true of energetic ideas generally, much more is it the case in matters of religion. Religion acts on the affections; who is to hinder these, when once roused, from gathering in their strength and running wild? They are not gifted with any connatural principle within them, which renders them self-governing, and self-adjusting. They hurry right on to their object, and often in their case it is, the more haste, the worse speed. Their object engrosses them, and they see nothing else. And of all passions love is the most unmanageable; nay more, I would not give much for that love which is never extravagant, which always observes the proprieties, and can move about in perfect good taste, under all emergencies. What mother, what husband or wife, what youth or maiden in love, but says a thousand foolish things, in the way of endearment, which the speaker would be sorry for strangers to hear; yet they are not on that account unwelcome to the parties to whom they are addressed. Sometimes by bad luck they are written down, sometimes they get into the newspapers; and what might be even graceful, when it was fresh from the heart, and interpreted by the voice and the countenance, presents but a melancholy exhibition when served up cold for the public eye. So it is with devotional feelings. Burning thoughts and words are as open to criticism as they are beyond it. What is abstractedly extravagant, may in particular persons be becoming and beautiful, and only fall under blame when it is found in others who imitate them. When it is formalized into meditations or exercises, it is as repulsive as love-letters in a police report. Moreover, even holy minds readily adopt and become familiar with language which they would never have originated themselves, when it proceeds from a writer who has the same objects of devotion as they have; and, if they find a stranger ridicule or reprobate supplication or praise which has come to them so recommended, they feel it as keenly as if a direct insult were offered to those to whom that homage is addressed. In the next place, what has

power to stir holy and refined souls is potent also with
the multitude; and the religion of the multitude is ever
vulgar and abnormal; it ever will be tinctured with
fanaticism and superstition, while men are what they
are. A people's religion is ever a corrupt religion, in
spite of the provisions of Holy Church. If she is to
be Catholic, you must admit within her net fish of
every kind, guests good and bad, vessels of gold, vessels
of earth. You may beat religion out of men, if you
will, and then their excesses will take a different
direction; but if you make use of religion to improve
them, they will make use of religion to corrupt it. And
then you will have effected that compromise of which
our countrymen report so unfavourably from abroad :—
a high grand faith and worship which compels their
admiration, and puerile absurdities among the people
which excite their contempt.

Nor is it any safeguard against these excesses in a
religious system, that the religion is based upon reason,
and developes into a theology. Theology both uses
logic and baffles it; and thus logic acts both for the protection and for the perversion of religion. Theology is
occupied with supernatural matters, and is ever running
into mysteries, which reason can neither explain nor
adjust. Its lines of thought come to an abrupt termina-
nation, and to pursue them or to complete them is to
plunge down the abyss. But logic blunders on, forcing
its way, as it can, through thick darkness and ethereal
mediums. The Arians went ahead with logic for their
directing principle, and so lost the truth; on the other
hand, St. Augustine intimates that, if we attempt to find

and tie together the ends of lines which run into infinity we shall only succeed in contradicting ourselves, when, in his Treatise on the Holy Trinity, he is unable to find the logical reason for not speaking of three Gods as well as of One, and of one Person in the Godhead as well as of Three. I do not mean to say that logic cannot be used to set right its own error, or that in the hands of an able disputant it may not trim the balance of truth. This was done at the Councils of Antioch and Nicæa, on occasion of the heresies of Paulus and Arius. But such a process is circuitous and elaborate ; and is conducted by means of minute subtleties which will give it the appearance of a game of skill in matters too grave and practical to deserve a mere scholastic treatment. Accordingly St. Augustine, in the Treatise above mentioned, does no more than simply lay it down that the statements in question are heretical, that is to say there are three Gods is Tritheism, and to say there is but one Person, Sabellianism. That is, good sense and a large view of truth are the correctives of his logic. And thus we have arrived at the final resolution of the whole matter, for good sense and a large view of truth are rare gifts ; whereas all men are bound to be devout, and most men busy themselves in arguments and inferences.

Now let me apply what I have been saying to the teaching of the Church on the subject of the Blessed Virgin. I have to recur to a subject of so sacred a nature, that, writing as I am for publication, I need the apology of my purpose for venturing to pursue it. I say then, when once we have mastered the idea, that

Mary bore, suckled, and handled the Eternal in the form of a child, what limit is conceivable to the rush and flood of thoughts which such a doctrine involves? What awe and surprise must attend upon the knowledge, that a creature has been brought so close to the Divine Essence? It was the creation of a new idea and of a new sympathy, of a new faith and worship, when the holy Apostles announced that God had become incarnate; then a supreme love and devotion to Him became possible, which seemed hopeless before that revelation. This was the first consequence of their preaching. But, besides this, a second range of thoughts was opened on mankind, unknown before, and unlike any other, as soon as it was understood that that Incarnate God had a mother. The second idea is perfectly distinct from the former, and does not interfere with it. He is God made low, she is a woman made high. I scarcely like to use a familiar illustration on the subject of the Blessed Virgin's dignity among created beings, but it will serve to explain what I mean, when I ask you to consider the difference of feeling, with which we read the respective histories of Maria Theresa and the Maid of Orleans; or with which the middle and lower classes of a nation regard a first minister of the day who has come of an aristocratic house, and one who has risen from the ranks. May God's mercy keep me from the shadow of a thought, dimming the purity or blunting the keenness of that love of Him, which is our sole happiness and our sole salvation! But surely when He became man, He brought home to us His incommunicable attributes

with a distinctiveness, which precludes the possibility
of our lowering Him merely by our exalting a creature.
He alone has an entrance into our soul, reads our
secret thoughts, speaks to our heart, applies to us
spiritual pardon and strength. On Him we solely depend. He alone is our inward life; He not only
regenerates us, but (to use the words appropriated to a
higher mystery) *semper gignit;* He is ever renewing
our new birth and our heavenly sonship. In this
sense He may be called, as in nature, so in grace, our
real Father. Mary is only our mother by divine appoint-
ment, given us from the Cross; her presence is above,
not on earth; her office is external, not within us. Her
name is not heard in the administration of the Sacraments. Her work is not one of ministration towards
us; her power is indirect. It is her prayers that avail,
and her prayers are effectual by the *fiat* of Him who is
our all in all. Nor need she hear us by any innate
power, or any personal gift; but by His manifestation
to her of the prayers which we make to her. When
Moses was on the Mount, the Almighty told him of
the idolatry of his people at the foot of it, in order that
he might intercede for them; and thus it is the Divine
Presence which is the intermediating Power by which
we reach her and she reaches us.

Woe is me, if even by a breath I sully these ineffable
truths! but still, without prejudice to them, there is,
I say, another range of thought quite distinct from
them, incommensurate with them, of which the Blessed
Virgin is the centre. If we placed our Lord in that

centre, we should only be dragging Him from His throne, and making Him an Arian kind of a God; that is, no God at all. He who charges us with making Mary a divinity, is thereby denying the divinity of Jesus. Such a man does not know what divinity is. Our Lord cannot pray for us, as a creature prays, as Mary prays; He cannot inspire those feelings which a creature inspires. To her belongs, as being a creature, a natural claim on our sympathy and familiarity, in that she is nothing else than our fellow. She is our pride,—in the poet's words, "Our tainted nature's solitary boast". We look to her without any fear, any remorse, any consciousness that she is able to read us, judge us, punish us. Our heart yearns towards that pure Virgin, that gentle Mother, and our congratulations follow her, as she rises from Nazareth and Ephesus, through the choirs of angels, to her throne on high, so weak, yet so strong; so delicate, yet so glorious; so modest and yet so mighty. She has sketched for us her own portrait in the Magnificat. "He hath regarded the low estate of His hand-maid; for, behold, from henceforth all generations shall call me blessed. He hath put down the mighty from their seat; and hath exalted the humble. He hath filled the hungry with good things, and the rich he hath sent empty away." I recollect the strange emotion which took by surprise men and women, young and old, when, at the Coronation of our present Queen, they gazed on the figure of one so like a child, so small, so tender, so shrinking, who had been exalted to so great an inherit-

ance and so vast a rule, who was such a contrast in
her own person to the solemn pageant which centred
in her. Could it be otherwise with the spectators, if
they had human affection? And did not the All-wise
know the human heart when He took to Himself a
Mother? did He not anticipate our emotion at the
sight of such an exaltation in one so simple and so
lowly? If He had not meant her to exert that wonderful influence in His Church, which she has in the event
exerted, I will use a bold word, He it is who has perverted us. If she is not to attract our homage, why
did He make her solitary in her greatness amid His
vast creation? If it be idolatry in us to let our
affections respond to our faith, He would not have
made her what she is, or He would not have told us
that He had so made her; but, far from this, He has
sent His Prophet to announce to us, "A Virgin shall
conceive and bear a Son, and they shall call His name
Emmanuel," and we have the same warrant for hailing
her as God's Mother, as we have for adoring Him as
God.

Christianity is eminently an objective religion. For
the most part it tells us of persons and facts in simple
words, and leaves that announcement to produce its
effect on such hearts as are prepared to receive it. This
at least is its general character; and Butler recognizes
it as such in his Analogy, when speaking of the Second
and Third Persons of the Holy Trinity:—"The internal
worship," he says, "to the Son and Holy Ghost is no
farther matter of pure revealed command than as

the relations they stand in to us are matters of pure
revelation; for the relations being known, the obligations to such internal worship are *obligations of reason
arising out of those relations themselves.*"⁶   It is in this
way that the revealed doctrine of the Incarnation
exerted a stronger and a broader influence on Christians,
as they more and more apprehended and mastered its
meaning and its bearings.   It is contained in the brief
and simple declaration of St. John, "The Word was
made flesh;" but it required century after century to
spread it out in its fulness, and to imprint it energetically on the worship and practice of the Catholic people
as well as on their faith.   Athanasius was the first and
the great teacher of it.   He collected together the inspired notices scattered through David, Isaias, St. Paul,
and St. John, and he engraved indelibly upon the imaginations of the faithful, as had never been before, that
man is God, and God is man, that in Mary they meet,
and that in this sense Mary is the centre of all things.
He added nothing to what was known before, nothing
to the popular and zealous faith that her Son was God;
he has left behind him in his works no such definite
passages about her as those of St. Irenæus or St. Epiphanius; but he brought the circumstances of the
Incarnation home to men's minds, by the multiform
evolutions of his analysis, and thereby secured it to us
for ever from perversion.   Still, however, there was
much to be done; we have no proof that Athanasius

---

⁶ Vid. Essay on Doctr. Dev., p. 50.

himself had any special devotion to the Blessed Virgin; but he laid the foundations on which that devotion was to rest, and thus noiselessly and without strife, as the first Temple was built in the Holy City, she grew up into her inheritance, and was "established in Sion and her power was in Jerusalem."

§ 5.—*Anglican Misconceptions and Catholic Excesses in
Devotion to the Blessed Virgin.*

Such was the origin of that august *cultus* which has
been paid to the Blessed Mary for so many centuries in
the East and in the West. That in times and places it
has fallen into abuse, that it has even become a superstition, I do not care to deny; for, as I have said above,
the same process which brings to maturity carries on to
decay, and things that do not admit of abuse have very
little life in them. This of course does not excuse such
excesses, or justify us in making light of them, when
they occur. I have no intention of doing so as regards
the particular instances which you bring against us,
though but a few words will suffice for what I need
say about them :—before doing so, however, I am
obliged to make three or four introductory remarks in
explanation.

1. I have almost anticipated my first remark already.
It is this : that the height of our offending in our devotion to the Blessed Virgin would not look so great in
your Volume as it does, had you not deliberately placed
yourself on lower ground than your own feelings towards her would have spontaneously prompted you to
take. I have no doubt you had some good reason for

adopting this course, but I do not know it; what I do know is, that, for the Fathers' sake who so exalt her, you really do love and venerate her, though you do not evidence it in your book. I am glad then in this place to insist on a fact which will lead those among us, who know you not, to love you from their love of her, in spite of what you refuse to give her; and lead Anglicans, on the other hand, who do know you, to think better of us, who refuse her nothing, when they reflect that, if you come short of us, you do not actually go against us in your devotion to her.

2. As you revere the Fathers, so you revere the Greek Church ; and here again we have a witness on our behalf, of which you must be aware as fully as we are, and of which you must really mean to give us the benefit. In proportion as the Greek ritual is known to the religious public, that knowledge will take off the edge of the surprise of Anglicans at the sight of our devotions to our Lady. It must weigh with them, when they discover that we can enlist on our side in this controversy those "seventy millions" (I think they do so consider them) of Orientals, who are separated from our communion. Is it not a very pregnant fact, that the Eastern Churches, so independent of us, so long separated from the West, so jealous for Antiquity, should even surpass us in their exaltation of the Blessed Virgin? That they go further than we do is sometimes denied, on the ground that the Western devotion towards her is brought out into system, and the Eastern is not; yet this only means really, that the Latins have more mental activity, more strength of intellect, less of routine, less

of mechanical worship among them, than the Greeks.
We are able, better than they, to give an account of
what we do ; and we seem to be more extreme. merely
because we are more definite.   But, after all, what have
the Latins done so bold, as that substitution of the
name of Mary for the Name of Jesus at the end of the
collects and petitions in the Breviary, nay, in the Ritual
and Liturgy ?   Not merely in local or popular, and in
semi-authorized devotions, which are the kind of sources
that supply you with your matter of accusation against
us, but in the formal prayers of the Greek Eucharistic
Service, petitions are offered, not in "the name of Jesus
Christ," but in that "of the Theotocos."   Such a phenomenon, in such a quarter, I think ought to make
Anglicans merciful towards those writers among ourselves, who have been excessive in singing the praises of
the Deipara.   To make a rule of substituting Mary with
all Saints for Jesus in the public service, has more
"Mariolatry" in it, than to alter the Te Deum to her
honour in private devotion.[7]

3. And thus I am brought to a third remark, supple-
mental to your accusation of us.   Two large views, as I
have said above, are opened upon our devotional thoughts
in Christianity ; the one centering in the Son of Mary,
the other in the Mother of Jesus.   Neither need obscure
the other ; and in the Catholic Church, as a matter of
fact, neither does.   I wish you had either frankly
allowed this in your Volume, or proved the contrary.   I
wish, when you report that "a certain proportion" of

[7] Vid. Note **IV.** infr.

Catholics, "it has been ascertained by those who have inquired, do," in their devotions, " stop short in her," p. 107, that you had added your belief, that the case was far otherwise with the great bulk of Catholics. Might I not have expected such an avowal? May I not, without sensitiveness, be somewhat pained at the omission? From mere Protestants, indeed, I expect nothing better. They content themselves with saying that our devotions to our Lady *must necessarily* throw our Lord into the shade; and thereby they relieve themselves of a great deal of trouble. Then they catch at any stray fact which countenances or seems to countenance their prejudice. Now I say plainly, I never will defend or screen any one from your just rebuke, who, through false devotion to Mary, forgets Jesus. But I should like the fact to be proved first; I cannot hastily admit it. There is this broad fact the other way ;— that, if we look through Europe, we shall find, on the whole, that just those nations and countries have lost their faith in the divinity of Christ, who have given up devotion to His Mother, and that those on the other hand, who had been foremost in her honour, have retained their orthodoxy. Contrast, for instance, the Calvinists with the Greeks, or France with the North of Germany, or the Protestant and Catholic communions in Ireland. As to England, it is scarcely doubtful what would be the state of its Established Church, if the Liturgy and Articles were not an integral part of its Establishment; and, when men bring so grave a charge against us, as is implied in your Volume, they cannot be surprised if we in turn say hard things of Anglicanism.[8] In the Catholic Church Mary has shown herself, not the rival, but the minister of her Son; she has protected Him, as in His infancy, so in the whole history of the Religion. There is then a plain historical truth in Dr. Faber's words, which you quote to condemn, "Jesus is obscured, because Mary is kept in the back-ground."

This truth, exemplified in history, might also be abundantly illustrated, did my space admit, from the lives and writings of holy men in modern times. Two of them, St. Alfonso Liguori and the Blessed Paul of the Cross, for all their notorious devotion to the Mother, have shown their supreme love of her Divine Son, in the names which they have given to their respective Congregations, viz. that " of the Redeemer," and that "of the Cross and Passion." However, I will do no more than refer to an apposite passage in the Italian translation of the work of a French Jesuit, Fr. Nepveu, " Christian Thoughts for every Day in the Year," which

[8] I have spoken more on this subject in my Essay on Development, p. 438, "Nor does it avail to object, that, in this contrast of devotional exercises, the human is sure to supplant the Divine, from the infirmity of our nature; for, I repeat, the question is one of fact, whether it has done so. And next, it must be asked, *whether the character of Pro-testant devotion towards our Lord, has been that of worship at all;* and not rather such as we pay to an excellent human being. . . . Carnal minds will ever create a carnal worship for themselves; and to forbid them the service of the saints, will have no tendency to teach them the worship of God. Moreover, . . . great and constant as is the devotion which the Catholic pays to St. Mary, it has a special pro-vince, and *has far more connexion with the public services and the festive aspect of Christianity,* and with certain extraordinary offices which she holds, *than with what is strictly personal and primary* in religion." Our late Cardinal, on my reception, singled out to me this last sentence, for the expression of his especial approbation.

was recommended to the friend who went with me to
Rome, by the same Jesuit Father there, with whom, as
I have already said, I stood myself in such intimate
relations; I believe it is a fair specimen of the teaching
of our spiritual books.

"The love of Jesus Christ is the most sure pledge of
our future happiness, and the most infallible token of our
predestination. Mercy towards the poor, devotion to
the Holy Virgin, are very sensible tokens of predestination; nevertheless they are not absolutely infallible;
but one cannot have a sincere and constant love of Jesus
Christ, without being predestinated. . . . The destroying angel, which bereaved the houses of the Egyptians
of their first-born, had respect to all the houses which
were marked with the blood of the Lamb."

And it is also exemplified, as I verily believe, not
only in formal and distinctive Confessions, not only in
books intended for the educated class, but also in the
personal religion of the Catholic populations. When
strangers are so unfavourably impressed with us, because
they see Images of our Lady in our churches, and
crowds flocking about her, they forget that there is a
Presence within the sacred walls, infinitely more awful,
which claims and obtains from us a worship transcen-
dently different from any devotion we pay to her. That
devotion to her might indeed tend to idolatry, if it
were encouraged in Protestant churches, where there is
nothing higher than it to attract the worshipper: but
all the images that a Catholic church ever contained, all
the Crucifixes at its Altars brought together, do not so
affect its frequenters, as the lamp which betokens the

presence or absence there of the Blessed Sacrament. Is
not this so certain, so notorious, that on some occasions
it has been even brought as a charge against us, that
we are irreverent in church, when what seemed to the
objector to be irreverence was but the necessary change
of feeling, which came over those who were in it, on their
knowing that their Lord was no longer there, but away?

The Mass again conveys to us the same lesson of the
sovereignty of the Incarnate Son; it is a return to
Calvary, and Mary is scarcely named in it. Hostile
visitors enter our churches on Sunday at midday, the
time of the Anglican Service. They are surprised to see
the High Mass perhaps poorly attended, and a body of
worshippers leaving the music and the mixed multitude
who may be lazily fulfilling their obligation, for the
silent or the informal devotions which are offered at an
Image of the blessed Virgin. They may be tempted,
with one of your informants, to call such a temple, not
a "Jesus church," but a "Mary church". But, if
they understood our ways, they would know that we
begin the day with our Lord and then go on to His
Mother. It is early in the morning that religious
persons go to Mass and Communion. The High Mass,
on the other hand, is the festive celebration of the day,
not the special devotional service; nor is there any
reason why those who have been at low Mass already,
should not at that hour proceed to ask the intercession
of the Blessed Virgin for themselves and all that is
dear to them.

Communion, again, which is given in the morning,
is a solemn unequivocal act of faith in the Incarnate

God, if any can be such; and the most gracious of admonitions, did we need one. of His sovereign and sole right to possess us. I knew a lady, who on her death-bed was visited by an excellent Protestant friend. The latter, with great tenderness for her soul's welfare, asked her whether her prayers to the Blessed Virgin did not, at that awful hour, lead to forgetfulness of her Saviour. "Forget Him?" she replied with surprise, "Why, He was just now here." She had been receiving Him in communion. When then, my dear Pusey, you read anything extravagant in praise of our Lady, is it not charitable to ask, even while you condemn it in itself, did the author write nothing else? Had he written on the Blessed Sacrament? had he given up "all for Jesus?" I recollect some lines, the happiest, I think, which that author wrote, which bring out strikingly the reciprocity. which I am dwelling on, of the respective devotions to Mother and Son :—

> " But scornful men have coldly said
>   Thy love was leading me from God ,
>   And yet in this I did but tread
>   The very path my Saviour trod.
>
> " They know but little of thy worth
>   Who speak these heartless words to me;
>   For what did Jesus love on earth
>   One half so tenderly as thee ?
>
> "Get me the grace to love thee more ;
>   Jesus will give, if thou wilt plead ;
>   And, Mother, when life's cares are o'er,
>   Oh, I shall love thee then indeed.
>
> " Jesus, when His three hours were run,
>   Bequeath'd thee from the Cross to me ,
>   And oh! how can I love thy Son,
>   Sweet Mother, if I love not thee."

4. Thus we are brought from the consideration of the sentiments themselves, of which you complain, to the persons who wrote, and the places where they wrote them. I wish you had been led, in this part of your work, to that sort of careful labour which you have employed in so masterly a way in your investigation of the circumstances of the definition of the Immaculate Conception. In the latter case you have catalogued the bishops who wrote to the Holy See, and analyzed their answers. Had you in like manner discriminated and located the Marian writers as you call them, and observed the times, places, and circumstances of their works, I think, they would not, when brought together, have had their present startling effect on the reader. As it is, they inflict a vague alarm upon the mind, as when one hears a noise, and does not know whence it comes and what it means. Some of your authors, I know are Saints; all, I suppose, are spiritual writers and holy men; but the majority are of no great celebrity, even if they have any kind of weight. Suarez has no business among them at all, for, when he says that no one is saved without the Blessed Virgin, he is speaking not of devotion to her, but of her intercession. The greatest name is St. Alfonso Liguori; but it never surprises me to read anything extraordinary in the devotions of a saint. Such men are on a level very different from our own, and we cannot understand them. I hold this to be an important canon in the Lives of the Saints, according to the words of the Apostle, "The spiritual man judges all things, and he himself is judged of no one." But we

H

may refrain from judging, without proceeding to imitate. I hope it is not disrespectful to so great a servant of God to say, that I never have read his Glories of Mary; but here I am speaking generally of all Saints, whether I know them or not;—and I say that they are beyond us, and that we must use them as patterns, not as copies. As to his practical directions, St. Alfonso wrote them for Neapolitans, whom he knew, and we do not know. Other writers whom you quote, as De Salazar, are too ruthlessly logical to be safe or pleasant guides in the delicate matters of devotion. As to De Montford and Oswald, I never even met with their names, till I saw them in your book; the bulk of our laity, not to say of our clergy, perhaps know them little better than I do. Nor did I know till I learnt it from your Volume, that there were two Bernardines. St. Bernardine of Sienna, I knew of course, and knew too that he had a burning love for our Lord. But about the other, "Bernardine de Bustis," I was quite at fault. I find from the Protestant Cave, that he, as well as his namesake, made himself also conspicuous for his zeal for the Holy Name, which is much to the point here. "With such devotion was he carried away," says Cave, "for the bare Name of Jesus, (which, by a new device of Bernardine of Sienna, had lately begun to receive divine honours,) that he was urgent with Innocent VIII. to assign it a day and rite in the Calendar."

One thing, however, is clear about all these writers; that not one of them is an Englishman. I have gone through your book, and do not find one English name among the various authors to whom you refer, except of course the name of the author whose lines I have been quoting, and who, great as are his merits, cannot, for the reasons I have given in the opening of my Letter[9] be considered a representative of English Catholic devotion. Whatever these writers may have said or not said, whatever they may have said harshly, and whatever capable of fair explanation, still they are foreigners; we are not answerable for their particular devotions; and as to themselves, I am glad to be able to quote the beautiful words which you use about them in your letter to the *Weekly Register* of November 25th last. "I do not presume," you say, "to prescribe to Italians or Spaniards, what they shall hold, or how they shall express their pious opinions; and least of all did I think of imputing to any of the writers whom I quoted that they took from our Lord any of the love which they gave to His Mother." In these last words too you have supplied one of the omissions in your Volume which I noticed above.

5. Now then we come to England itself, which after all, in the matter of devotion, alone concerns you and me; for though doctrine is one and the same everywhere, devotions, as I have already said, are matters of the particular time and the particular country. I suppose we owe it to the national good sense, that English Catholics have been protected from the extravagances which are elsewhere to be found. And we owe it also to the wisdom and moderation of the Holy See, which, in giving us the pattern for our devotion, as well as the

---

[9] Supra, p. 22.

rule of our faith, has never indulged in those curiosities
of thought which are both so attractive to undisciplined
imaginations and so dangerous to grovelling hearts.
In the case of our own common people I think such a
forced style of devotion would be simply unintelligible;
as to the educated, I doubt whether it can have more
than an occasional or temporary influence. If the Catholic faith spreads in England, these peculiarities will not
spread with it. There is a healthy devotion to the
Blessed Mary, and there is an artificial; it is possible to
love her as a Mother, to honour her as a Virgin, to seek
her as a Patron, and to exalt her as a Queen, without
any injury to solid piety and Christian good sense:—I
cannot help calling this the English style. I wonder
whether you find anything to displease you in the
Garden of the Soul, the Key of Heaven, the Vade
Mecum, the Golden Manual, or the Crown of Jesus.
These are the books to which Anglicans ought to
appeal, who would be fair to us in this matter. I do
not observe anything in them which goes beyond the
teaching of the Fathers, except so far as devotion goes
beyond doctrine.

There is one collection of Devotions besides, of the
highest authority, which has been introduced from
abroad of late years. It consists of prayers of very
various kinds which have been indulgenced by the
Popes; and it commonly goes by the name of the
Raccolta. As that word suggests, the language of
many of the prayers is Italian, while others are in Latin.
This circumstance is unfavourable to a translation,
which. however skilful, must ever savour of the words

and idioms of the original; but, passing over this necessary disadvantage, I consider there is hardly a clause in
the goodsized volume in question which even the sensitiveness of English Catholicism would wish changed.
Its anxious observance of doctrinal exactness is almost
a fault. It seems afraid of using the words " give me,"
" make me," in its addresses to the Blessed Virgin,
which are as natural to adopt in speaking to her, as in
addressing a parent or friend. Surely we do not
disparage Divine Providence when we say that we are
indebted to our parents for our life, or when we ask their
blessing; we do not show any atheistical leaning,
because we say that a man's recovery must be left to
nature, or that nature supplies brute animals with
instincts. In like manner it seems to me a simple purism,
to insist upon minute accuracy of expression in devotional
and popular writings. However, the *Raccolta*, as coming
from responsible authority, for the most part observes it.
It commonly uses the phrases " gain for us by thy
prayers," " obtain for us," " pray to Jesus for me,"
" speak for me, Mary," " carry thou our prayers," " ask
for us grace,' " intercede for the people of God," and
the like, marking thereby with great emphasis that she
is nothing more than an Advocate, and not a source of
mercy. Nor do I recollect in this book more than one
or two ideas to which you would be likely to raise an
objection. The strongest of these is found in the Novena
before her Nativity, in which, *apropos* of her Birth, we
pray that she " would come down again, and be reborn
spiritually in our souls;"—but it will occur to you that
St. Paul speaks of his wish to impart to his converts,

"not only the gospel, but his own soul;" and writing
to the Corinthians, he says he has "begotten them by
the gospel," and to Philemon, that he had "begotten
Onesimus, in his bonds;" whereas St. James, with
greater accuracy of expression, says "of His own will
hath God begotten us with the word of truth." Again,
we find the petitioner saying to the Blessed Mary, "In
thee I place all my hope;" but this is explained by
another passage, "Thou art my best hope after Jesus."
Again, we read elsewhere, "I would I had a greater
love for thee, since to love thee is a great mark of predestination;" but the prayer goes on, "Thy Son
deserves of us an immeasurable love; pray that I may
have this grace, a great love for Jesus," and further
on, "I covet no good of the earth, but to love my God
alone."

Then again, as to the lessons which our Catholics
receive, whether by catechising or instruction, you
would find nothing in our received manuals to which
you would not assent, I am quite sure. Again, as to
preaching, a standard book was drawn up three centuries ago, to supply matter for the purpose to the
parochial clergy. You incidentally mention, p. 153,
that the comment of Cornelius à Lapide on Scripture is
"a repertorium for sermons;" but I never heard of this
work being so used, nor indeed can it, because of its
size. The work provided for the purpose by the Church
is the "Catechism of the Council of Trent," and nothing
extreme about our Blessed Lady is propounded there.
On the whole I am sanguine that you will come to the
conclusion, that Anglicans may safely trust themselves

to us English Catholics, as regards any devotions to the
Blessed Virgin which might be required of them over
and above the rule of the Council of Trent.

6. And, now at length coming to the statements,
not English, but foreign, which offend you in works
written in her honour, I will allow that I like some
of those which you quote as little as you do. I will
frankly say that, when I read them in your volume,
they affected me with grief and almost anger; for they
seemed to me to ascribe to the Blessed Virgin a power
of " searching the reins and hearts," which is the attribute of God alone; and I said to myself, how can we
any longer prove our Lord's divinity from Scripture, if
those cardinal passages which invest Him with divine
prerogatives, after all invest Him with nothing beyond
what His Mother shares with Him? And how, again,
is there anything of incommunicable greatness in His
death and passion, if He who was alone in the garden,
alone upon the cross, alone in the resurrection, after all
is not alone, but shared His solitary work with His
Blessed Mother,—with her to whom, when He entered
on His ministry, He said for our instruction, not as
grudging her her proper glory, "Woman, what have I
to do with thee?" And then again, if I hate those
perverse sayings so much, how much more must she, in
proportion to her love of Him? and how do we show
our love for her, by wounding her in the very apple of
her eye? This I felt and feel; but then on the other
hand I have to observe that these strange words after
all are but few in number, out of the many passages
you cite; that most of them exemplify what I said

above about the difficulty of determining the exact
point where truth passes into error, and that they are
allowable in one sense or connection, though false in
another. Thus to say that prayer (and the Blessed
Virgin's prayer) is omnipotent, is a harsh expression
in every-day prose; but, if it is explained to mean that
there is nothing which prayer may not obtain from God,
it is nothing else than the very promise made us in
Scripture. Again, to say that Mary is the centre of all
being, sounds inflated and profane; yet after all it is
only one way, and a natural way, of saying that the
Creator and the creature met together, and became one
in her womb; and as such, I have used the expression
above. Again, it is at first sight a paradox to say that
"Jesus is obscured, because Mary is kept in the back-
ground;" yet there is a sense, as I have shown above,
in which it is a simple truth.

And so again certain statements may be true, under
circumstances and in a particular time and place, which
are abstractedly false; and hence it may be very unfair
in a controversialist to interpret by an English or a
modern rule, whatever may have been asserted by a
foreign or medieval author. To say, for instance, dogmatically, that no one can be saved without personal
devotion to the Blessed Virgin, would be an untenable
proposition; yet it might be true of this man or that,
or of this or that country at this or that date; and, if
that very statement has ever been made by any writer of
consideration (and this has to be ascertained), then
perhaps it was made precisely under these exceptional
circumstances. If an Italian preacher made it, I should

feel no disposition to doubt him, at least if he spoke of
Italian youths and Italian maidens.

Next I think you have not always made your quota-
tions with that consideration and kindness which is
your rule. At p. 106, you say, "It is commonly said
that, if any Roman Catholic acknowledges that 'it is
good and useful to pray to the saints,' he is not bound
himself to do so. Were the above teaching true, it
would be cruelty to say so; because, according to it,
he would be forfeiting what is morally necessary to his
salvation." But now, as to the fact, by whom is it
said that to pray to our Lady and the Saints is
necessary to salvation? The proposition of St. Alfonso
is, that "God gives no grace except through Mary;"
that is through her intercession. But intercession is
one thing, devotion is another. And Suarez says, "It
is the universal sentiment that the intercession of Mary
is not only useful, but also in a certain manner necessary;" but still it is the question of her intercession,
not of our invocation of her, not of devotion to her. If
it were so, no Protestant could be saved; if it were so,
there would be grave reasons for doubting of the salvation of St. Chrysostom or St. Athanasius, or of the
primitive Martyrs; nay, I should like to know whether
St. Augustine, in all his voluminous writings, invokes
her once. Our Lord died for those heathens who did
not know Him; and His Mother intercedes for those
Christians who do not know her; and she intercedes
according to His will, and, when He wills to save a
particular soul, she at once prays for it. I say, He
wills indeed according to her prayer, but then she prays

according to His will. Though then it is natural and prudent for those to have recourse to her, who from the Church's teaching know her power, yet it cannot be said that devotion to her is a *sine-quâ-non* of salvation. Some indeed of the authors, whom you quote, go further; they do speak of devotion; but even then, they do not enunciate the general proposition which I have been disallowing. For instance, they say, "It is morally impossible for those to be saved who *neglect* the devotion to the Blessed Virgin;" but a simple omission is one thing, and neglect another. "It is impossible for any to be saved who *turns away* from her," yes; but to "turn away" is to offer some positive disrespect or insult towards her, and that with sufficient knowledge; and I certainly think it would be a very grave act, if in a Catholic country (and of such the writers were speaking, for they knew of no other), with Ave-Marias sounding in the air, and images of the Madonna in every street and road, a Catholic broke off or gave up a practice that was universal, and in which he was brought up, and deliberately put her name out of his thoughts.

7. Though, then, common sense may determine for us, that the line of prudence and propriety has been certainly passed in the instance of certain statements about the Blessed Virgin, it is often not easy to convict them of definite error logically; and in such cases authority, if it attempt to act, would be in the position which so often happens in our courts of law, when the commission of an offence is morally certain, but the government prosecutor cannot find legal evidence suffi-

cient to insure conviction. I am not denying the right
of sacred Congregations, at their will, to act peremp-
torily, and without assigning reasons for the judgment
they pass upon writers; but, when they have found it
inexpedient to take this severe course, perhaps it may
happen from the circumstances of the case, that there
is no other that they can take, even if they would. It
is wiser then for the most part to leave these excesses
to the gradual operation of public opinion, that is, to
the opinion of educated and sober Catholics; and this
seems to me the healthiest way of putting them down.
Yet in matter of fact I believe the Holy See has interfered from time to time, when devotion seemed running
into superstition; and not so long ago. I recollect
hearing in Gregory the XVI.'s time, of books about
the Blessed Virgin, which had been suppressed by
authority; and in particular of a pictorial representation
of the Immaculate Conception which he had forbidden;
and of measures taken against the shocking notion that
the Blessed Mary is present in the Holy Eucharist, in
the sense in which our Lord is present; but I have no
means of verifying the information I then received.[1]

Nor have I time, any more than you have had, to
ascertain how far great theologians have made protests
against those various extravagances of which you so
rightly complain. Passages, however, from three well-
known Jesuit Fathers have opportunely come in my
way, and in one of them is introduced in confirmation,
the name of the great Gerson. They are Canisius,
Petavius, and Raynaudus; and as they speak very

[1] Vid. Note V. infr.

appositely, and you do not seem to know them, I will here make some extracts from them :—

(1.) Canisius :—

" We confess that in the *cultus* of Mary it has been, and is possible for corruptions to creep in ; and we have a more than ordinary desire that the Pastors of the Church should be carefully vigilant here, and give no place to Satan, whose characteristic office it has ever been, while men sleep, to sow the cockle amid the Lord's wheat. . . . For this purpose it is his wont gladly to avail himself of the aid of heretics, fanatics, and false Catholics, as may be seen in the instance of this *Marianus cultus.* This *cultus*, heretics, suborned by Satan, attack with hostility. . . . Thus too, certain mad heads are so demented by Satan, as to embrace superstitions and idolatries instead of the true *cultus*, and neglect altogether the true measures whether in respect to God or to Mary. Such indeed were the Collyridians of old. . . . Such that German herdsman a hundred years ago, who gave out publicly that he was a new prophet, and had had a vision of the Deipara, and told the people in her name to pay no more tributes and taxes to princes. . . . Moreover, how many Catholics does one see who, by great and shocking negligence, have neither care nor regard for her *cultus;* but, given to profane and secular objects, scarce once a year raise their earthly minds to sing her praises or to venerate her."—*De Mariâ Deiparâ*, p. 518.

(2.) Father Petau says, when discussing the teaching of the Fathers about the Blessed Virgin (*de Incarn.* xiv. 8) :—

" I will venture to give this advice to all who would be devout and panegyrical towards the Holy Virgin, viz., not to exceed in their piety and devotion to her, but to be content with true and solid praises, and to cast aside what is otherwise. This kind of idolatry, lurking, as St. Augustine says, nay implanted in human hearts, is greatly abhorrent from Theology, that is, from the gravity of heavenly wisdom, which never thinks or asserts anything, but what is measured by certain and accurate rules. What that rule should be, and what caution is to be used in our present subject, I will not determine of myself; but according to the mind of a most weighty and most learned theologian, John Gerson, who in one of his Epistles proposes certain canons, which he calls truths, by means of which are to be measured the assertions of theologians concerning the Incarnation. . . . By these truly golden precepts Gerson brings within bounds the immoderate licence of praising the Blessed Virgin, and restrains it within the measure of sober and healthy piety. And from these it is evident that that sort of reasoning is frivolous and nugatory, in which so many indulge, in order to assign any sort of grace they please, however unusual, to the Blessed Virgin. For they argue thus; ' Whatever the Son of God could bestow for the glory of His Mother, that it became Him in fact to furnish ;' or again, ' Whatever honours or ornaments He has poured out on other saints, those altogether hath He heaped upon His Mother;' whence they draw their chain of reasoning to their desired conclusion; a mode of argumentation which Gerson treats with contempt as captious and sophistical."

He adds, what of course we all should say, that, in thus speaking, he has no intention to curtail the liberty of pious persons in such meditations and conjectures, on the mysteries of faith, sacred histories, and the Scripture text, as are of the nature of comments, supplements, and the like.

(3.) Raynaud is an author, full of devotion, if any one is so, to the Blessed Virgin; yet in the work which he has composed in her honour (*Diptycha Mariana*), he says more than I can quote here, to the same purpose as Petau. I abridge some portions of his text :—

" Let this be taken for granted, that no praises of ours can come up to the praises due to the Virgin Mother. But we must not make up for our inability to reach her true praise, by a supply of lying embellishment and false honours. For there are some whose affection for religious objects is so imprudent and lawless, that they transgress the due limits even towards the saints. This Origen has excellently observed upon in the case of the Baptist, for very many, instead of observing the measure of charity, considered whether he might not be the Christ," p. 9. . . . "St. Anselm, the first, or one of the first champions of the public celebration of the Blessed Virgin's Immaculate Conception, says, *de Excell. Virg.*, that the Church considers it indecent, that anything that admits of doubt should be said in her praise, when the things which are certainly true of her supply such large materials for laudation. It is right so to interpret St. Epiphanius also, when he says that human tongues should not pronounce anything lightly of the Deipara; and who is more justly to be charged with speaking lightly of the most Holy Mother of God, than he, who, as if what is certain and evident did not suffice for her full investiture, is wiser than the aged, and obtrudes on us the toadstools of his own mind, and devotions unheard of by those Holy Fathers who loved her best? Plainly, as St. Anselm says, that she is the Mother of God, this by itself exceeds every elevation which can be named or imagined, short of God. About so sublime a majesty we should not speak hastily from prurience of wit, or flimsy pretext of promoting piety; but with great maturity of thought; and whenever the maxims of the Church and the oracles of faith do not suffice, then not without the suffrages of the Doctors. . . . Those who are subject to this prurience of innova-tion, do not perceive how broad is the difference between subjects of human science, and heavenly things. All novelty concerning the objects of our faith is to be put far away; except so far as by diligent investigation of God's Word, written and unwritten, and a well-founded inference from what is thence to be elicited, something is brought to light which though already indeed there, has not hitherto been recognized. The innovations which we condemn are those which rest neither on the written nor unwritten Word, nor on conclusions from it, nor on the judgment of ancient sages, nor sufficient basis of reason, but on the sole colour and pretext of doing more honour to the Deipara," p. 10.

In another portion of the same work, he speaks in particular of one of those imaginations to which you especially refer, and for which, without strict necessity (as it seems to me) you allege the authority of à Lapide.

"Nor is that honour of the Deipara to be offered, viz. that the elements of the body of Christ, which the Blessed Virgin supplied to it, remain perpetually unaltered in Christ, and thereby are found also in the Eucharist. . . . This solicitude for the Virgin's glory must, I consider, be discarded; since, if rightly considered, it involves an injury towards Christ, and such honour the Virgin loveth not. And first, dismissing philosophical bagatelles about the animation of blood, milk, &c., who can endure the proposition that a good portion of the substance of Christ in the Eucharist should be worshipped with a *cultus* less than *latria*? viz. by the inferior *cultus* of *hyperdulia*? The preferable class of theologians contend that not even the humanity of Christ, is to be materially abstracted from the Word of God, and worshipped by itself; how then shall we introduce a *cultus* of the Deipara in Christ, which is inferior to the *cultus* proper to Him? How is this other than a casting down of the substance of Christ from His Royal Throne, and a degradation of it to some inferior sitting place? It is nothing to the purpose to refer to such Fathers, as say that the flesh of Christ is the flesh of Mary, for they speak of its origin. What will hinder, if this doctrine be admitted, our also admitting that there is something in Christ which is detestable? for, as the first elements of a body which were communicated by the Virgin to Christ, have (as these authors say) remained perpetually in Christ, so the same *materia*, at least in part, which belonged originally to the ancestors of Christ, came down to the Virgin from her father, unchanged, and taken from her grandfather, and so on.

And thus, since it is not unlikely that some of these ancestors were reprobate, there would now be something actually in Christ, which had belonged to a reprobate, and worthy of detestation."—p. 237.

8. After such explanation, and with such authorities, to clear my path, I put away from me, as you would wish, without any hesitation, as matters in which my heart and reason have no part, (when taken in their literal and absolute sense, as any Protestant would naturally take them, and as the writers doubtless did not use them), such sentences, and phrases, as these :— that the mercy of Mary is infinite ; that God has resigned into her hands His omnipotence ; that it is safer to seek her than to seek her Son ; that the Blessed Virgin is superior to God ; that our Lord is subject to her command ; that His present disposition towards sinners, as well as His Father's, is to reject them, while the Blessed Mary takes His place as an Advocate with Father and Son ; that the Saints are more ready to intercede with Jesus than Jesus with the Father ; that Mary is the only refuge of those with whom God is angry ; that Mary alone can obtain a Protestant's conversion ; that it would have sufficed for the salvation of men if our Lord had died, not in order to obey His Father, but to defer to the decree of His Mother ; that she rivals our Lord in being God's daughter, not by adoption, but by a kind of nature ; that Christ fulfilled the office of Saviour by imitating her virtues ; that, as the Incarnate God bore the image of His Father, so He bore the image of His Mother ; that

I

redemption derived from Christ indeed its sufficiency, but
from Mary its beauty and loveliness; that, as we are
clothed with the merits of Christ, so we are clothed with
the merits of Mary; that, as He is Priest, in a like sense
is she Priestess; that His Body and Blood in the Eucharist are truly hers and appertain to her; that as He is
present and received therein, so is she present and received therein; that Priests are ministers as of Christ,
so of Mary; that elect souls are born of God and Mary;
that the Holy Ghost brings into fruitfulness His action
by her, producing in her and by her Jesus Christ in His
members; that the kingdom of God in our souls, as our
Lord speaks, is really the kingdom of Mary in the soul;
that she and the Holy Ghost produce in the soul extraordinary things; and that when the Holy Ghost finds
Mary in a soul He flies there.

Sentiments such as these I freely surrender to your
animadversion; I never knew of them till I read your
book, nor, as I think, do the vast majority of English
Catholics know them. They seem to me like a bad
dream. I could not have conceived them to be said.
I know not to what authority to go for them, to Scripture, or to the Fathers, or to the decrees of Councils,
or to the consent of schools, or to the tradition of the
faithful, or to the Holy See, or to Reason. They defy
all the *loci theologici*. There is nothing of them in the
Missal, in the Roman Catechism, in the Roman *Raccolta*,
in the Imitation of Christ, in Gother, Challoner, Milner
or Wiseman, as far as I am aware. They do but scare
and confuse me. I should not be holier, more spiritual,
more sure of perseverance, if I twisted my moral being

into the reception of them; I should but be guilty of
fulsome frigid flattery towards the most upright and
noble of God's creatures, if I professed them,—and of
stupid flattery too; for it would be like the compliment
of painting up a young and beautiful princess with the
brow of a Plato and the muscle of an Achilles. And I
should expect her to tell one of her people in waiting
to turn me off her service without warning. Whether
thus to feel be the *scandalum parvulorum* in my case,
or the *scandalum Pharisæorum*, I leave others to decide;
but I will say plainly that I had rather believe (which is
impossible) that there is no God at all, than that Mary
is greater than God. I will have nothing to do with
statements, which can only be explained, by being
explained away. I do not, however, speak of these
statements, as they are found in their authors, for I
know nothing of the originals, and cannot believe that
they have meant what you say; but I take them as
they lie in your pages. Were any of them the sayings
of Saints in ecstasy, I should know they had a good
meaning; still I should not repeat them myself; but
I am looking at them, not as spoken by the tongues of
Angels, but according to that literal sense which they
bear in the mouths of English men and English women.
And, as spoken by man to man, in England, in the
nineteenth century, I consider them calculated to prejudice inquirers, to frighten the unlearned, to unsettle
consciences, to provoke blasphemy, and to work the loss
of souls.

9. And now, after having said so much as this, bear
with me, my dear Friend, if I end with an expostula-

I 2

tion. Have you not been touching us on a very tender
point in a very rude way? is it not the effect of what you
have said to expose her to scorn and obloquy, who is
dearer to us than any other creature? Have you even
hinted that our love for her is anything else than an
abuse? Have you thrown her one kind word yourself
all through your book? I trust so, but I have not
lighted upon one. And yet I know you love her well.
Can you wonder, then, — can I complain much, much as
I grieve,—that men should utterly misconceive of you,
and are blind to the fact that you have put the whole
argument between you and us on a new footing ; and
that, whereas it was said twenty-five years ago in
the British Critic, "Till Rome ceases to be what
practically she is, union is *impossible* between her and
England," you declare on the contrary, "Union *is
possible*, as soon as Italy and England, having the same
faith and the same centre of unity, are allowed to hold
severally their own theological opinions"? They have
not done you justice here ; because in truth, the honour
of our Lady is dearer to them than the conversion of
England.

Take a parallel case, and consider how you would
decide it yourself. Supposing an opponent of a doctrine
for which you so earnestly contend, the eternity of punishment, instead of meeting you with direct arguments
against it, heaped together a number of extravagant
descriptions of the place, mode, and circumstances of its
infliction, quoted Tertullian as a witness for the primitive
Fathers, and the Covenanters and Ranters for these last
centuries ; brought passages from the Inferno of Dante,

and from the Sermons of Wesley and Whitfield; nay, supposing he confined himself to the chapter on the subject in the work, which has the sanction of Jeremy Taylor, on "The State of Man," or to his Sermon on "The Foolish Exchange," or to particular passages in Leighton, South, Beveridge, and Barrow, would you think this a fair and becoming method of reasoning? and if he avowed that he should ever consider the Anglican Church committed to all these accessories of the doctrine, till its authorities formally denounced Beveridge, and Whitfield, and a hundred others, would you think this an equitable determination, or the procedure of a theologian?

So far concerning the Blessed Virgin; the chief but not the only subject of your Volume. And now, when I could wish to proceed,[2] she seems to stop all controversy, for the Feast of her Immaculate Conception is upon us; and close upon its Octave, which is kept with special solemnities in the Churches of this town, come the great Antiphons, the heralds of Christmas. That joyful season, joyful for all of us, while it centres in Him who then came on earth, also brings before us in peculiar prominence that Virgin Mother, who bore and nursed Him. Here she is not in the background, as at Easter-tide, but she brings Him to us in her arms. Two great Festivals, dedicated to her honour, to-morrow's and the Purification, mark out and keep the

[2] The sequel to this letter never was written. Vid. supr., note p. 17.

ground, and, like the towers of David, open the way to and fro, for the high holiday season of the Prince of Peace. And all along it her image is upon it, such as we see it in the typical representation of the Catacombs. May the sacred influences of this tide bring us all together in unity! May it destroy all bitterness on your side and ours! May it quench all jealous, sour, proud, fierce antagonism on our side; and dissipate all captious, carping, fastidious refinements of reasoning on yours! May that bright and gentle Lady, the Blessed Virgin Mary, overcome you with her sweetness, and revenge herself on her foes by interceding effectually for their conversion!

I am,

Yours, most affectionately,

JOHN H. NEWMAN.

THE ORATORY, BIRMINGHAM,
Dec. 7, 1865.

NOTES.

NOTE I. Page 33.

TESTIMONIES OF THE FATHERS TO THE DOCTRINE THAT
MARY IS THE SECOND EVE.

St. Justin :—Υἱὸν Θεοῦ γεγραμμένον αὐτὸν ἐν τοῖς
ἀπομνημονεύμασι τῶν ἀποστόλων αὐτοῦ ἔχοντες, καὶ υἱὸν
αὐτὸν λέγοντες, νενοήκαμεν, καὶ πρὸ πάντων ποιημάτων
ἀπὸ τοῦ πατρὸς δυνάμει αὐτοῦ καὶ βουλῇ προελθόντα
. . . . καὶ διὰ τῆς παρθένου ἄνθρωπος [ον] γεγονέναι, ἵνα
καὶ δι' ἧς ὁδοῦ ἡ ἀπὸ τοῦ ὄφεως παρακοὴ τὴν ἀρχὴν ἔλαβε,
καὶ διὰ ταύτης τῆς ὁδοῦ καὶ κατάλυσιν λάβῃ· παρθένος
γὰρ οὖσα Εὔα καὶ ἄφθορος τὸν λόγον τὸν ἀπὸ τοῦ ὄφεως
συλλαβοῦσα, παρακοὴν καὶ θάνατον ἔτεκε· πίστιν δὲ καὶ
χαρὰν λαβοῦσα Μαρία ἡ παρθένος, εὐαγγελιζομένου αὐτῇ
Γαβριὴλ ἀγγέλου, ὅτι Πνεῦμα Κυρίου ἐπ' αὐτὴν ἐπελεύ-
σεται, &c. . . . ἀπεκρίνατο, Γένοιτό μοι κατὰ τὸ ῥῆμά
σου. — Tryph. 100.

2. Tertullian :—"Ne mihi vacet incursus nominis
Adæ, unde Christus Adam ab Apostolo dictus est, si
terreni non fuit census homo ejus? Sed et hic ratio
defendit, quod Deus imaginem et similitudinem suam a
diabolo captam æmula operatione recuperavit. In virginem enim adhuc Evam irrepserat verbum ædificatorium

mortis. In virginem æque introducendum erat Dei
verbum extructorium vitæ; ut quod per ejusmodi sexum
abierat in perditionem, per eundem sexum redigeretur
in salutem. Crediderat Eva serpenti; credidit Maria
Gabrieli; quod illa credendo deliquit, hæc credendo
delevit."—*De Carn. Chr.* 17.

3. St. Irenæus:—"Consequenter autem et Maria virgo
obediens invenitur, dicens, Ecce ancilla tua, Domine, fiat
mihi secundum verbum tuum. Eva vero inobediens:
non obedivit enim, adhuc quum esset virgo. Quemadmodum illa, virum quidem habens Adam, virgo tamen
adhuc existens (erant enim utrique nudi in Paradiso, et
non confundebantur, quoniam, paullo ante facti, non
intellectum habebant filiorum generationis; oportebat
enim illos primo adolescere, dehinc sic multiplicari),
inobediens facta, et sibi et universo generi humano causa
facta est mortis: sic et Maria, habens prædestinatum
virum, et tamen virgo, obediens, et sibi et universo
generi humano causa facta est salutis. Et propter hoc
Lex eam, quæ desponsata erat viro, licet virgo sit adhuc,
uxorem ejus, qui desponsaverat, vocat; eam quæ est à
Maria in Evam recirculationem significans: quia non
aliter quod colligatum est solveretur, nisi ipsæ com-
pagines alligationis reflectantur retrorsus; ut primæ
conjunctiones solvantur per secundas, secundæ rursus
liberent primas. Et evenit primam quidem compaginem
à secundâ colligatione solvere, secundam vero colliga-
tionem primæ solutionis habere locum. Et propter hoc
Dominus dicebat, primos quidem novissimos futuros, et
novissimos primos. Et propheta autem hoc idem signi-
ficat, dicens, 'Pro patribus nati sunt tibi filii.' 'Pri-

mogenitus' enim 'mortuorum' natus Dominus et in
sinum suum recipiens pristinos patres, regeneravit eos in
vitam Dei, ipse initium viventium factus, quoniam Adam
initium morientium factus est. Propter hoc et Lucas
initium generationis a Domino inchoans, in Adam retulit,
significans, quoniam non illi hunc, sed hic illos in Evan-
gelium vitæ regeneravit. Sic autem et Evæ inobedientiæ
nodus solutionem accepit per obedientiam Mariæ. Quod
enim alligavit virgo Eva per incredulitatem, hoc virgo
Maria solvit per fidem."—*S. Iren. contr. Hær.* iii. 22.

"Quemadmodum enim illa per Angeli sermonem
seducta est, ut effugeret Deum, prævaricata verbum
ejus; ita et hæc per Angelicum sermonem evangelizata
est, ut portaret Deum, obediens ejus verbo. Et si ea
inobedierat Deo; sed hæc suasa est obedire Deo, uti Virginis Evæ Virgo Maria fieret advocata. Et quemadmodum adstrictum est morti genus humanum per Virginem, salvatur [solvatur] per Virginem, æqua lance
disposita, virginalis inobedientia, per virginalem obedientiam."—*Ibid.* v. 19.

4. St. Cyril :—Διὰ παρθένου τῆς Εὔας ἦλθεν ὁ θάνατος,
ἔδει διὰ παρθένου, μᾶλλον δὲ ἐκ παρθένου, φανῆναι τὴν
ζωήν· ἵνα ὥσπερ ἐκείνην ὄφις ἠπάτησεν, οὕτω καὶ ταύτην
Γαβριὴλ εὐαγγελίσηται.—*Cat.* xii. 1.

5. St. Ephrem. :—"Per Evam nempe decora et
amabilis hominis gloria extincta est, quæ tamen rursus
per Mariam refloruit."—*Opp. Syr.* ii. p. 318.

"Initio protoparentum delicto in omnes homines
mors pertransiit; hodie vero per Mariam translati sumus
de morte ad vitam. Initio serpens, Evæ auribus occu-
patis, inde virus in totum corpus dilatavit; hodie Maria

ex auribus perpetuæ felicitatis assertorem excepit. Quod
ergo mortis fuit, simul et vitæ extitit instrumentum."—
iii. p. 607.

6. St. Epiphanius :—Αὐτὴ ἐστὶν ἡ παρὰ μὲν τῇ Εὔᾳ
σημαινομένη δι' αἰνίγματος λαβοῦσα τὸ καλεῖσθαι μήτηρ
ζωντων. . . . καὶ ἦν θαῦμα ὅτι μετὰ τὴν παράβασιν ταύτην
τὴν μεγάλην ἔσχεν ἐπωνυμίαν. καὶ κατὰ μὲν τὸ αἰσθητὸν
ἀπ' ἐκείνης τῆς Εὔας πᾶσα τῶν ἀνθρώπων ἡ γέννησις ἐπὶ
γῆς γεγέννηται· ὧδε δὲ ἀληθῶς ἀπὸ Μαρίας αὐτὴ ἡ ζωὴ
τῷ κόσμῳ γεγέννηται· ἵνα ζῶντα γεννήσῃ, καὶ γέννηται ἡ
Μαρία μήτηρ ζώντων· δι' αἰνίγματος οὖν ἡ Μαρία μήτηρ
ζώντων κέκληται . . . ἀλλὰ καὶ ἕτερον περὶ τούτων δια-
νοεῖσθαι ἐστι θαυμαστὸν, περὶ δὲ τῆς Εὔας καὶ τῆς Μαρίας.
ἡ μὲν γὰρ Εὔα πρόφασις γενέννηται θανάτου τοῖς ἀνθρώ-
ποις· . . . ἡ δὲ Μαρία πρόφασις ζωῆς . . . ἵνα ζωὴ ἀντὶ
θανάτου γέννηται, ἐκκλείσασα τὸν θάνατον τὸν ἐκ γυναικὸς
πάλιν ὁ διὰ γυναικὸς ἡμῖν ζωὴ γεγεννημένος.—*Hær.* 78. 18.

7. St. Jerome :—"Postquam vero Virgo concepit in
utero, et peperit nobis puerum . . . soluta maledictio
est. Mors per Evam, vita per Mariam."—*Ep.* 22. *ad
Eustochium,* 21.

8. St. Augustine :—"Huc accedit magnum sacra-
mentum, ut, quoniam per feminam nobis mors acciderat,
vita nobis per feminam nasceretur : ut de utrâque naturâ,
id est, femininâ et masculinâ, victus diabolus cruciaretur,
quoniam de ambarum subversione lætabatur, cui parum
fuerat ad pœnam si ambæ naturæ in nobis liberarentur,
nisi etiam perambas liberaremur".—*De Agone Christ.* 24.

9. St. Peter Chrysologus :—"Benedicta tu in mulie-
ribus. Quia in quibus Eva maledicta puniebat viscera ;
tunc in illis gaudet, honoratur, suspicitur Maria bene-

dicta. Et facta est vere nunc mater viventium per gratiam quæ mater extitit morientium per naturam. . . . Quantus sit Deus satis ignorat ille, qui hujus Virginis mentem non stupet, animum non miratur : pavet cœlum, tremunt Angeli, creatura non sustinet, natura non sufficit, et una puella sic Deum in sui pectoris capit, recipit, oblectat hospitio, ut pacem terris, cœlis glor'am, salutem perditis, vitam mortuis, terrenis cum cœlestibus parentelam, ipsius Dei cum carne commercium, pro ipsa domus exigat pensione, pro ipsius uteri mercede conquirat, et impleat illud Prophetæ : Ecce hæreditas Domini, filii merces fructus ventris. Sed jam se concludat sermo ut de partu Virginis, donante Deo, et indulgente tempore, gratius proloquamur."—*Serm.* 140.

10. St. Fulgentius :—" In primi hominis conjuge, nequitia diaboli seductam depravavit mentem : in secundi autem hominis matre, gratia Dei et mentem integram servavit, et carnem : menti contulit firmissimam fidem, carni abstulit omnino libidinem. Quoniam igitur miserabiliter pro peccato damnatus est homo, ideo sine peccato mirabiliter natus est Deus homo."—*Serm.* ii.

" Venite, virgines, ad virginem ; venite, concipientes, ad concipientem ; venite, parturientes, ad parturientem ; venite, matres, ad matrem ; venite, lactantes, ad lactantem ; venite, juvenculæ, ad juvenculam. Ideo omnes istos cursus naturæ virgo Maria in Domino nostro Jesu Christo suscepit, ut omnibus ad se confugientibus fœminis subveniret, et sic restauraret omne genus fœminarum ad se advenientium nova Eva servando virginitatem, sicut omne genus virorum Adam novus recuperat dominus Jesus Christus."—*Ibid.* iii.

I have omitted, among the instances of the comparison
of Eve with Mary, the passage at the end of the Epistle
to Diognetus, a testimony which would be most important from the great antiquity of that work, from the
religious beauty of its composition, and the stress laid
upon it by Protestants.   But I cannot construe it satisfactorily as it stands in the received text.   Should not
the semicolon be placed after φθείρεται, not, as in the
editions, after πιστεύεται? thus :—ὃν ὄφις οὐχ ἅπτεται
οὐδὲ πλάνη συγχωρίζεται, οὐδὲ Εὖα φθείρεται· ἀλλὰ
παρθένος πιστεύεται. καὶ σωτήριον δείκνυται, καὶ ἀπό-
στολοι κ.τ.λ.

NOTE II. Page 48.

SUAREZ ON THE IMMACULATE CONCEPTION.

ABRIDGED from Suarez. Opp. t. 17, p. 7—Ed. Venet. 1746 :—

" 1. Statuendum est B. Virginem fuisse a Christo redemptam, quia Christus fuit universalis redemptor totius generis humani, et pro omnibus hominibus mortuus est."—p. 15.

" 2. Præterea constat indiguisse Virginem redemptione, quia nimirum descendebat ex Adamo per seminalem generationem."—p. 7.

" 3. Tanquam certum statuendum est, B. Virginem procreatam esse ex viri et fœminæ commixtione carnali, ad modum aliorum hominum. Habetur certâ traditione et communi consensu totius Ecclesiæ."—p. 7.

" 4. Absolute et simpliciter fatendum B. Virginem in Adam peccasse."—p. 16.

" 5. B. Virgo peccavit in Adamo, ex quo tanquam ex radice infecta per seminalem rationem est orta ; hæc est tota ratio contrahendi originale peccatum, quod est ex vi conceptionis, nisi gratia Dei præveniat."—p. 16.

" 6. Certum est B. Virginem fuisse mortuam saltem in Adamo. Sicut in Christo vitam habuit, ita et in

Adam fuit mortua. Alias B. Virgo non contraxisset mortem aliasve corporis pœnalitates ex Adamo ; consequens [autem] est omnino falsum. Habuit B. Virgo meritum mortis saltem in Adamo. Illa vere habuit mortem carnis ex peccato Adami contractam."—p. 16.

"7. B. Virgo, ex vi suæ conceptionis fuit obnoxia originali peccato, seu debitum habuit contrahendi illud, nisi divinâ gratiâ fuisset impeditum."—p. 16.

"8. Si B. Virgo non fuisset (ut ita dicam) vendita in Adamo, et de se servituti peccati obnoxia, non fuisset vere redempta."—p. 16.

"9. Dicendum est, potuisse B. Virginem præservari ab originali peccato, et in primo suæ conceptionis instanti sanctificari."—p. 17.

"10. Potuit B. Virgo ex vi suæ originis esse obnoxia culpæ, et ideo indigere redemptione, et nihilominus in eodem momento, in quo erat obnoxia, præveniri, ne illam contraheret."—p. 14.

"11. Dicendum B. Virginem in ipso primo instanti conceptionis suæ fuisse sanctificatam, et ab originali peccato præservatam."—p. 19.

"12. Carnem Virginis fuisse carnem peccati . . . . verum est, non quia illa caro aliquando fuit subdita peccato aut informata anima 'carente gratia, sed quia fuit mortalis et passibilis ex debito peccati, cui de se erat obnoxia, si per Christi gratiam non fuisset præservata."—p. 22.

"13. Quod B. Virgo de se fuerit obnoxia peccato, (si illud revera nunquam habuit) non derogat perfectæ ejus sanctitati et puritati."—pp. 16, 17.

Cornelius à Lapide, Comment. in Ep. ad Rom. v. 12, says :—

"The Blessed Virgin sinned in Adam, and incurred this necessity of contracting original sin ; but original sin itself she did not contract in herself in fact, nor had it ; for she was anticipated by the grace of God, which excluded all sin from her, in the first moment of her conception."

In 2 Ep. ad Corinth. v. 15 :—

" All died, namely, in Adam, for in him all contracted the necessity of sin and death, even the Deipara ; so that both herself and man altogether needed Christ as a Redeemer and His death. Therefore the Blessed Virgin sinned and died in Adam, but in her own person she contracted not sin and the death of the soul, for she was anticipated by God and God's grace."

If any one wishes to see our doctrine drawn out in a Treatise of the present day, he should have recourse to Dr. Ullathorne's Exposition of the Immaculate Conception, a work full of instruction and of the first authority.

NOTE III. PAGE 50.

THE ANOMALOUS STATEMENTS OF ST. BASIL, ST. CHRYSOSTOM,
AND ST. CYRIL ABOUT THE BLESSED VIRGIN.

I HAVE admitted that several great Fathers of the
Church of the fourth and fifth centuries speak of the
Blessed Virgin in terms which we never should think of
using now, and which at first sight are inconsistent with
the belief and sentiment concerning her, which I have
ascribed to their times. These Fathers are St. Basil,
St. Chrysostom, and St. Cyril of Alexandria; and the
occasion of their speaking is furnished by certain passages of Scripture on which they are commenting. It
may in consequence be asked of me, why I do not
take these three, instead of St. Justin, St. Irenæus, and
Tertullian, as my authoritative basis for determining the
doctrine of the primitive times concerning the Blessed
Mary : why, instead of making St. Irenæus, &c., the
rule, and St. Basil, &c., the exception, I do not make the
earlier Fathers the exception, and the latter the rule.
Since I do not, it may be urged against me that I am
but making a case for my own opinion, and playing the
part of an advocate.

Now I do not see that it would be illogical or nugatory, though I did nothing more than make a case;

indeed I have worded myself in my Letter as if I wished
to do little more.   For so much as this would surely be
to the purpose, considering that the majority of Anglicans have a supreme confidence that no case whatever can
be made in behalf of our doctrine concerning the Blessed
Virgin from the ancient Fathers.   I should have gained a
real point if I did anything to destroy this imagination;
but I intend to attempt something more than this.   I shall
attempt to invalidate the only grounds on which any
teaching contrary to the Catholic can be founded on
Antiquity.

1.

First, I set down the passages which create the difficulty, as they are found in the great work of Petavius,
a theologian too candid and fearless to put out of sight
or explain away adverse facts, from fear of scandal, or
from the expedience of controversy.

1. St. Basil then writes thus, in his 260th Epistle,
addressed to Optimus :—

"[Symeon] uses the word 'sword,' meaning the word
which is tentative and critical of the thoughts, and
reaches unto the separation of soul and spirit, of the
joints and marrow.   Since then every soul, at the time
of the Passion, was subjected in a way to some unsettle-
ment ($\delta\iota\alpha\kappa\rho\acute{\iota}\sigma\epsilon\iota$), according to the Lord's word, who
said, 'All ye shall be scandalized in Me,' Symeon pro-
phesies even of Mary herself, that, standing by the Cross,
and seeing what was doing, and hearing the words, after
the testimony of Gabriel, after the secret knowledge of
the divine conception, after the great manifestation of
miracles, Thou wilt experience, he says, a certain tossing

K

(σάλος) of thy soul.   For it beseemed the Lord to taste
death for every one, and to become a propitiation of the
world, in order to justify all in His blood.   And thee
thyself who hast been taught from above the things concerning the Lord, some unsettlement (διάκρισις) will
reach.   This is the sword; 'that out of many hearts
thoughts may be revealed.'   He obscurely signifies, that,
after the scandalizing which took place upon the Cross
of Christ, both to the disciples and to Mary herself,
some quick healing should follow upon it from the Lord,
confirming their heart unto faith in Him."

2. St. Chrysostom, in Matth. Hom. iv. :—

" 'Wherefore,' a man may say, 'did not the Angel do
in the case of the Virgin [what he did to Joseph?'"
viz., appear to her after, not before, the Incarnation],
" ' why did he not bring her the good tidings after her
conception?' lest she should be in great disturbance and
trouble.   For the probability was, that, had she not
known the clear fact, she would have resolved something
strange (ἄτοπον) about herself, and had recourse to rope
or sword, not bearing the disgrace.   For the Virgin was
admirable, and Luke shows her virtue when he says
that, when she heard the salutation, she did not at once
become extravagant, nor appropriated the words, but
was troubled, searching what was the nature of the
salutation.   One then of so refined a mind (διηκριβωμένη)
would be made beside herself with despondency, considering the disgrace, and not expecting, whatever she
may say, to persuade any one who hears her, that adul-
tery had not been the fact.   Lest then these things
should occur, the Angel came before the conception; for

it beseemed that that womb should be without disorder,
which the Creator of all entered, and that that soul
should be rid of all perturbation, which was counted
worthy to become the minister of such mysteries."

In Matth. Hom. xliv. (vid. also in Joann. Hom.
xxi.) : —

"To-day we learn something else even further, viz.,
that not even to bear Christ in the womb, and to have
that wonderful childbirth, has any gain without virtue.
And this is especially true from this passage, ' As He was
yet speaking to the multitude, behold His Mother and
His brethren stood without, seeking to speak to Him,'
&c. This He said, not as ashamed of His Mother, nor as
denying her who bore Him ; for, had He been ashamed,
He had not passed through that womb ; but as showing
that there was no profit to her thence, unless she did all
that was necessary. For what she attempted, came of
overmuch love of honour ; for she wished to show to the
people that she had power and authority over her
Son, in nothing ever as yet having given herself airs
(φανταζομένη) about Him. Therefore she came thus
unseasonably. Observe then her and their rashness
(ἀπόνοιαν). . . . Had He wished to deny His Mother,
then He would have denied, when the Jews taunted Him
with her. But no : He shows such care of her as to
commit her as a legacy on the Cross itself to the disciple whom He loved best of all, and to take anxious
oversight of her. But does He not do the same now,
by caring for her and His brethren ? . . . And consider,
not only the words which convey the considerate rebuke,
but also . . . who He is who utters it . . . and what He

aims at in uttering it; not, that is, as wishing to cast
her into perplexity, but to release her from a most
tyrannical affection, and to bring her gradually to the
fitting thought concerning Him, and to persuade her
that He is not only her Son, but also her Master."

3. St. Cyril, in Joann. lib. xii. 1064 :—

" How shall we explain this passage ?   He introduces
both His Mother and the other women with her standing
at the Cross, and, as is plain, weeping. For somehow the
race of women is ever fond of tears ; and especially given
to laments, when it has rich occasions for weeping. How
then did they persuade the blessed Evangelist to be so
minute in his account, as to make mention of this abidance
of the women ?   For it was his purpose to teach even
this, viz., that probably even the Mother of the Lord
herself was scandalized at the unexpected Passion, and
that the death upon the Cross, being so very bitter, was
near unsettling her from her fitting mind ; and in addition to this, the mockeries of the Jews, and the soldiers
too, perhaps, who were sitting near the Cross and making
a jest of Him who was hanging on it, and daring, in the
sight of His very mother, the division of His garments.
Doubt not that she admitted (εισεδέξατο) some such
thoughts as these :—I bore Him who is laughed at on the
wood ; but, in saying He was the true son of the Omnipotent God, perhaps somehow He was mistaken. He
said He was the Life, how then has He been crucified ?
how has He been strangled by the cords of His mur-
derers ? how prevailed He not over the plot of His
persecutors ? why descends He not from the Cross,
though He bade Lazarus to return to life, and amazed all

Judæa with His miracles? And it is very natural that the woman in her (τὸ γύναιον), not knowing the mystery, should slide into some such trains of thought. For we must conclude, if we judge well, that the gravity of the circumstances was enough to overturn even a self-possessed mind; it is no wonder then if a woman (τὸ γύναιον) slipped into this reasoning. For if Peter himself, the chosen one of the holy disciples, once was scandalized . . . so as to cry out hastily, Be it far from Thee, Lord . . . what paradox is it, if the soft mind of womankind was carried off to weak ideas? And this we say, not idly conjecturing, as it may strike one, but entertaining the suspicion from what is written concerning the Mother of the Lord. For we remember that Simeon the Just, when he received the Lord as a little child into his arms, . . . said to her, 'A sword shall go through thine own soul, that out of many hearts thoughts may be revealed.' By sword he meant the sharp excess of suffering cutting down a woman's mind into extravagant thoughts. For temptations test the hearts of those who suffer them, and make bare the thoughts which are in them."

Now what do these three Fathers say in these passages?

1. St. Basil imputes to the Blessed Virgin, not only doubt, but the sin of doubt. On the other hand, 1. he imputes it only on one occasion; 2. he does not consider it to be a grave sin; 3. he implies that, in point of spiritual perfection, she is above the Apostles.

2. St. Chrysostom, in his first passage, does not im-

pute sin to her at all. He says God so disposed things
for her as to shield her from the chance of sinning; that
she was too admirable to be allowed to be betrayed by
her best and purest feelings into sin.   All that is implied
repugnant to a Catholic's reverence for her, is, that her
woman's nature, viewed in itself and apart from the
watchful providence of God's grace over her, would not
have had strength to resist a hypothetical temptation,—
a position which a Catholic will not care to affirm or
deny, though he will feel great displeasure at having to
discuss it at all.   This, moreover, at least is distinctly
brought out in the passage, viz., that in St. Chrysostom's mind, our Lady was not a mere physical instrument of the Incarnation, but that her soul, as well as
her body, " ministered to the mystery," and needed to
be duly prepared for it.

As to his second most extraordinary passage, I should
not be candid, unless I simply admitted that it is as
much at variance with what we hold, as it is solitary
and singular in the writings of Antiquity.   The saint
distinctly and (*pace illius*) needlessly, imputes to the
Blessed Virgin, on the occasion in question, the sin or
infirmity of vainglory.   He has a parallel passage in
commenting on the miracle at the marriage-feast.   All
that can be said to alleviate the startling character of
these passages is, that it does not appear that St. Chrysostom would account such vainglory in a woman as any
great failing.

3. Lastly, as to St. Cyril, I do not see that he declares
that Mary actually doubted at the Crucifixion, but that,
considering she was a woman, it is likely she was tempted

to doubt, and nearly doubted. Moreover, St. Cyril does not seem to consider such doubt, had it occurred, as any great sin.

Thus on the whole, all three Fathers, St. Basil and St. Cyril explicitly, and St. Chrysostom by implication, consider that on occasions she was, or might be, exposed to violent temptation to doubt; but two Fathers consider that she actually did sin, though she sinned lightly;—the sin being doubt, and on one occasion, according to St. Basil; and on two occasions, the sin being vainglory, according to St. Chrysostom.

However, the strong language of these Fathers is not directed against our Lady's person, so much as against her nature. They seem to have participated with Ambrose, Jerome, and other Fathers, in that low estimation of woman's nature which was general in their times. In the broad imperial world, the conception entertained of womankind was not high; it seemed only to perpetuate the poetical tradition of the " Varium et mutabile semper." Little was then known of that true nobility, which is exemplified in the females of the Gothic and German races, and in those of the old Jewish stock, Miriam, Deborah, Judith, and Susanna, the forerunners of Mary. When then St. Chrysostom imputes vainglory to her, he is not imputing to her anything worse than an infirmity, the infirmity of a nature, inferior to man's, and intrinsically feeble; as though the Almighty could have created a more excellent being than Mary, but could not have made a greater woman. Accordingly Chrysostom does not say that she sinned. He does not deny that she had all the perfections which woman could have ; but he seems to have thought the capabilities of her nature were bounded, so that the utmost grace bestowed upon it could not raise it above that standard of perfection in which its elements resulted, and that to attempt more, would have been to injure, not to benefit it. Of course I am not stating this as brought out in any part of his writings, but it seems to me to be the real sentiment of many of the ancients.

I will add that such a belief on the part of these Fathers, that the Blessed Virgin had committed a sin or a weakness, was not in itself inconsistent with the exercise of love and devotion to her (though I am not pretending that there is proof of any such exercise on their part in fact) ; and for this simple reason, that if sinlessness were a condition of inspiring devotion, we should not feel devotion to any but our Lady, not to St. Joseph, or to the Apostles, or to our Patron saints.

Such then is the teaching of these three Fathers ; now how far is it in antagonism to ours? On the one hand, we will not allow that our Blessed Lady ever sinned ; we cannot bear the notion, entering, as we do, into the full spirit of St. Augustine's words, "Concerning the Holy Virgin Mary, I wish no question to be raised at all, when we are treating of sins." On the other hand, we admit, rather we maintain, that, except for the grace of God, she might have sinned ; and that she may have been exposed to temptation in the sense in which our Lord was exposed to it, though as His Divine Nature made it impossible for Him to yield to it, so His grace preserved her under its assaults also. While then we do

not hold that St. Simeon prophesied of temptation, when
he said a sword would pierce her, still, if any one likes to
say he did, we do not consider him heretical, provided he
does not impute to her any sinful or inordinate emotion as
the consequence to it. In this way St. Cyril may be let
off altogether; and we have only to treat of the *paradoxa*
or *anomala* of those great Saints, St. Basil and St.
Chrysostom. I proceed to their controversial value.

2.

I mean, that having determined what the Three
Fathers say, and how far they are at issue with what
Catholics hold now, I now come to the main question,
viz., What is the authoritative force in controversy of
what they thus say in opposition to Catholic teaching?
I think I shall be able to show that it has no controversial force at all.

1. I begin by observing, that the main force of passages which can be brought from any Father or Fathers
in controversy, lies in the fact that such passages represent the judgment or sentiment of their own respective
countries; and again, I say that the force of that local
judgment or sentiment lies in its being the existing expression of an Apostolical tradition. I am far, of course,
from denying the claim of the teaching of a Father on
our deference, arising out of his personal position and
character; or the claims of the mere sentiments of a
Christian population on our careful attention, as a fact
carrying with it, under circumstances, especial weight;
but, in a question of doctrine, we must have recourse to
the great source of doctrine, Apostolical Tradition, and a

Father must represent his own people, and that people must be the witnesses of an uninterrupted Tradition from the Apostles, if anything decisive is to come of any theological statement which is found in his writings; and if, in a particular case, there is no reason to suppose that he does echo the popular voice, or that that popular voice is transmitted from Apostolic times,—or (to take another channel of Tradition) unless the Father in question receives and reports his doctrine from the Bishops and Priests who instructed him on the very under-standing and profession that it is Apostolical,—then, though it was not one Father but ten who said a thing, it would weigh nothing against the assertion of only one Father to the contrary, provided it was clear that that one Father witnessed to an Apostolical Tradition. Now I do not say that I can decide the question by this issue with all the exactness which is conceivable, but still this is the issue by which it must be tried, and the issue by which I shall be enabled, as I think, to come to a satis-factory conclusion upon it.

2. Such, I say, being the issue, viz., that a doctrine reported by the Fathers, in order to have dogmatic force, must be a Tradition in its *source* or *form*, next, what is a Tradition, considered in its *matter?* It is a belief, which, be it *affirmative* or *negative*, is *positive.* The mere absence of a tradition in a country, is not a tradition the other way. If, for instance, there was no tradition in Syria and Asia Minor that the phrase "consubstantial with the Father," came from the Apostles, that would not be a tradition that it did not come from the Apostles; though of course it would be necessary for those who

said that it did, to account for the ignorance of those countries as to the real fact.

3. The proposition " Christ is God," serves as an example of what I mean by an affirmative tradition ; and " no one born of woman is born in God's favour," is an example of a negative tradition. I observe then, in the third place, that a tradition does not carry its own full explanation with it ; it does but land (so to say) a proposition at the feet of the Apostles, and its interpretation has still to be determined,—as the Apostles' words in Scripture, however much theirs, need an interpretation. Thus I may accept the above negative Tradition, that " no one woman-born is born in God's favour," yet question its strict universality, as a point of criticism, saying that a general proposition admits of exceptions, that our Lord was born of woman, yet was the sinless and acceptable priest and sacrifice for all men. So again the Arians allowed that " Christ was God," but they disputed about the meaning of the word " God."

4. Further, there are *explicit* traditions and *implicit*. By an explicit tradition I mean a doctrine which is conveyed in the letter of the proposition which has been handed down ; and by implicit, one which lies in the force and virtue, not in the letter of the proposition. Thus it might be an Apostolical tradition that our Lord was the very Son of God, of one nature with the Father, and in all things equal to Him ; and again a tradition that there was but one God : these would be explicit, but in them would necessarily be conveyed, moreover, the implicit tradition, that the Father and the Son were numerically one. Implicit traditions are

positive traditions, as being strictly conveyed in positive.

5. Lastly, there are at least two ways of determining an Apostolical tradition :—(1.) When credible witnesses declare that it *is* Apostolical; as when three hundred Fathers at Nicæa stopped their ears at Arius's blasphemies: (2.) When, in various places, independent witnesses enunciate one and the same doctrine, as St. Irenæus, St. Cyprian, and Eusebius assert, that the Apostles founded a Church, Catholic and One.

3.

Now to apply these principles to the particular case on account of which I have laid them down.

1. That " Mary is the new Eve," is a proposition answering to the *idea* of a Tradition. I am not prepared to say that it can be shown to have the first of the above two tests of its Apostolicity, viz. that the writers who record it, profess to have received it from the Apostles; but I conceive it has the second test, viz. that the writers are independent witnesses, as I have shown at length in the course of my Letter.

It is an explicit tradition ; and by the force of it follow two others, which are implicit:—first (considering the condition of Eve in paradise), that Mary had no part in sin, and indefinitely large measures of grace; secondly (considering the doctrine of merits), that she has been exalted to glory proportionate to that grace.

This is what I have to observe on the argument in behalf of the Blessed Virgin. St. Justin, St. Irenæus, Tertullian, are witnesses of an Apostolical tradition, because in three distinct parts of the world they enunciate one and the same definite doctrine. And it is remarkable that they witness just for those three seats of Catholic teaching, where the truth in this matter was likely to be especially lodged. St. Justin speaks for Jerusalem, the see of St. James; St. Irenæus for Ephesus, the dwelling-place, the place of burial, of St. John; and Tertullian, who made a long residence at Rome, for the city of St. Peter and St. Paul.

2. Now, what can be produced on the other side, parallel to an argument like this? A tradition in its matter is a positive statement of belief; in its form it is a statement which comes from the Apostles: (1.) now, first in point of matter, what definite statement of belief at all, is witnessed to by St. Basil, St. Chrysostom, and St. Cyril? I cannot find any. They do but interpret certain passages in the Gospels to our Lady's disadvantage; is an interpretation a distinct statement of belief? but even if it was, there is no joint interpretation in this case; they do not all three interpret one and the same passage. Nor do they agree together in their interpretation of those passages, which either one or other of them interprets so harshly; for, while St. Chrysostom holds that our Lord spoke in correction of His Mother at the wedding feast, St. Cyril on the contrary says that He wrought a miracle which He was Himself unwilling to work, in order to show " reverence to His Mother," and that she " having great authority for the working of the miracle, got the victory, persuading the Lord, as being her Son, as was fitting." But, taking the statements which are in her disparagement as we find them, can we

generalize them into one proposition? Shall we make
it such as this, viz. "The Blessed Virgin during her
earthly life committed actual sin"? If we mean by
this, that there was a positive recognition of such a
proposition in the country of St. Basil or St. Chrysostom,
this surely is not to be gathered merely from their separate
and independent comments on passages of Scripture.
All that can be gathered thence legitimately is, that, had
there been a positive belief in her sinlessness in those
countries, the Fathers in question would not have spoken
of her in the terms which they have used; in other words,
that there was no belief in her sinlessness then and there;
but the absence of a belief is not a belief to the contrary,
it is not that positive statement, which, as I have said,
is required for the matter of a tradition.

(2.) Nor do the passages which I have quoted from
these Fathers, supply us with any tradition, viewed in
its form, that is, as a statement which has come down
from the Apostles. I have suggested two tests of such
a statement:—one, when the writers who make it so
declare that it was from the Apostles; and the other
when, being independent of one another, they bear
witness to one and the same positive statement of
doctrine. Neither test is fulfilled in this case. The
three Fathers of the 4th and 5th centuries are but commenting on Scripture; and comments, though carrying
with them of course, and betokening. the tone of thought
of the place and time to which they belong, are, *primâ
facie*, of a private and personal character. If they are
more than this, the *onus probandi* lies with those who so
maintain. Exegetical theology is one department of

divine science, and dogmatic is another. On the other hand, the three Fathers of the 2nd century are all writing on dogmatic subjects, when they compare Mary to Eve.

4.

Now to take the Three later Fathers, viewed as organs of tradition, one by one:—

1. As to St. Cyril, as I have said, he does not, strictly speaking, say more than that our Lady was grievously tempted. This does not imply sin, for our Lord was "tempted in all things like as we are, yet without sin." Moreover, it is this St. Cyril who spoke at Ephesus of the Blessed Virgin in terms of such high panegyric, as to make it more consistent in him to suppose that she was sinless, than that she was not.

2. St. Basil derives his notion from Origen, that the Blessed Virgin at the time of the Passion admitted a doubt about our Lord's mission, and Origen, so far from professing to rest it on Tradition, draws it as a theological conclusion from a received doctrine. Origen's characteristic fault was to prefer scientific reasonings to authority; and he exemplifies it in the case before us. In the middle age, the great obstacle to the reception of the doctrine of the Blessed Mary's immaculate conception, was the notion that, unless she had been in some sense a sinner, she could not have been redeemed. By an argument parallel to this, Origen argues, that since she was one of the redeemed, she must at one time or another have committed an actual sin. He says: "Are we to think, that the Apostles were scandalized, and not the Lord's Mother? If she suffered not scandal at

our Lord's passion, then Jesus died not for her sins.
If all have sinned and need the glory of God, being
justified by His grace, and redeemed, certainly Mary
at that time was scandalized." This is precisely the
argument of Basil, as contained in the passage given
above; his statement then of the Blessed Virgin's
wavering in faith, instead of professing to be the tradition of a doctrine, carries with it an avowal of its being
none at all.

However, I am not unwilling to grant that, whereas
Scripture tells us that all were scandalized at our Lord's
passion, there was some sort of traditional interpretation
of Simeon's words, to the effect that she was in some
sense included in that trial. How near the Apostolic
era the tradition existed, cannot be determined; but
such a belief need not include the idea of sin in the
Blessed Virgin, but only the presence of temptation and
darkness of spirit. This tradition, whatever its authority, would be easily perverted, so as actually to impute
sin to her, by such reasonings as that of Origen. Origen
himself, in the course of the passage to which I have
referred, speaks of "the sword" of Simeon, and is the
first to do so. St. Cyril, who, though an Alexandrian
as well as Origen, represents a very different school of
theology, has, as we have seen, the same interpretation
for the piercing sword. It is also found in a Homily
attributed to St. Amphilochius; and in that sixth Oration
of Proclus, which, according to Tillemont and Ceillier,
is not to be considered genuine. It is also found in a
work incorrectly attributed to St. Augustine.

3. St. Chrysostom is, *par excellence*, the Commentator

of the Church. As Commentator and Preacher, he, of all the Fathers, carries about him the most intense personality. In this lies his very charm, peculiar to himself. He is ever overflowing with thought, and he pours it forth with a natural engaging frankness, and an unwearied freshness and vigour. If he really was in the practice of deeply studying and carefully criticizing what he delivered in public, he had in perfection the rare art of concealing his art. He ever speaks from himself, not of course without being impregnated with the fulness of a Catholic training, but, still, not speaking by rule, but as if, " trusting the lore of his own loyal heart." On the other hand, if it is not a paradox to say it, no one carries with him so little of the science, precision, consistency, gravity of a Doctor of the Church, as he who is one of the greatest. The difficulties are well known which he has occasioned to school theologians : his *obiter dicta* about our Lady are among them.

On the whole then I conclude that these three Fathers supply no evidence that, in what they say about her having failed in faith or humility on certain occasions mentioned in Scripture, they are reporting the enunciations of Apostolical Tradition.

5.

Moreover, such difficulties as the above are not uncommon in the writings of the Fathers. I will mention several :—

1. St. Gregory Nyssen is a great dogmatic divine; he too, like St. Basil, is of the school of Origen ; and, in several passages of his works, he, like Origen, declares or

L

suggests that future punishment will not be eternal. Those Anglicans who consider St. Chrysostom's passages in his Commentary on the Gospels to be a real argument against the Catholic belief of the Blessed Virgin's sinlessness, should explain why they do not feel St. Gregory Nyssen's teaching in his Catechetical Discourse, an argument against their own belief in the eternity of punishment.

2. Again, Anglicans believe in the proper Divinity of our Lord, in spite of Bull's saying of the Ante-Nicene Fathers, "Nearly all the ancient Catholics, who preceded Arius, have the appearance of being ignorant of the invisible and incomprehensible (*immensam*) nature of the Son of God;" an article of faith expressly contained in the Athanasian Creed, and enforced by its anathema.

3. The Divinity of the Holy Ghost is an integral part of the fundamental doctrine of Christianity; yet St. Basil, in the fourth century, apprehending the storm of controversy which its assertion would raise, refrained from asserting it on an occasion when the Arians were on watch as to what he would say. And, on his keeping silence, St. Athanasius took his part. Such inconsistencies take place continually, and no Catholic doctrine but suffers from them at times, until what has been preserved by Tradition is formally pronounced to be Apostolical by definition of the Church.

6.

Before concluding, I shall briefly take notice of two questions which may be asked me.

1. How are we to account for the absence, at Antioch

or Cæsarea, of a tradition of our Lady's sinlessness? I answer that it was obliterated or confused for the time by the Arian troubles in the countries in which those Sees are situated.

It is not surely wonderful, if, in Syria and Asia Minor, the seat in the fourth century of Arianism and Semi-Arianism, the prerogatives of the Mother were obscured together with the essential glory of the Son, or if they who denied the tradition of His divinity, forgot the tradition of her sinlessness. Christians in those countries and times, however religious themselves, however orthodox their teachers, were necessarily under peculiar disadvantages.

Now let it be observed that Basil grew up in the very midst of Semi-Arianism, and had direct relations with that portion of its professors who had been reconciled to the Church and accepted the Homoüsion. It is not wonderful then, if he had no firm habitual hold upon a doctrine which (though Apostolical) in his day was as yet so much in the background all over Christendom, as our Lady's sinlessness.

As to Chrysostom, not only was he in close relations with the once Semi-Arian Cathedra of Antioch, to the disowning of the rival succession there, recognized by Rome and Alexandria, but, as his writings otherwise show, he came under the teaching of the celebrated Antiochene School, celebrated, that is, at once for its method of Scripture criticism, and (orthodox as it was itself) for the successive outbreaks of heresy among its members. These outbreaks began in Paul of Samosata, were continued in the Semi-Arian pupils of Lucian, and ended in Nestorius. The famous Theodore, and Diodorus, of the same school, who, though not heretics themselves, have a bad name in the Church, were, Diodorus the master, and Theodore the fellow-pupil, of St. Chrysostom. (Vid. *Essay on Doctr. Devel.* chap. v. § 2.) Here then is a natural explanation, why St. Chrysostom, even more than St. Basil, might be wanting, great doctor as he was, in a clear perception of the place of the Blessed Virgin in the Evangelical Dispensation.

2. How are we to account for the passages in the Gospels which are the occasion of the three Fathers' remarks to her disparagement? I answer, they were intended to discriminate between our Lord's work who is our Teacher and Redeemer, and the ministrative office of His Mother.

As to the words of Simeon, indeed, as interpreted by St. Basil and St. Cyril, there is nothing in the sacred text which obliges us to consider the "sword" to mean doubt rather than anguish; but Matth. xii. 46—50, with its parallels Mark iii. 31—35, and Luke viii. 19—21: and with Luke xi. 27, 28, and John ii. 4, requires some explanation.

I observe then, that, when our Lord commenced His ministry, and during it, as one of His chief self-sacrifices, He separated Himself from all ties of earth, in order to fulfil the typical idea of a teacher and priest; and to give an example to His priests after Him; and especially to manifest by this action the cardinal truth, as expressed by the Prophet, "I am the Lord, and there is no Saviour besides Me." As to His Priests, they, after Him, were to be of the order of that Melchizedech, who was "without father and without mother;" for "no man, being a soldier to God, entangleth himself with secular business:" and "no man putting his hand to the plough, and looking back, is fit for the kingdom of God." Again, as to the Levites, who were His types in the Old Law, there was that honourable history of their zeal for God, when they even slew their own brethren and companions who had committed idolatry; "who said to his father and to his mother, I do not know you, and to his brethren, I know you not, and their own children they have not known." To this His separation even from His Mother He refers by anticipation at twelve years old in His words, "How is it that you sought Me? Did you not know that I must be about My Father's business?"

The separation from her, with whom He had lived thirty years and more, was not to last beyond the time of His ministry. She seems to have been surprised when she first heard of it, for St. Luke says, on occasion of His staying in the Temple, "they understood not the word that He spoke to them." Nay, she seems hardly to have understood it at the marriage-feast; but He, in dwelling on it more distinctly then, implied also that it was not to last long. He said, "Woman, what have I to do with thee? My hour is not yet come,"— that is, the hour of His triumph, when His Mother was to take her predestined place in His kingdom. In saying the hour was not yet come, He implied that the hour would come, when He would have to "do with her," and she might ask and obtain from Him miracles. Accordingly, St. Augustine thinks that that hour had come, when He said upon the Cross, "*Consummatum est,*" and, after this ceremonial estrangement of years, He recognized His Mother and committed her to the beloved disciple. Thus, by marking out the beginning and the end of the period of exception, during which she could not exert her influence upon Him, He signifies more clearly by the contrast, that her presence with Him, and Her power, was to be the rule of His kingdom. In a higher sense than He spoke to the Apostles, He seems to address her in the words, "Because I have spoken these things, sorrow hath filled your heart. But I will see you again, and your heart shall rejoice, and your joy no man shall take from you." (*Vid. Sermon* iii. *in Sermons on Subjects of the Day.* Also the comment of St. Irenæus, &c., upon John ii. 4, in my note on Athanas. Orat. iii. 41.)

Also, I might have added the passage in Tertullian, Carn. Christ. § 7, as illustrating, by its contrast with § 17 (quoted above, p. 34), the distinction between doctrinal tradition and personal opinion, if it were clear to me that he included the Blessed Virgin in the unbelief which he imputes to our Lord's brethren; on the contrary, he expressly separates her off from them. The passage runs thus on the text, "Who is My Mother? and who are My Brethren?"

"The Lord's brothers had not believed in Him, as is contained in the Gospel published before Marcion. His Mother, equally, *is not described* (non demonstratur) *as having adhered to Him,* whereas other Marthas and Maries are frequent in intercourse with him. In this place at length, their (corum) incredulity is evident;

while He was teaching the way of life, was preaching the kingdom of God, was working for the cure of ailments and diseases, though strangers were riveted to Him, these, so much the nearest to Him (tam proximi), were away. At length they come upon Him, and stand without, nor enter, not reckoning forsooth on what was going on within."

Additional Note, Ed. 5.—It may be added to the above, that Fr. Hippolyto Maracci, in his " Vindicatio Chrysostomica," arguing in behalf of St. Chrysostom's belief in the Blessed Virgin's Immaculate Conception, maintains that a real belief in that doctrine is compatible with an admission that she was not free from venial sin, granting for argument's sake that St. Chrysostom held the latter doctrine. If this be so, it follows that we cannot at once conclude that either he or the other two Fathers deny the doctrine of the Immaculate Conception, because here and there in their writings they impute to the Blessed Virgin infirmities or faults. He writes as follows :—

" Demus, quod dandum non est, scilicet Chrysostomum tribuisse Deiparæ Virgini peccatum actuale veniale, nunquid ex hoc potest solidè inferri ipsum eidem tribuisse etiam peccatum originale ? Minimè quidem. Non enim apparet necessaria connexio inter carentiam peccati venialis et carentiam originalis, ita ut ex unâ possit inferri alia. Potuit Chrysostomus liberare B. Virginem à peccato originali, licet non liberaverit à veniali. Peccatum veniale, juxta doctrinam Angelici Doctoris, non causat maculam in animâ, nec spiritualem pulchritudinem in eâ demolitur, stareque potest cum elogiis 'immaculatæ,' 'incontaminatæ,' 'impollutæ,' &c. Cæterùm peccatum originale, cùm penitus omnem gratiæ ornatum explodat, cum decore immaculatæ, incontaminatæ, impollutæ &c., minimè potest consistere. Chrysostomus arbitratus est, minùs indecorum fuisse Christo nasci ex matre, quæ levi veniali maculâ afficeretur, quam quæ originali ignominiâ dehonestaretur. Præservare Virginem à peccato originali majus privilegium et excellentius beneficium est ex parte Dei, quàm eam non permittere maculâ veniali aliquantulum opacari. Stante enim præservatione à peccato originali, nec anima Dei inimicitiam contrahit, nec diaboli mancipium evadit, nec denique redditur inepta ad recipienda plura auxilia gratiæ annexa, quibus plura peccata venialia declinare posset. Ex aliâ parte, peccatum veniale ex se his bonis recipiendis obicem non adeo ponit, nec animæ pulchritudini, nec amicitiæ, nec charitati machinatur exilium."

NOTE IV. PAGE 91.

ON THE TEACHING OF THE GREEK CHURCH ABOUT
THE BLESSED VIRGIN.

CANISIUS, in his work *de Mariâ Deiparâ Virgine*, p. 514.
while engaged in showing the carefulness with which
the Church distinguishes the worship of God from the
cultus of the Blessed Virgin, observes, " Lest the
Church should depart from *Latria* (i.e. the worship of
God) she has instituted the public supplications in the
Liturgy in perpetuity in such wise as to address them
directly to God the Father, and not to the Saints, according to that common form of praying, ' Almighty, everlasting God,' &c. ; and the said prayers which they also
call ' Collects,' she generally ends in this way, ' through
Jesus Christ, Thy Son, our Lord.' " He says more to
the same purpose, but the two points here laid down are
sufficient ; viz. that as to the Latin Missal, Ritual, and
Breviary, (1.) Saints are not directly addressed in these
authoritative books : and (2.) in them prayers end with
the name of Jesus. An apposite illustration of both of
these, that is, in what is omitted and what is introduced,
is supplied by the concluding prayer of the Offertory in
the Latin Mass. If in any case the name of " our Lady
and all Saints" might at the end of a prayer be sub-

stituted for our Lord's name, it would be when the object addressed is, not God the Father, but the Son, or the Holy Trinity; but let us observe how the prayer in question runs :—

"Suscipe, Sancta Trinitas"—"Receive, *O Holy Trinity,* this oblation which we make to Thee, in memory of the Passion, Resurrection, and Ascension of our Lord Jesus Christ, and *in honour of* the Blessed Mary, Ever-Virgin, of Blessed John Baptist, and of the Holy Apostles Peter and Paul, and of these and all Saints, that it may avail for their honour and our salvation, and that they may vouchsafe to intercede for us in heaven, whose memory we celebrate on earth, *Through the same Christ our Lord.* Amen."

When in occasional Collects the intercession of the Blessed Mary is introduced, it does not supersede mention of our Lord as the Intercessor. Thus in the Post-Communion on the Feast of the Circumcision,—

"May this Communion, O Lord, purify us from guilt; and at the intercession of the Blessed Virgin Mary, Mother of God, make us partakers of the heavenly remedy, through the same our Lord Jesus Christ. Amen."

In like manner, when the Son is addressed, and the intercession of Mary and the Saints is supplicated, His atoning passion is introduced at the close, as on the Feast of the Seven Dolours :—

"God, at whose passion, according to the prophecy of Simeon, the most sweet soul of the glorious Virgin-Mother Mary was pierced through with the sword of sorrow, mercifully grant, that we, who reverently commemorate her piercing and passion, may, by the intercession of the glorious merits and prayers of the Saints who faithfully stood by the Cross, *obtain the happy fruit of Thy Passion*, who livest and reignest, &c."

"We offer to Thee, Lord Jesus Christ, our prayers and sacrifices, humbly supplicating, that we, who renew in our prayers the piercing of the most sweet soul of Thy Blessed Mother Mary, by the manifold compassionate intervention of both her and her holy companions under the Cross, *by the merits of Thy death*, may merit a place with the Blessed, who livest, &c."

Now let us observe how far less observant of dogmatic exactness, how free and fearless in its exaltation of the Blessed Virgin, is the formal Greek devotion :—

1. "We have risen from sleep, and we fall down before Thee, O good God ; and we sing to Thee the Angelic Hymn, O powerful God. Holy, holy, holy art Thou, God ; have mercy on us through the Theotocos.

"Thou hast raised me from my bed and slumber, O God. Lighten my mind. and open my heart and lips, to sing of Thee, Holy Trinity. Holy, holy, holy art Thou, God ; have mercy on us through the Theotocos.

"Soon will come the Judge, and the deeds of all will be laid bare . . . Holy, holy, holy art Thou, God ; have mercy on us through the Theotocos."—*Horologium*, p. 2, *Venet.* 1836: vide also, pp. 34. 48. 52. Also *Eucholog. Venet.* p. 358.

2. "O God, who lookest on the earth, and makest it tremble, deliver us from the fearful threatenings of earthquake, Christ our God ; and send down on us Thy rich mercies, and save us, at the intercessions (πρεσβείαις)

of the Theotocos."—*Ibid.* p. 224. Vid. also *Pentecostar* p. 14.

3. "O Holy God. . . . visit us in Thy goodness, pardon us every sin, sanctify our souls, and grant us to serve Thee in holiness all the days of our life, at the intercessions (πρεσβείαις) of the Holy Theotocos and all the Saints, &c."—*Euchologium*, p. 64. *Venet.* 1832.

4. "Again, and still again, let us beseech the Lord in peace. Help, save, pity, preserve us, O God [through] her, the all-holy, Immaculate, most Blessed, and glorious (διαφύλαξον ἡμᾶς ὁ Θεὸς, τῆς παναγίας), &c."—*Euchologium*, p. 92 *Venet.* 1832. Vid. also *Pentecostar.* p. 232; and *passim.*

5. "Lord, Almighty Sovereign, . . . restore and raise from her bed this Thy servant, &c. . . . at the intercession (πρεσβείαις) of the all-undefiled Theotocos and all the Saints."—*Ibid.* p. 142.

6. "Have mercy and pardon, (for Thou alone hast power to remit sins and iniquities,) at the intercession of Thy all-holy Mother and all the Saints."—*Ibid.* p. 150.

7. "O Lord God Almighty, . . . bless and hallow Thy place . . . at the intercession (πρεσβείαις) of our glorious Lady, Mary, Mother of God and Ever-Virgin."—*Eucholog.* p. 389.

Is the Blessed Virgin ever called "our Lady," as here, in the Latin Prayers? whereas it is a frequent title of her in the Greek.

8. "Save me, my God, from all injury and harm, Thou who art glorified in Three Persons . . . and guard Thy flock at the intercessions (ἐντεύξεσιν) of the Theo-

tocos."—*Pentecostarium*, p. 59. *Venet.* 1820. Vid. also Goar, *Eucholog.* p. 30.

9. " In the porch of Solomon there lay a multitude of sick . . . Lord, send to us Thy great mercies at the intercession (πρεσβείαις) of the Theotocos."—*Pente-costar.* p. 84. Vid. also Goar, *Eucholog.* pp. 488. 543.

10. " O great God, the Highest, who alone hast immortality . . . prosper our prayer as the incense before Thee . . . that we may remember even in the night Thy holy Name, . . . and rise anew in gladness of soul . . . bringing our prayers and supplications to Thy loving kindness in behalf of our own sins and of all Thy people, whom visit in mercy at the intercessions (πρεσβείαις) of the Holy Theotocos."—*Ibid.* p. 232. Vid. *Horolog.* p. 192. *Venet.* 1836.

11. Between the Trisagion and Epistle in Mass. "O Holy God, who dwellest in the holy place, whom with the voice of their Trisagion the Seraphim do praise, &c. . . . sanctify our souls and bodies, and grant us to serve Thee in holiness all the days of our life, at the intercession (πρεσβείαις) of the Holy Theotocos and all the Saints."—*Eucholog.* p. 64. *Venet.* 1832.

12. In the early part of Mass. " Lift up the horn of Christians, and send down on us Thy rich mercies, by the power of the precious and life-giving Cross, by the grace of Thy light-bringing, third-day resurrection from the dead, at the intercession (πρεσβείαις) of our All-holy Blessed Lady, Mother of God and Ever-Virgin, and all Thy Saints."—Assemani, *Codex Liturg.* t. v. p. 71. *Rite of St. James.*

13. At the Offertory at Mass. " In honour and

memory of our singularly blessed and glorious Queen, Mary Theotocos and Ever-Virgin; at whose intercession, O Lord, receive, O Lord, this sacrifice unto Thy altar which is beyond the heavens."—Goar, *Euchol.* p. 58. *Rite of St. Chrysostom.*

14. In the Commemoration at Mass. "*Cantors.* Hail, Mary, full of grace, &c. &c. . . . for thou hast borne the Saviour of our souls. *Priest.* [Remember, Lord] especially the most Holy Immaculate, &c. . . . Mary. *Cantors.* It is meet truly to bless ($\mu\alpha\kappa\alpha\rho\iota\zeta\epsilon\iota\nu$) thee, the Theotocos . . . more honourable than the Cherubim, &c. . . . thee we magnify, who art truly the Theotocos. O Full of Grace, in thee the whole creation rejoices, the congregation of Angels, and the race of men, O sanctified shrine, and spiritual Paradise, boast of virgins," &c.—Assemani, t. v. p. 44. *Jerusalem Rite.*

15. In the Commemoration at Mass. "*Priest.* Especially and first of all, we make mention of the Holy, glorious, and Ever-Virgin Mary, &c. *Deacon.* Remember her, Lord God, and at her holy and pure prayers be propitious, have mercy upon us, and favourably hear us. *Priest.* Mother of our Lord Jesus Christ, pray for me to thy Son Only-begotten, who came of thee, that, having remitted my sins and debts, He may accept from my humble and sinful hands this sacrifice, which is offered by my vileness on this altar, through thy intercession, Mother most holy."—*Ibid.* p. 186. *Syrian Rite.*

16. Apparently, after the Consecration. "*The Priest incenses thrice before the Image (or Picture, imagine) of the Virgin and says:* Rejoice, Mary, beautiful dove, who

hast borne for us God, the Word; thee we salute with the Angel Gabriel, saying, Hail, full of grace, the Lord is with thee, Hail, Virgin, true Queen; hail, glory of our race, thou hast borne Emmanuel. We ask, remember us, O faithful advocate, in the sight of our Lord Jesus Christ, that He put away from us our sins."— *Ibid.* t. vii., *pars 2da. in fin.* p. 20. *Alexandrian Rite.*

17. At the Communion in Mass. "Forgive, our God, remit, pardon me my trespasses as many as I have committed, whether in knowledge or in ignorance, whether in word or in deed. All these things pardon me, as Thou art good and kind to men, at the intercession ($\pi\rho\epsilon\sigma\beta\epsilon\acute{\iota}\alpha\iota\varsigma$) of Thy all-undefiled and Ever-Virgin Mother. Preserve me uncondemned, that I may receive Thy precious and undefiled Body, for the healing of my body and soul."—Goar, *Euchologium*, p. 66.

18. After Communion at Mass. "O Lord, be merciful to us, bless us, let Thy countenance be seen upon us, and pity us, Lord, save Thy people, bless Thine heritage, &c., . . . through the prayers and addresses (orationes) which the Lady of us all, Mother of God, the divine (diva) and Holy Mary, and the four bright holy ones, Michael," &c., &c.—Renaudot, *Liturg. Orient.* t. i. p. 29. *Coptic Rite of St. Basil.* Vid. also *ibid.* pp. 29. 37. 89. 515, *of St. Basil, Coptic; of St. Gregory, Coptic; of Alexandria, Greek; and of Ethiopia.*

19. After Communion at Mass. "We have consummated this holy service ($\lambda\epsilon\iota\tau o\upsilon\rho\gamma\acute{\iota}\alpha\nu$), as we have been ordered, O Lord . . . we, sinners, and Thine unworthy servants, who have been made worthy to serve at Thy holy altar, in offering to Thee the bloodless sacrifice, the

immaculate Body, and the precious Blood of the Great
God, our Saviour Jesus Christ, to Thy glory, the unori-
ginate Father, and to the glory of Him, Thy only-
begotten Son, and of the Holy Ghost, good, life-giving,
and consubstantial with Thee. We ask a place on Thy
right hand in Thy fearful and just day through the intercession (διὰ τῶν πρεσβειῶν) and prayers of our most
glorious Lady, Mary, Mother of God, and Ever-Virgin,
and of all saints."—Assemani, *Cod. Liturg.* t. vii. p. 85,
Rite of Alexandria.

20. After Communion at Mass. "We thank Thee,
Lord, Lover of men, Benefactor of our souls, that also on
this day Thou hast vouchsafed us Thy heavenly and
immortal mysteries. Direct our way aright, confirm us
all in Thy fear, &c., . . . at the prayers and supplications of the glorious Theotocos and Ever-Virgin Mary,
and of all Thy saints."—*Eucholog.* p. 86. *Venet.* 1832.

21. Concluding words of Mass. "Blessed is He who
has given us His holy Body and precious Blood. We
have received grace and found life, by virtue of the Cross
of Jesus Christ. To Thee, O Lord, we give thanks, &c.
Praise to Mary, who is the glory of us all, who has
brought forth for us the Eucharist."—Renaudot, *Liturg.
Orient.* t. i. p. 522. *Rite of Ethiopia.*

I will add some of the instances, which have caught
my eye in these ecclesiastical books, of expressions used
of the Blessed Virgin, which, among Latins, though
occurring in some Antiphons, belong more to the
popular than to the formal and appointed devotions
paid to her.

22. "Thee we have as a tower and harbour, and an

acceptable ambassadress (πρέσβιν) to the God whom thou didst bear, Mother of God who hadst no spouse, the salvation of believers."—*Pentecostar.* p. 209. *Venet.* 1820.

23. " O Virgin alone holy and undefiled, who hast miraculously (ἀσπόρως) conceived God, intercede (πρεσβεύε) for the salvation of the soul of thy servant."—*Eucholog.* p. 439. *Venet.* 1832.

24. " Show forth thy speedy protection and aid and mercy on thy servant, and still the waves, thou pure one, of vain thoughts, and raise up my fallen soul, O Mother of God. For I know, O Virgin, I know that thou hast power for whatever thou willest."—*Ibid.* p. 679.

25. " Joachim and Anna were set free from the reproach of childlessness, and Adam and Eve from the corruption of death, O undefiled, in thy holy birth. And thy people keeps festival upon it, being ransomed from the guilt of their offences in crying to thee. The barren bears the Theotocos, and the nurse of Life."— *Horolog.* p. 198. *Venet.* 1836.

26. " Let us now run earnestly to the Theotocos, sinners as we are, and low, and let us fall in repentance, crying from the depths of our souls, Lady, aid us, taking compassion on us. Make haste, we perish under the multitude of our offences. Turn us not, thy servants, empty away; for we have thee as our only hope."—*Ibid.* p. 470. Vid. " My whole hope I repose in thee."—*Triodion*, p. 94. *Venet.* 1820.

27. " We have gained thee for a wall of relief, and the all-perfect salvation of souls, and a relief (πλατυσμὸν)

M

in afflictions, and in thy light we ever rejoice; O Queen, even now through suffering and danger preserve us."— *Ibid*. p. 474.

28. "By thy mediation, Virgin, I am saved."—*Triod.* p. 6. *Venet.* 1820.

29. "The relief of the afflicted, the release of the sick, O Virgin Theotoços, save this city and people; the peace of those who are oppressed by war, the calm of the tempest-tost, the sole protection of the faithful." —Goar, *Eucholog.* p. 478.

30. All through the Office Books are found a great number of Collects and Prayers to the Blessed Virgin, called Theotocia, whereas in the Latin Offices addresses to her scarcely get beyond the Antiphons. There are above 100 of them in the Euchology, above 170 in the Pentecostarium, close upon 350 in the Triodion. These, according to Renaudot, are sometimes collected together into separate volumes. (*Liturg. Orient.* t. ii. p. 98.)

31. At p. 424 of the *Horologium* there is a collection of 100 invocations in her honour, arranged for the year.

32. At page 271 of the *Euchologium*, is a form of prayer to her "in the confession of a sinner," consisting of thirty-six collects, concluding with a Gospel, supplication, &c. If there were any doubt of the difference which the Greeks make between her and the Saints, one of these would be evidence of it. "*Take with you* (παράλαβε) the multitude of Archangels and of the heavenly hosts, and the Forerunner, &c., . . . and make intercession (πρεσβειαν), Holy one, in my behalf with God," p. 275. *Vid.* also *ibid.* p. 390, &c.

33. There is another form of prayer to her at p. 640,

of forty-three collects or verses, "in expectation of war," arranged to form an Iambic acrostic, "O undefiled, be the ally of my household." Among other phrases we read here, "Thou art the head commander (ὁ ἀρχιστράτηγος) of Christians; . . . . "They in their chariots and horses, we, thy people, in thy name;" "with thy spiritual hand cast down the enemies of thy people;" "Thy power runs with thy will (σύνδρομον ἔχεις)," &c. "Deliver not thine heritage, O holy one, into the hands of the heathen, lest they shall say, Where is the Mother of God in whom they trusted?" "Hear from thy holy Temple, thy servants, O pure one, and pour out God's wrath upon the Gentiles that do not know thee, and the kingdoms that have not faithfully called upon thy glorious name."

34. It is remarkable, that, not only the Jacobites, but even the Nestorians agree with the Orthodox in the unlimited honours they pay to the Blessed Virgin. "No one," says Renaudot, "has accused the Orientals of deficiency in the legitimate honours, which are the right of the Deipara; but many have charged them with having sometimes been extravagant in that devotion, and running into superstition, which accusation is not without foundation."—t. i. p. 257.

Another remark of his is in point here. The extracts above made are in great measure from Greek service-books of the day; but even those which are not such are evidence, according to their date and place, of opinions and practices, then and there existing. "Their weight does not depend on the authority of the writers, but on the use of the Churches. Those prayers had their authors, who indeed were not known; but, when once it was clear that they had been used in Mass, who their authors were ceased to be a question."—t. i. p. 173. The existing manuscripts can hardly be supposed to be mere compositions, but are records of rites.

I say then, first:—That usage, which, after a split has taken place in a religious communion, is found to obtain equally in each of its separated parts, may fairly be said to have existed before the split occurred. The concurrence of Orthodox, Nestorian, and Jacobite in the honours they pay to the Blessed Virgin, is an evidence that those honours were in the substance paid to her in their "Undivided Church."

Next:—Passages such as the above, taken from the formal ritual of the Greeks, are more compromising to those who propose entering into communion with them, than such parallel statements as occur in unauthoritative emotions of the Latins.

NOTE V. Page 107.

ON A SCANDALOUS TENET CONCERNING THE BLESSED
VIRGIN.

I find the following very apposite passage at note t,
p. 390, of vol. i. of Mr. Morris's "Jesus the Son of
Mary," a work full of learning, which unhappily I forgot to consult, till my Letter was finished and in type.

"An error of this sort [that our Lady is in the Holy
Eucharist] was held by some persons, and is condemned
in the following language by Benedict XIV. [i.e. by Cardinal Lambertini], as has been pointed out to me by my
old and valued friend, Father Faber: 'This doctrine was
held to be erroneous, dangerous, and scandalous, and the
cultus was reprobated, which in consequence of it they
asserted was to be paid to· the most Blessed Virgin in
the Sacrament of the Altar.'

"Lambertini de Canonizatione Sanctorum, lib. iv.
p. 2, c. 31, n. 32.

"De cultu erga Deiparam in Sacramento Altaris.

"Non multis abhinc annis prodiit Liber de cultu erga
Deiparam in Sacramento altaris, auctore Patre Zephy-
rino de Someire Recollecto Sancti Francisci, in quo
asserebatur, in Sacramento altaris aliquam illius partem
adesse, eandem videlicet carnem, quam olim ejus sanctis-
sima anima vivificavit, eumdemque illum sanguinem,

qui in ejus venis continebatur, et ipsum lac, quo ejus ubera plena erant. Addebatur, nos habere in Sacramento non tantum sanguinem Deiparæ, quatenus in carnem et ossa Christi mutatus est, sed etiam partem sanguinis in propria specie ; neque solum veram carnem ipsius, sed etiam aliquid singulorum membrorum, quia sanguis, et lac, ex quibus formatum et nutritum fuit corpus Christi, missa fuerunt ab omnibus et singulis membris Beatissimæ Virginis.

Etiam Christophorus de Vega in volumine satis amplo, quod inscribitur "Theologia Mariana," Lugduni edito ann. 1653, fusius ea omnia prosecutus est: sed Theophilus Raynaudus in suis Diptychis Marianis, t. 7, p. 65, ea reprobat, asseritque hæresim sapere juxta Guidonem Carmelitam in Summa de hæresibus tract. de hæresi Græcorum, c. 13, cujus verba sunt hæc : "Tertius decimus error Græcorum est. Dicunt enim, quod reliquiæ Panis consecrati sunt reliquiæ corporis Beatæ Virginis. Hic error stultitiæ et amentiæ plenus est. Nam corpus Christi sub qualibet parte hostiæ consecratæ integrum manet. Itaque quælibet pars, a tota consecrata hostia divisa et separata, est verum corpus Christi. Hæreticum autem est et fatuum dicere, quod corpus Christi sit corpus Virginis matris suæ, sicut hæreticum esset dicere, quod Christus esset Beata Virgo : quia distinctorum hominum distincta sunt corpora, nec tantus honor debetur corpori virginis, quantus debetur corpori Christi, cui ratione Divini Suppositi debetur honor latriæ, non corpori Virginis. Igitur dicere, reliquias hostiæ consecratæ esse reliquias corporis Beatæ Virginis est hæreticum manifeste."

Porro Theologorum Princeps D. Thomas, 3 part.
quæst. 31, art. 5, docet primo, Christi corpus conceptum
fuisse ex Beatæ Virginis castissimis et purissimis
sanguinibus non quibuscunque, sed "perductis ad
quamdam ampliorem digestionem per virtutem genera-
tivam ipsius, ut essent materia apta ad conceptum,"
cum Christi conceptio fuerit secundum conditionem
naturæ; materiamque aptam, sive purissimum sanguinem in conceptione Christi sola Spiritus Sancti operatione in utero Virginis adunatum, et in prolem formatum
fuisse; ita ut vere dicatur corpus Christi ex purissimis et
castissimis sanguinibus Beatæ Virginis fuisse formatum.
Docet secundo, non potuisse corpus Christi formari de
aliqua substantia, videlicet de carne et ossibus Beatissimæ
Virginis, cum sint partes integrantes corpus ipsius:
ideoque subtrahi non potuissent sine corruptione, et ejus
diminutione: illud vero, quod aliquando dicitur, Christum de Beata Virgine carnem sumpsisse, intelligendum
esse et explicandum, non quod materia corporis ejus
fuerit actu caro, sed sanguis qui est potentia caro.
Docet demum tertio, quomodo subtrahi potuerit ex
corpore Adam aliqua ejus pars absque ipsius diminutione, cum Adam institutus ut principium quoddam
humanæ naturæ, aliquid habuerit ultra partes sui corporis personales, quod ab eo subtractum est pro formanda
Heva, salva ipsius integritate in ratione perfecti corporis
humani: quæ locum habere non potuerunt in Beatis-
sima Virgine, quæ uti singulare individuum habuit
perfectissimum corpus humanum, et aptissimam materiam ad Christi corpus formandum, quantum est ex
parte feminæ, et ad ejus naturalem generationem.   Ex

quo fit, ut non potuerit, salva integritate Beatæ Virginis, aliquid subtrahi, quod dici posset de substantia corporis ipsius.

Itaque, cum per hanc doctrinam, Fidei principiis conjunctissimam, directe et expressis verbis improbata remanserint asserta in citato libro Patris Zephyrini, ejus doctrina habita est tanquam "erronea, periculosa, et scandalosa," reprobatusque fuit cultus, quem ex ea præstandum Beatissimæ Virgini in Sacramento altaris asserebat. Loquendi autem formulæ a nonnullis Patribus adhibitæ, Caro Mariæ est caro Christi etc. Nobis carnem Mariæ manducandum ad salutem dedit, ita explicandæ sunt, non ut dicamus, in Christo aliquid esse, quod sit Mariæ; sed Christum conceptum esse ex Maria Virgine, materiam ipsa ministrante in similitudinem naturæ et speciei, et ideo filium ejus esse. Sic, quia caro Christi fuit sumpta de David, ut expresse dicitur ad Romanos 1: "Qui factus est ex semine David secundum carnem," David dicitur Christus, ut notat S. Augustinus enarrat, in Psalm. 144, num. 2: "Intelligitur laus ipsi David, laus ipsi Christo." Christus autem secundum carnem David, quia Filius David." Et infra: "Quia itaque ex ipso Christus secundum carnem, ideo David." Est item solemnis Scripturæ usus, loquendo de parentibus, ut caro unius vocitetur caro alterius. Sic Laban, Gen. 29, dixit Jacob: "Os meum es, et caro mea;" et Judas, loquendo de fratre suo Joseph, Gen. 27, ait: "Frater enim, et caro nostra est;" et Lev. 18 legitur: "Soror patris tui caro est patris tui, et soror matris tuæ caro est matris tuæ;" absque eo quod hinc inferri possit, ut in Jacob fuerit aliqua actualis pars corporis Laban, aut in Joseph pars Judæ, aut in filio pars aliqua patris. Igitur id solum affirmare licet, in Sacramento esse carnem Christi assumptam ex Maria, ut ait Sanctus Ambrosius relatus in canone Omnia, de Consecrat. distinct. 2 his verbis : "Hæc caro mea est pro mundi vita, et, ut mirabilius loquar, non alia plane quam quæ nata est de Maria, et passa in cruce, et resurrexit de sepulcro; hæc, inquam, ipsa est." Et infra loquens de corpore Christi : " Illud vere, illud sane, quod sumptum est de Virgine, quod passum est, et sepultum."

So much for Fr. de Someire's wild notion. As to Oswald, his work is on the Index. Vide page 5 of " Appendix Librorum Prohibitorum a die 6 Septembris, 1852, ad mensem Junium, 1858."

Additional Note, Ed. 5.—As another and recent instance of the jealousy with which the Holy See preserves the bounds, within which both tradition and theology confine the *cultus* of the Blessed Virgin, I refer to a Decree of Inquisition of February 28, 1875, addressed to the Bishop of Presmilia, in which the title of " *Queen* of the Heart of Jesus," as well as a certain novelty in the representation of Madonna and Child, as in use in a certain Sodality, are condemned, on the ground that they may be understood in a sense inconsistent with the true faith. It will be found in the " Irish Ecclesiastical Record " for April. 1875.

The Bishop had forbidden the above innovations, and the Sacred Congregation, " to which the examination of the matter was committed by the Holy Father," says to the Bishop, it cannot but "acknowledge and praise your Excellency's zeal and care in defending the purity of the faith, especially in these days, when it seems not to be held in much account by men, who, whatever their piety, are led by a sovereign love of novelty to neglect the danger, incurred in consequence by the simple among the faithful, of deviating from the right sense of piety and devotion by means of strange and foreign doctrines.

"To obviate this danger," the letter proceeds to say, the Sacred Congregation has at other times (*altre volte*) interposed, "to warn and reprehend" those who, by such language about the Blessed Virgin, "have not sufficiently conformed to the right Catholic sense," but "ascribe power to her, as issuing from her divine maternity, beyond its due limits; as if this new title had brought her an accession of greatness and glory hitherto unknown, and, in the notion of her sublime dignity hitherto held by the Church according to the doctrine of the Holy Fathers, there were something still wanting, not considering that, although she has the greatest influence (*possa moltissimo*) with her Son, still it cannot be piously affirmed that she exercises command over Him (*eserciti impero*)."

Further, in order apparently to mark the ministrative office of the Blessed Virgin, and her dependence as a creature on her Son, "it has been ruled by the Sovereign Pontiff, that the images or pictures to be consecrated to the *cultus* in question, must represent the Virgin as carrying the infant Jesus, not placed before her knees, but in her arms."

A LETTER ADDRESSED TO
HIS GRACE THE DUKE OF NORFOLK ON OCCASION OF
MR. GLADSTONE'S RECENT EXPOSTULATION.

CONTENTS.

TO HIS GRACE THE DUKE OF NORFOLK

HEREDITARY EARL MARSHAL OF ENGLAND, ETC., ETC.

————◆————

My dear Duke of Norfolk,

When I yielded to the earnest wish which you, together with many others, urged upon me, that I should reply to Mr. Gladstone's recent expostulation, a friend suggested that I ought to ask your Grace's permission to address my remarks to you.   Not that for a moment he or I thought of implicating you, in any sense or measure, in a responsibility which is solely and entirely my own; but on a very serious occasion, when such heavy charges had been made against the Catholics of England by so powerful and so earnest an adversary, it seemed my duty, in meeting his challenge, to gain the support, if I could, of a name, which is the special representative and the fitting sample of a laity, as zealous for the Catholic Religion as it is patriotic.

You consented with something of the reluctance which I had felt myself when called upon to write ; for it was hard to be summoned at any age, early or late, from a peaceful course of life and the duties of one's station, to a scene of war. Still, you consented; and for myself, it is the compensation for a very unpleasant task, that I, who belong to a generation that is fast flitting away, am thus enabled, in what is likely to be my last publication, to associate myself with one, on many accounts so dear to me,—so full of young promise—whose career is before him.

I deeply grieve that Mr. Gladstone has felt it his duty to speak with such extraordinary severity of our Religion and of ourselves. I consider he has committed himself to a representation of ecclesiastical documents which will not hold, and to a view of our position in the country which we have neither deserved nor can be patient under. None but the *Schola Theologorum* is competent to determine the force of Papal and Synodal utterances, and the exact interpretation of them is a work of time. But so much may be safely said of the decrees which have lately been promulgated, and of the faithful who have received them, that Mr. Gladstone's account, both of them and of us, is neither trustworthy nor charitable.

Yet not a little may be said in explanation of a step, which so many of his admirers and well-wishers deplore. I own to a deep feeling, that Catholics may in good measure thank themselves, and no one else, for having alienated from them so religious a mind. There are those among us, as it must be confessed, who for years past have conducted themselves as if no responsibility attached to wild words and overbearing deeds; who have stated truths in the most paradoxical form, and stretched principles till they were close upon snapping; and who at length, having done their best to set the house on fire, leave to others the task of putting out the flame. The English people are sufficiently sensitive of the claims of the Pope, without having them, as if in defiance, flourished in their faces. Those claims most certainly I am not going to deny; I have never denied them. I have no intention, now that I have to write upon them, to conceal any part of them. And I uphold them as heartily as I recognize my duty of loyalty to the constitution, the laws and the government of England. I see no inconsistency in my being at once a good Catholic and a good Englishman. Yet it is one thing to be able to satisfy myself as to my consistency, quite another to satisfy others; and, undisturbed as I am in my own conscience, I have great difficulties in the task before me. I have one difficulty to overcome in the present excitement of the public mind against our Religion, caused partly by the chronic extravagances of knots of Catholics here and there, partly by the vehement rhetoric which is the occasion and subject of this Letter. A worse difficulty lies in getting people, as they are commonly found, to put off the modes of speech and language which are usual with them, and to enter into scientific distinctions and traditionary rules of interpretation, which as being new to them, appear evasive and unnatural. And a third difficulty, as I may call it, is this—that in so very wide a subject, opening as great a variety of questions, and of opinions upon them, while it will be simply necessary to take the objections made against us and our faith, one by

N

one, readers may think me trifling with their patience, because they do not find those points first dealt with, on which they lay most stress themselves.

But I have said enough by way of preface; and without more delay turn to Mr. Gladstone's pamphlet.

§ 1. *Introductory Remarks.*

THE main question which Mr. Gladstone has started I consider to be this:—Can Catholics be trustworthy subjects of the State? has not a foreign Power a hold over their consciences such, that it may at any time be used to the serious perplexity and injury of the civil government under which they live? Not that Mr. Gladstone confines himself to these questions, for he goes out of his way, I am sorry to say, to taunt us with our loss of mental and moral freedom, a vituperation which is not necessary for his purpose at all. He informs us too that we have " repudiated ancient history," and are rejecting modern " thought," and that our Church has been " refurbishing her rusty tools," and has been lately aggravating, and is likely still more to aggravate, our state of bondage. I think it unworthy of Mr. Gladstone's high character thus to have inveighed against us ; what intellectual manliness is left to us according to him ? yet his circle of acquaintance is too wide, and his knowledge of his countrymen on the other hand too accurate, for him not to know that he is bringing a great amount of odium and bad feeling upon excellent men, whose only offence is their religion. The more intense is the prejudice with which we are regarded by whole classes of men, the less is there of generosity in his pouring upon us superfluous reproaches. The graver the charge which is the direct occasion of his writing against us, the more careful should he be not to prejudice judge and jury to our disadvantage. No rhetoric is needed in England against an unfortunate Catholic at any time; but so little is Mr. Gladstone conscious of his treatment of us, that in one place of his Pamphlet, strange as it may seem, he makes it his boast that he has been careful to " do nothing towards importing passion into what is matter of pure argument," pp. 15, 16. I venture to think he will one day be sorry for what he has said.

However, we must take things as we find them; and what I propose to do is this—to put aside, unless it comes directly in my way, his accusation against us of repudiating ancient history, rejecting modern thought, and renouncing our mental freedom, and to confine myself for the most part to what he principally insists upon, that Catholics, if they act consistently with their principles, cannot be loyal subjects;—I shall not, however, omit notice of his attack upon our moral uprightness.

The occasion and the grounds of Mr. Gladstone's impeachment of us, if I understand him, are as follows :—He was alarmed, as a statesman, ten years ago by the Pope's Encyclical of December 8, and by the Syllabus of Erroneous Propositions which, by the Pope's authority, accompanied its transmission to the bishops. Then came the Definitions of the Vatican Council in 1870, upon the universal jurisdiction and doctrinal infallibility of the Pope. And lastly, as the event which turned alarm into indignation, and into the duty of public remonstrance, "the Roman Catholic Prelacy of Ireland thought fit to procure the rejection of" the Irish University Bill of February, 1873, "by the direct influence which they exercised over a certain number of Irish Members of Parliament," &c. p. 60. This step on the part of the bishops showed, if I understand him, the new and mischievous force which had been acquired at Rome by the late acts there, or at least left him at liberty, by causing his loss of power, to denounce it. "From that time forward the situation was changed," and an opening was made for a "broad political discussion" on the subject of the Catholic religion and its professors, and "a debt to the country had to be disposed of." That debt, if I am right, will be paid, if he can ascertain, on behalf of the country, that there is nothing in the Catholic Religion to hinder its professors from being as loyal as other subjects of the State, and that the See of Rome cannot interfere with their civil duties so as to give the civil power trouble or alarm. The main ground on which he relies for the necessity of some such inquiry is, first, the text of the authoritative documents of 1864 and 1870; next, and still more, the *animus* which they breathe, and the sustained aggressive spirit which they disclose; and thirdly, the daring deed of aggression in 1873, when the Pope, acting (as it is alleged) upon the Irish Members of Parliament, succeeded in ousting from their seats a ministry who, besides past benefits, were at that very time doing for Irish Catholics, and therefore ousted for doing, a special service.

Now, it would be preposterous and officious in me to put myself forward as champion for the Venerable Prelacy of Ireland, or to take upon myself the part of advocate and representative of the Holy See. " Non tali auxilio ;" in neither character could I come forward without great presumption ; not the least for this reason, because I cannot know the exact points which are really the *gist* of the affront, which Mr. Gladstone conceives he has sustained, whether from the one quarter or from the other ; yet in a question so nearly interesting myself as that February bill, which he brought into the House, in great sincerity and kindness, for the benefit of the Catholic University in Ireland, I may be allowed to say thus much—that I, who now have no official relation to the Irish Bishops, and am not in any sense in the counsels of Rome, felt at once, when I first saw the outline of that bill, the greatest astonishment on reading one of its provisions, and a dread which painfully affected me, lest Mr. Gladstone perhaps was acting on an understanding with the Catholic Prelacy. I did not see how in honour they could accept it. It was possible, did the question come over again, to decide in favour of the Queen's Colleges, and to leave the project of a Catholic University alone. The Holy See might so have decided in 1847. But at or about that date, three rescripts had come from Rome in favour of a distinctively Catholic Institution ; a National Council had decided in its favour ; large offers of the Government had been rejected ; great commotions had been caused in the political world ; munificent con-

tributions had been made ;—all on the sole principle
that Catholic teaching was to be upheld in the country
inviolate. If, then, for the sake of a money grant, or
other secular advantage, this ground of principle was
deserted, and Catholic youths after all were allowed to
attend the lectures of men of no religion, or of the Protestant, the contest of thirty years would have been
stultified, and the Pope and the Bishops would seem to
have been playing a game, while putting forward the
plea of conscience and religious duty. I hoped that the
clause in the Bill, which gave me such uneasiness, could
have been omitted from it; but, anyhow, it was an
extreme relief to me when the papers announced that the
Bishops had expressed their formal dissatisfaction with it.

They determined to decline a gift laden with such a
condition, and who can blame them for so doing ? who
can be surprised that they should now do what they did
in 1847 ? what new move in politics was it, if they so
determined? what was there in it of a factious character?
Is the Catholic Irish interest the only one which is not
to be represented in the House of Commons ? Why is
not that interest as much a matter of right as any other?
I fear to expose my own ignorance of Parliamentary
rules and proceedings, but I had supposed that the rail-
way interest, and what is called the publican interest,
were very powerful there : in Scotland, too, I believe, a
government has a formidable party to deal with ; and, to
revert to Ireland, there are the Home-rulers, who have
objects in view quite distinct from, or contrary to, those
of the Catholic hierarchy. As to the Pope, looking at
the surface of things, there is nothing to suggest that he

interfered, there was no necessity of interference, on so plain a point ; and, when an act can be sufficiently accounted for without introducing an hypothetical cause, it is bad logic to introduce it. Speaking according to my lights, I altogether disbelieve the interposition of Rome in the matter. In the proceedings which they adopted, the Bishops were only using civil rights, common to all, which others also used and in their own way. Why might it not be their duty to promote the interests of their religion by means of their political opportunities ? Is there no Exeter Hall interest ? I thought it was a received theory of our Reformed Constitution that Members of Parliament were representatives, and in some sort delegates of their constituents, and that the strength of each interest was shown, and the course of the nation determined, by the divisions in the House of Commons. I recollect the *Times* intimating its regret, after one general election, that there was no English Catholic in the new House, on the ground that every class and party should be represented there. Surely the Catholic religion has not a small party in Ireland ; why then should it not have a corresponding number of exponents and defenders at Westminster ? So clear does this seem to me, that I think there must be some defect in my knowledge of facts to explain Mr. Gladstone's surprise and displeasure at the conduct of the Irish Prelacy in 1873 ; yet I suspect none ; and, if there be none, then his unreasonableness in this instance of Ireland makes it not unlikely that he is unreasonable also in his judgment of the Encyclical, Syllabus, and Vatican Decrees.

However, the Bishops, I believe, not only opposed Mr. Gladstone's bill, but, instead of it, they asked for some money grant towards the expenses of their University. If so, their obvious argument was this—that Catholics formed the great majority of the population of Ireland, and it was not fair that the Protestant minority should have all that was bestowed in endowment or otherwise upon education. To this the reply, I suppose, would be, that it was not Protestantism, but liberal education that had the money, and that, if the Bishops chose to give up their own principles and act as Liberals, they might have the benefit of it too. I am not concerned here with these arguments, but I wish to notice the position which the Bishops would occupy in urging such a request :—I must not say that they were Irishmen first and Catholics afterwards, but I do say that in such a demand they spoke not simply as Catholic Bishops, but as the Bishops of a Catholic nation. They did not speak from any promptings of the Encyclical, Syllabus, or Vatican Decrees. They claimed as Irishmen a share in the endowments of the country; and has not Ireland surely a right to speak in such a matter, and might not her Bishops fairly represent her? It seems to me a great mistake to think that everything that is done by the Irish Bishops and clergy is done on an ecclesiastical motive; why not on a national? but if so, such acts have nothing to do with Rome. I know well what simple firm faith the great body of the Irish people have, and how they put the Catholic Religion before anything else in the world. It is their comfort, their joy, their treasure, their boast, their compensation for a hundred worldly disadvantages; but who can deny that in politics their conduct at times—nay, more than at times—has had a flavour rather of their nation than of their Church? Only in the last general election this was said, when they were so earnest for Home Rule. Why, then, must Mr. Gladstone come down upon the Catholic Religion, because the Irish love dearly the Green Island, and its interests? Ireland is not the only country in which politics, or patriotism, or party, has been so closely associated with religion in the nation or a class, that it is difficult to say which of the various motive principles was uppermost. "The Puritan," says Macaulay, "prostrated himself in the dust before his Maker, but he set his foot on the neck of his king:" I am not accusing such a man of hypocrisy on account of this; having great wrongs, as he considered, both in religious and temporal matters, and the authors of these distinct wrongs being the same persons, he did not nicely discriminate between the acts which he did as a patriot and the acts which he did as a Puritan. And so as regards Irishmen, they do not, cannot, distinguish between their love of Ireland and their love of religion; their patriotism is religious, and their religion is strongly tinctured with patriotism; and it is hard to recognize the abstract and Ideal Ultramontane, pure and simple, in the concrete exhibition of him in flesh and blood as found in the polling-booth or in his chapel. I do not see how the Pope can be made answerable for him in any of his political acts during the last fifty years.

This leads me to a subject, of which Mr. Gladstone makes a good deal in his pamphlet. I will say of a

great man, whom he quotes, and for whose memory I
have a great respect, I mean Bishop Doyle, that there
was just a little tinge of patriotism in the way in which,
on one occasion, he speaks of the Pope. I dare say any
of us would have done the same, in the heat of a great
struggle for national liberty, for he said nothing but
what was true and honest; I only mean that the energetic language which he used was not exactly such as
would have suited the atmosphere of Rome. He says to
Lord Liverpool, "We are taunted with the proceedings
of Popes. What, my Lord, have we Catholics to do
with the proceedings of Popes, or why should we be
made accountable for them?" p. 27. Now, with some
proceedings of Popes, we Catholics have very much to do
indeed; but, if the context of his words is consulted, I
make no doubt it would be found that he was referring
to certain proceedings of certain Popes, when he said that
Catholics had no part of their responsibility. Assuredly
there are certain acts of Popes in which no one would
like to have part. Then, again, his words require some
pious interpretation when he says that "the allegiance
due to the king and the allegiance due to the Pope, are
as distinct and as divided in their nature as any two
things can possibly be," p. 30. Yes, in their nature, in
the abstract, but not in the particular case; for a heathen
State might bid me throw incense upon the altar of
Jupiter, and the Pope would bid me not to do so. I
venture to make the same remark on the Address of the
Irish Bishops to their clergy and laity in 1826, quoted
at p. 31, and on the Declaration of the Vicars Apostolic
in England, *ibid.*

But I must not be supposed for an instant to mean, in what I have said, that the venerable men, to whom I have referred, were aware of any ambiguity either in such statements as the above, or in others which were denials of the Pope's infallibility. Indeed, one of them at an earlier date, 1793, Dr. Troy, Archbishop of Dublin, had introduced into onè of his Pastorals the subject which Mr. Gladstone considers they so summarily disposed of. The Archbishop says, "Many Catholics contend that the Pope, when teaching the universal Church, as their supreme visible head and pastor, as successor to St. Peter, and heir to the promises of special assistance made to him by Jesus Christ, is infallible; and that his decrees and decisions in that capacity are to be respected as rules of faith, when they are dogmatical or confined to doctrinal points of faith and morals. Others deny this, and require the expressed or tacit acquiescence of the Church, assembled or dispersed, to stamp infallibility on his dogmatical decrees. Until the Church shall decide upon this question of the Schools, either opinion may be adopted by individual Catholics, without any breach of Catholic communion or peace. The Catholics of Ireland have lately declared, that it is not an article of the Catholic faith; nor are they thereby required to believe or profess that the Pope is infallible, without adopting or abjuring either of the recited opinions which are open to discussion, while the Church continues silent about them." The Archbishop thus addressed his flock, at the time when he was informing them that the Pope had altered the oath which was taken by the Catholic Bishops.

As to the language of the Bishops in 1826, we must recollect that at that time the clergy, both of Ireland and England, were educated in Gallican opinions. They took those opinions for granted, and they thought, if they went so far as to ask themselves the question, that the definition of Papal Infallibility was simply impossible. Even among those at the Vatican Council, who themselves personally believed in it, I believe there were Bishops who, until the actual definition had been passed, thought that such a definition could not be made. Perhaps they would argue that, though the historical evidence was sufficient for their own personal conviction, it was not sufficiently clear of difficulties to be made the ground of a Catholic dogma. Much more would this be the feeling of the Bishops in 1826. "How," they would ask, "can it ever come to pass that a majority of our order should find it their duty to relinquish their prime prerogative, and to make the Church take the shape of a pure monarchy?" They would think its definition as much out of the question, as the prospect that, in twenty-five years after their time, there would be a hierarchy of thirteen Bishops in England, with a cardinal for Archbishop.

But, all this while, such modes of thinking were foreign altogether to the minds of the *entourage* of the Holy See. Mr. Gladstone himself says, and the Duke of Wellington and Sir Robert Peel must have known it as well as he, "The Popes have kept up, with comparatively little intermission, for well-nigh a thousand years, their claim to dogmatic infallibility," p. 28. Then, if the Pope's claim to infallibility was so patent a fact, could they ever suppose that he could be brought to admit that it was hopeless to turn that claim into a dogma? In truth, Wellington and Peel were very little interested in that question; as was said in a Petition or Declaration, signed among others by Dr. Troy, it was "immaterial in a political light;" but, even if they thought it material, or if there were other questions they wanted to ask, why go to Bishop Doyle? If they wanted to obtain some real information about the probabilities of the future, why did they not go to head-quarters? Why did they potter about the halls of Universities in this matter of Papal exorbitances, or rely upon the pamphlets or examinations of Bishops whom they never asked for their credentials? Why not go at once to Rome?

The reason is plain: it was a most notable instance, with a grave consequence, of what is a fixed tradition with us the English people, and a great embarrassment to every administration in its dealings with Catholics. I recollect, years ago, Dr. Griffiths, Vicar Apostolic of the London District, giving me an account of an interview he had with the late Lord Derby, then I suppose Colonial Secretary. I understood him to say that Lord Derby was in perplexity at the time, on some West India matter, in which Catholics were concerned, because he could not find their responsible representative. He wanted Dr. Griffiths to undertake the office, and expressed something of disappointment when the Bishop felt obliged to decline it. A chronic malady has from time to time its paroxysms, and the history on which I am now engaged is a serious instance of it. I think it is impossible that the British government could have entered into formal negotiations with the Pope, without its transpiring in the course of them, and its becoming perfectly clear, that Rome could never be a party to such a pledge as England wanted, and that no pledge from Catholics was of any value to which Rome was not a party.

But no; they persisted in an enterprise which was hopeless in its first principle, for they thought to break the indissoluble tie which bound together the head and the members,—and doubtless Rome felt the insult, though she might think it prudent not to notice it. France was not the keystone of the ecumenical power, though her Church was so great and so famous; nor could the hierarchy of Ireland, in spite of its fidelity to the Catholic faith, give any pledge of the future to the statesmen who required one; there was but one See, whose word was worth anything in the matter, "that church" (to use the language of the earliest of our Doctors) "to which the faithful all round about are bound to have recourse." Yet for three hundred years it has been the official rule with England to ignore the existence of the Pope, and to deal with Catholics in England, not as his children, but as sectaries of the Roman Catholic persuasion. Napoleon said to his envoy, "Treat with the Pope as if he was master of 100,000 men." So clearly did he, from mere worldly sagacity, comprehend the Pope's place in the then state of European affairs, as to say that, "if the Pope had not existed, it would have been well to have created him for that occasion, as the Roman consuls created a dictator in difficult

circumstances." (Alison's *Hist.* ch. 35.) But we, in
the instance of the greatest, the oldest power in Europe,
a church whose grandeur in past history demanded, one
would think, some reverence in our treatment of her, the
mother of English Christianity, who, whether her subsequent conduct had always been motherly or not, had
been a true friend to us in the beginning of our history,
her we have not only renounced, but, to use a familiar
word, we have absolutely cut. Time has gone on and
we have no relentings ; to-day, as little as yesterday, do
we understand that pride was not made for man, nor the
cuddling of resentments for a great people. I am entering into no theological question : I am speaking all
along of mere decent secular intercourse between England and Rome. A hundred grievances would have
been set right on their first uprising, had there been a
frank diplomatic understanding between two great
powers ; but, on the contrary, even within the last few
weeks, the present Ministry has destroyed any hope of
a better state of things by withdrawing from the Vatican
the makeshift channel of intercourse which had of late
years been permitted there.

The world of politics has its laws ; and such abnormal
courses as England has pursued have their *Nemesis.*
An event has taken place which, alas, already makes
itself felt in issues, unfortunate for English Catholics
certainly, but also, as I think, for our country. A great
Council has been called ; and as England has for so long a
time ignored Rome, Rome, I suppose, it must be said, has
in turn ignored England. I do not mean of set purpose
ignored, but as the natural consequence of our act,

Bishops brought from the corners of the earth, in 1870, what could they know of English blue books and Parliamentary debates in the years 1826 and 1829 ? It was an extraordinary gathering, and its possibility, its purpose, and its issue, were alike marvellous, as depending on a coincidence of strange conditions, which, as might be said beforehand, never could take place. Such was the long reign of the Pope, in itself a marvel, as being the sole exception to a recognized ecclesiastical tradition. Only a Pontiff so unfortunate, so revered, so largely loved, so popular even with Protestants, with such a prestige of long sovereignty, with such claims on the Bishops around him, both of age and of paternal gracious acts, only such a man could have harmonized and guided to the conclusion which he pointed out, an assembly so variously composed. And, considering the state of theological opinion seventy years before, not less marvellous was the concurrence of all but a few out of so many hundred Bishops in the theological judgment, so long desired at Rome; the protest made by some eighty or ninety, at the termination of the Council, against the proceedings of the vast majority lying, not against the truth of the doctrine then defined, but against the fact of its definition. Nor less to be noted is the neglect of the Catholic powers to send representatives to the Council, who might have laid before the Fathers its political bearings. For myself, I did not call it inopportune, for times and seasons are known to God alone, and persecution may be as opportune, though not so pleasant as peace; nor, in accepting as a dogma what I had ever held as a truth, could I be

o

doing violence to any theological view or conclusion of my own; nor has the acceptance of it any logical or practical effect whatever, as I consider, in weakening my allegiance to Queen Victoria; but there are few Catholics, I think, who will not deeply regret, though no one be in fault, that the English and Irish Prelacies of 1826 did not foresee the possibility of the Synodal determinations of 1870, nor can we wonder that Statesmen should feel themselves aggrieved that stipulations, which they considered necessary for Catholic emancipation, should have been, as they may think, rudely cast to the winds.

And now I must pass from the mere accidents of the controversy to its essential points, and I cannot treat them to the satisfaction of Mr. Gladstone, unless I go back a great way, and be allowed to speak of the ancient Catholic Church.

§ 2. *The Ancient Church.*

WHEN Mr. Gladstone accuses us of "repudiating ancient history," he means the ancient history of the Church: also, I understand him to be viewing that history under a particular aspect. There are many aspects in which Christianity presents itself to us ; for instance, the aspect of social usefulness, or of devotion, or again of theology ; but, though he in one place glances at the last of these aspects, his own view of it is its relation towards the civil power. He writes " as one of the world at large ; " as a " layman who has spent most and the best years of his life in the observation and practice of politics " (p. 7) ; and, as a statesmen, he naturally looks at the Church on its political side. Accordingly, in his title-page, in which he professes to be expostulating with us for accepting the Vatican Decrees, he does so, not for any reason whatever, but because of their incompatibility with our civil allegiance. This is the key-note of his impeachment of us. As a public man, he has only to do with the public action and effect of our Religion, its aspect upon national affairs, on our civil duties, on our foreign interests ; and he tells us that our Religion has a bearing and behaviour towards the State utterly unlike that of ancient Christianity, so unlike that we may be even said to repudiate what Christianity was in its first centuries, so unlike to what it was then, that we have actually forfeited the proud boast of being " Ever one and the same;" unlike, I say, in this, that our action is so antagonistic to the State's action, and our claims so menacing to civil peace and prosperity.

Indeed ! then I suppose that St. Ignatius of Antioch, and St. Polycarp of Smyrna, and St. Cyprian of Carthage, and St. Laurence of Rome, that St. Alexander and St. Paul of Constantinople, that St. Ambrose of Milan, that Popes Leo, John, Sylverian, Gregory, and Martin, all members of the " undivided Church," cared supremely, and laboured successfully, to cultivate peaceful relations with the government of Rome. They had no doctrines and precepts, no rules of life, no isolation and aggressiveness, which caused them to be considered, in spite of themselves, the enemies of the human race ! May I not, without disrespect, submit to Mr. Gladstone that this is very paradoxical ? Surely it is our fidelity to the history of our forefathers, and not its repudiation, which Mr. Gladstone dislikes in us. When, indeed, was it in ancient times that the State did not show jealousy of the Church ? Was it when Decius and Dioclesian slaughtered their thousands who had abjured the religion of old Rome ? or, was it when Athanasius was banished to Treves ? or when Basil, on the Imperial Prefect's crying out, " Never before did any man make so free with me," answered, " Perhaps you never before fell in with a Bishop " ? or when Chrysostom was sent off to Cucusus, to be worried to death by an Empress? Go through the long annals of Church History, century after century, and say, was there ever a time when her Bishops, and notably the Bishop of Rome, were slow to give their testimony in behalf of the moral and revealed law and to suffer for their obedience to it? ever a time when they forgot that they had a message to deliver to the world,—not the task merely of administering spiritual consolation, or of making the sick-bed easy, or of training up good members of society, or of " serving tables " (though all this was included in their range of duty),—but specially and directly, a definite message to high and low, from the world's Maker, whether men would hear or whether they would forbear? The history surely of the Church in all past times, ancient as well as medieval, is the very embodiment of that tradition of Apostolical independence and freedom of speech which in the eyes of man is her great offence now.

Nay, that independence, I may say, is even one of her Notes or credentials; for where shall we find it except in the Catholic Church? " I spoke of Thy testimonies," says the Psalmist, " even before kings, and I was not ashamed." This verse, I think Dr. Arnold used to say, rose up in judgment against the Anglican Church, in spite of its real excellences. As to the Oriental Churches, every one knows in what bondage they lie, whether they are under the rule of the Czar or of the Sultan. Such is the actual fact that, whereas it is the very mission of Christianity to bear witness to the Creed and Ten Commandments in a

world which is averse to them, Rome is now the one
faithful representative, and thereby is heir and successor,
of that free-spoken dauntless Church of old, whose
political and social traditions Mr. Gladstone says the
said Rome has repudiated.

I have one thing more to say on the subject of the
"semper eadem." In truth, this fidelity to the ancient
Christian system, seen in modern Rome, was the
luminous fact which more than any other turned men s
minds at Oxford forty years ago to look towards her
with reverence, interest, and love. It affected individual
minds variously of course; some it even brought on
eventually to conversion, others it only restrained from
active opposition to her claims; but none of us could read
the Fathers, and determine to be their disciples, without
feeling that Rome, like a faithful steward, had kept in
fulness and in vigour what our own communion had let
drop. The Tracts for the Times were founded on a
deadly antagonism to what in these last centuries has
been called Erastianism or Cæsarism. Their writers considered the Church to be a divine creation, "not of men,
neither by man, but by Jesus Christ," the Ark of Salvation, the Oracle of Truth, the Bride of Christ, with a
message to all men everywhere, and a claim on their
love and obedience; and, in relation to the civil power,
the object of that promise of the Jewish prophets,
"Behold, I will lift up My Hand to the Gentiles, and
will set up My standard to the peoples: kings and their
queens shall bow down to thee with their face toward
the earth, and they shall lick up the dust of thy feet."
No Ultramontane (so called) could go beyond those

writers in the account which they gave of her from the
Prophets, and that high notion is recorded beyond
mistake in a thousand passages of their writings.

There is a fine passage of Mr. Keble's in the *British
Critic*, in animadversion upon a contemporary reviewer.
Mr. Hurrell Froude, speaking of the Church of England,
had said that " she was 'united' to the State as Israel
to Egypt." This shocked the reviewer in question,
who exclaimed in consequence, "The Church is *not*
united to the State as Israel to Egypt; it is united as a
believing *wife* to a *husband* who threatened to apostatize;
and, as a Christian wife so placed would act . . cling-
ing to the connexion . . so the Church must struggle
even now, and save, not herself, but the State, from the
crime of a *divorce*." On this Mr. Keble says, " We
had thought that the Spouse of the Church was a very
different Person from any or all States, and her relation
to the State through Him *very unlike that of hers, whose
duties are summed up in ' love, service, cherishing, and
obedience.'* And since the one is exclusively of this
world, the other essentially of the eternal world, *such
an Alliance* as the above sentence describes, would have
seemed to us, *not only fatal, but monstrous !* "[1] And he
quotes the lines,—

> " Mortua quinetiam jungebat corpora vivis,
> Componens manibusque manus, atque oribus ora :
> Tormenti genus ! "

It was this same conviction that the Church had rights
which the State could not touch, and was prone to

[1] Review of Gladstone's " The State in its Relations with the
Church," October, 1839.

ignore, and which in consequence were the occasion of
great troubles between the two, that led Mr. Froude at
the beginning of the movement to translate the letters
of St. Thomas Becket, and Mr. Bowden to write the
Life of Hildebrand. As to myself, I will but refer, as
to one out of many passages with the same drift, in the
books and tracts which I published at that time, to my
Whit-Monday and Whit-Tuesday Sermons.

I believe a large number of members of the Church
of England at this time are faithful to the doctrine
which was proclaimed within its pale in 1833, and
following years; the main difference between them and
Catholics being, not as to the existence of certain high
prerogatives and spiritual powers in the Christian
Church, but that the powers which we give to the Holy
See, they lodge in her Bishops and Priests, whether as
a body or individually. Of course, this is a very important difference, but it does not interfere with my
argument here. It does seem to me preposterous to
charge the Catholic Church of to-day with repudiating
ancient history by certain political acts of hers, and
thereby losing her identity, when it was her very likeness in political action to the Church of the first
centuries, that has in our time attracted even to her
communion, and at least to her teaching, not a few
educated men, who made those first centuries their
special model.

But I have more to say on this subject, perhaps too
much, when I go on, as I now do, to contemplate the
Christian Church, when persecution was exchanged for

establishment, and her enemies became her children. As she resisted and defied her persecutors, so she ruled her convert people. And surely this was but natural, and will startle those only to whom the subject is new. If the Church is independent of the State, so far as she is a messenger from God, therefore, should the State, with its high officials and its subject masses, come into her communion, it is plain that they must at once change hostility into submission. There was no middle term ; either they must deny her claim to divinity or humble themselves before it,—that is, as far as the domain of religion extends, and that domain is a wide one. They could not place God and man on one level. We see this principle carried out among ourselves in all sects every day, though with greater or less exactness of application, according to the supernatural power which they ascribe to their ministers or clergy. It is a sentiment of nature, which anticipates the inspired command, "Obey them that have the rule over you, and submit yourselves, for they watch for your souls."

As regards the Roman Emperors, immediately on their becoming Christians, their exaltation of the hierarchy was in proportion to its abject condition in the heathen period. Grateful converts felt that they could not do too much in its honour and service. Emperors bowed the head before the Bishops, kissed their hands and asked their blessing. When Constantine entered into the presence of the assembled Prelates at Nicæa, his eyes fell, the colour mounted up into his cheek, and his mien was that of a suppliant ; he would not sit, till the Bishops bade him, and he kissed the wounds of the

Confessors. Thus he set the example for the successors
of his power, nor did the Bishops decline such honours.
Royal ladies served them at table ; victorious generals
did penance for sin and asked forgiveness. When they
quarrelled with them, and would banish them, their hand
trembled when they came to sign the order, and after
various attempts they gave up their purpose. Soldiers
raised to sovereignty asked their recognition and were
refused it. Cities under imperial displeasure sought
their intervention, and the master of thirty legions found
himself powerless to withstand the feeble voice of some
aged travel-stained stranger.

Laws were passed in favour of the Church ; Bishops
could only be judged by Bishops, and the causes of their
clergy were withdrawn from the secular courts. Their
sentence was final, as if it were the Emperor's own, and
the governors of provinces were bound to put it in
execution. Litigants everywhere were allowed the liberty
of referring their causes to the tribunal of the Bishops,
who, besides, became arbitrators on a large scale in
private quarrels ; and the public, even heathens, wished
it so. St. Ambrose was sometimes so taken up with
business of this sort, that he had time for nothing else.
St. Austin and Theodoret both complain of the weight of
such secular engagements, as were forced upon them by
the importunity of the people. Nor was this all ; the
Emperors showed their belief in the divinity of the
Church and of its creed by acts of what we should now
call persecution. Jews were forbidden to proselytize a
Christian ; Christians were forbidden to become pagans ;
pagan rights were abolished, the books of heretics and

infidels were burned wholesale ; their chapels were razed to the ground, and even their private meetings were made illegal.

These characteristics of the convert Empire were the immediate, some of them the logical, consequences of its new faith. Had not the Emperors honoured Christianity in its ministers and in its precepts, they would not properly have deserved the name of converts. Nor was it unreasonable in litigants voluntarily to frequent the episcopal tribunals, if they got justice done to them there better than in the civil courts. As to the prohibition of heretical meetings, I cannot get myself quite to believe that Pagans, Marcionites, and Manichees had much tenderness of conscience in their religious profession, or were wounded seriously by the Imperial rescripts to their disadvantage. Many of these sects were of a most immoral character, whether in doctrine or practice ; others were forms of witchcraft ; often they were little better than paganism. The Novatians certainly stand on higher ground ; but on the whole, it would be most unjust to class such wild, impure, inhuman rites with even the most extravagant and grotesque of American sectaries now. They could entertain no bitter feeling that injustice was done them in their repression. They did not make free thought or private judgment their watch-words. The populations of the Empire did not rise in revolt when its religion was changed. There were two broad conditions which accompanied the grant of all this ecclesiastical power and privilege, and made the exercise of it possible ; first, that the people con- sented to it, secondly, that the law of the Empire enacted

and enforced it. Thus high and low opened the door to it.
The Church of course would say that such prerogatives
were justly hers, as being at least congruous grants
made to her, on the part of the State, in return for the
benefits which she bestowed upon it. It was her right
to demand them, and the State's duty to concede them.
This seems to have been the basis of the new state of
society.   And in fact these prerogatives were in force
and in exercise all through those troublous centuries
which followed the break-up of the Imperial sway : and,
though the handling of them at length fell into the
hands of one see exclusively (on which I shall remark presently), the see of Peter, yet the substance and character of these prerogatives, and the
Church's claim to possess them, remained untouched.
The change in the internal allocation of power did
not affect the existence and the use of the power
itself.

Ranke, speaking of this development of ecclesiastical
supremacy upon the conversion of the Empire, remarks
as follows :—

"It appears to me that this was the result of an
internal necessity.   The rise of Christianity involved the
liberation of religion from all political elements. From
this followed the growth of a distinct ecclesiastical class
with a peculiar constitution.   In this separation of the
Church from the State consists, perhaps the greatest, the
most pervading and influential peculiarity of all Christian times.   The spiritual and secular powers may come
into near contact, may even stand in the closest community ; but they can be thoroughly incorporated only at

rare conjunctures and for a short period. Their mutual relations, their positions with regard to each other, form, from this time forward, one of the most important considerations in all history."—*The Popes,* vol. i. p. 10, *transl.*

§ 3. *The Papal Church.*

Now we come to the distinctive doctrine of the Catholic Religion, the doctrine which separates us from all other denominations of Christians however near they may approach to us in other respects, the claims of the see of Rome, which have given occasion to Mr. Gladstone's Pamphlet and to the remarks which I am now making upon it. Of those rights, prerogatives, privileges, and duties, which I have been surveying in the ancient Church, the Pope is historically the heir. I shall dwell now upon this point, as far as it is to my purpose to do so, not treating it theologically (else I must define and prove from Scripture and the Fathers the "Primatus jure divino Romani Pontificis," which of course I firmly hold), but historically,[1] because Mr. Gladstone appeals to history. Instead of treating it theologically I wish to look with (as it were) secular, or even non-Catholic eyes at the powers claimed during the last thousand years by the Pope—that is, only as they lie in the nature of the case, and on the surface of the facts which come before us in history.

[1] History never serves as the measure of dogmatic truth in its fulness. *Vid. infr.* § 8.

I. I say the Pope is the heir of the Ecumenical Hierarchy of the fourth century, as being, what I may call, heir by default. No one else claims or exercises its rights or its duties. Is it possible to consider the Patriarch of Moscow or of Constantinople, heir to the historical pretensions of St. Ambrose or St. Martin? Does any Anglican Bishop for the last 300 years recall to our minds the image of St. Basil? Well, then, has all that ecclesiastical power, which makes such a show in the Christian Empire, simply vanished, or, if not, where is it to be found? I wish Protestants would throw themselves into our minds upon this point; I am not holding an argument with them; I am only wishing them to understand where we stand and how we look at things. There is this great difference of belief between us and them: they do not believe that Christ set up a visible society, or rather kingdom, for the propagation and maintenance of His religion, for a necessary home and a refuge for His people; but we do. We know the kingdom is still on earth: where is it? If all that can be found of it is what can be discerned at Constantinople or Canterbury, I say, it has disappeared; and either there was a radical corruption of Christianity from the first, or Christianity came to an end, in proportion as the type of the Nicene Church faded out of the world: for all that we know of Christianity, in ancient history, as a concrete fact, is the Church of Athanasius and his fellow Bishops: it is nothing else historically but that bundle of phenomena, that combination of claims, prerogatives, and corresponding acts, some of which I have recounted above. There is no help for it then; we cannot take as much as we please, and no more, of an institution which has a monadic existence. We must either give up the belief in the Church as a divine institution altogether, or we must recognize it at this day in that communion of which the Pope is the head. With him alone and round about him are found the claims, the prerogatives, and duties which we identify with the kingdom set up by Christ. We must take things as they are; to believe in a Church, is to believe in the Pope. And thus this belief in the Pope and his attributes, which seems so monstrous to Protestants, is bound up with our being Catholics at all; as our Catholicism is bound up with our Christianity. There is nothing then of wanton opposition to the powers that be, no dinning of novelties in their startled ears in what is often unjustly called Ultramontane doctrine; there is no pernicious servility to the Pope in our admission of his pretensions. I say, we cannot help ourselves—Parliament may deal as harshly with us as it will; we should not believe in the Church at all, unless we believe in its visible head.

So it is; the course of ages has fulfilled the prophecy and promise, "Thou art Peter, and upon this rock I will build My Church; and whatsoever thou shalt bind on earth, shall be bound in heaven, and whatsoever thou shalt loose on earth shall be loosed in heaven." That which in substance was possessed by the Nicene Hierarchy, that the Pope claims now. I do not wish to put difficulties in my way: but I cannot conceal or smooth over what I believe to be a simple truth, though the avowal of it will be very unwelcome to Protestants, and, as I fear, to some

Catholics. However, I do not call upon another to believe all that I believe on the subject myself. I declare it, as my own judgment, that the prerogatives, such as, and in the way in which, I have described them in substance, which the Church had under the Roman Power, those she claims now, and never, never will relinquish; claims them, not as having received them from a dead Empire, but partly by the direct endowment of her Divine Master, and partly as being a legitimate outcome of that endowment; claims them, but not except from Catholic populations, not as if accounting the more sublime of them to be of every-day use, but holding them as a protection or remedy in great emergencies or on supreme occasions, when nothing else will serve, as extraordinary and solemn acts of her religious sovereignty. And our Lord, seeing what would be brought about by human means, even had He not willed it, and recognizing, from the laws which He Himself had imposed upon human society, that no large community could be strong which had no head, spoke the word in the beginning, as He did to Judah, "Thou art he whom thy brethren shall praise," and then left it to the course of events to fulfil it.

2. Mr. Gladstone ought to have chosen another issue for attack upon us, than the Pope's special power. His real difficulty lies deeper; as little permission as he allows to the Pope, would he allow to any ecclesiastic who would wield the weapons of St. Ambrose and St. Augustine. That concentration of the Church's powers which history brings before us ought not to be the simple object of his indignation. It is not the existence of a Pope, but of

P

a Church, which is his aversion. It is the powers them
selves, and not their distribution and allocation in the
ecclesiastical body which he writes against. A triangle
is the same in its substance and nature, whichever
side is made its base. "The Pontiffs," says Mr. Bowden,
who writes as an Anglican, "exalted to the kingly
throne of St. Peter, did not so much claim new privileges
for themselves, as deprive their episcopal brethren of
privileges originally common to the hierarchy. Even
the titles by which those autocratical prelates, in the
plenitude of their power, delighted to style themselves,
'Summus Sacerdos,' 'Pontifex Maximus,' 'Vicarius
Christi,' ' Papa' itself, had, nearer to the primitive times,
been the honourable appellations of every bishop; as
'Sedes Apostolica' had been the description of every
Bishop's throne. The ascription of these titles, therefore,
to the Pope only gave to the terms new force, because
that ascription became exclusive; because, that is, the
bishops in general were stripped of honours, to which
their claims were as well founded as those of their Roman
brother, who became, by the change, not so strictly
universal as sole Bishop." (*Greg. VII.* vol. i. p. 64.)

Say that the Christian polity now remained, as history
represents it to us in the fourth century, or that it was,
if that was possible, now to revert to such a state, would
politicians have less trouble with 1800 centres of power
than they have with one? Instead of one, with traditionary rules, the trammels of treaties and engagements,
public opinion to consult and manage, the responsibility
of great interests, and the guarantee for his behaviour
in his temporal possessions, there would be a legion of

ecclesiastics, each bishop with his following, each in-dependent of the others, each with his own views, each with extraordinary powers, each with the risk of misusing them, all over Christendom. It would be the Anglican theory, made real. It would be an ecclesiastical communism; and, if it did not benefit religion, at least it would not benefit the civil power. Take a small illustration:—what interruption at this time to Parliamentary proceedings, does a small zealous party occasion, which its enemies call a mere "handful of clergy;" and why? Because its members are responsible for what they do to God alone and to their conscience as His voice. Even suppose it was only here or there that episcopal autonomy was vigorous; yet consider what zeal is kindled by local interests and national spirit. One John of Tuam, with a Pope's full apostolic powers, would be a greater trial to successive ministries than an Ecumenical Bishop at Rome. Parliament understands this well, for it exclaims against the Sacerdotal principle. Here, for a second reason, if our Divine Master has given those great powers to the Church, which ancient Christianity testifies, we see why His Providence has also brought it about that the exercise of them should be concentrated in one see.

But, anyhow, the progress of concentration was not the work of the Pope; it was brought about by the changes of times and the vicissitudes of nations. It was not his fault that the Vandals swept away the African sees, and the Saracens those of Syria and Asia Minor, or that Constantinople and its dependencies became the creatures of Imperialism, or that France, England, and

Germany would obey none but the author of their own Christianity, or that clergy and people at a distance were obstinate in sheltering themselves under the majesty of Rome against their own fierce kings and nobles or imperious bishops, even to the imposing forgeries on the world and on the Pope in justification of their proceedings. All this will be fact, whether the Popes were ambitious or not; and still it will be fact that the issue of that great change was a great benefit to the whole of Europe. No one but a Master, who was a thousand bishops in himself at once, could have tamed and controlled, as the Pope did, the great and little tyrants of the middle age.

3. This is generally confessed now, even by Protestant historians, viz., that the concentration of ecclesiastical power in those centuries was simply necessary for the civilization of Europe. Of course it does not follow that the benefits rendered then to the European commonwealth by the political supremacy of the Pope, would, if he was still supreme, be rendered in time to come. I have no wish to make assumptions; yet conclusions short of this will be unfavourable to Mr. Gladstone's denunciation of him. We reap the fruit at this day of his services in the past. With the purpose of showing this I make a rather long extract from Dean Milman's "Latin Christianity;" he is speaking of the era of Gregory I., and he says, the Papacy "was the only power which lay not entirely and absolutely prostrate before the disasters of the times—a power which had an inherent strength, and might resume its majesty. It was this power which was most imperatively required

to preserve all which was to survive out of the crumbling wreck of Roman civilization. To Western Christianity was absolutely necessary a centre, standing alone, strong in traditionary reverence, and in acknowledged claims to supremacy. Even the perfect organization of the Christian hierarchy might in all human probability have fallen to pieces in perpetual conflict : it might have degenerated into a half-secular feudal caste, with hereditary benefices more and more entirely subservient to the civil authority, a priesthood of each nation or each tribe, gradually sinking to the intellectual or religious level of the nation or tribe. On the rise of a power both controlling and conservative hung, humanly speaking, the life and death of Christianity—of Christianity as a permanent, aggressive, expansive, and, to a certain extent, uniform system. There must be a counterbalance to barbaric force, to the unavoidable anarchy of Teutonism, with its tribal, or at the utmost national independence, forming a host of small, conflicting, antagonistic kingdoms. All Europe would have been what England was under the Octarchy, what Germany was when her emperors were weak; and even her emperors she owed to Rome, to the Church, to Christianity. Providence might have otherwise ordained; but it is impossible for man to imagine by what other organizing or consolidating force the commonwealth of the Western nations could have grown up to a discordant, indeed, and conflicting league, but still a league, with that unity and conformity of manners, usages, laws, religion, which have made their rivalries, oppugnancies, and even their long ceaseless wars, on the whole to issue in the noblest, highest, most intellectual form of civilization known to man. . . . It is impossible to conceive what had been the confusion, the lawlessness, the chaotic state of the middle ages, without the medieval Papacy; and of the medieval Papacy the real father is Gregory the Great. In all his predecessors there was much of the uncertainty and indefiniteness of a new dominion. . . . Gregory is the Roman altogether merged in the Christian Bishop. It is a Christian dominion of which he lays the foundations in the Eternal City, not the old Rome, associating Christian influence to her ancient title of sovereignty." (Vol. i. p. 401, 402.)

4. From Gregory I. to Innocent III. is six hundred years; a very fair portion of the world's history, to have passed in doing good of primary importance to a whole continent, and that the continent of Europe; good, by which all nations and their governors, all statesmen and legislatures, are the gainers. And, again, should it not occur to Mr. Gladstone that these services were rendered to mankind by means of those very instruments of power on which he thinks it proper to pour contempt as "rusty tools"? The right to warn and punish powerful men, to excommunicate kings, to preach aloud truth and justice to the inhabitants of the earth, to denounce immoral doctrines, to strike at rebellion in the garb of heresy, were the very weapons by which Europe was brought into a civilized condition; yet he calls them "rusty tools" which need "refurbishing." Does he wish then that such high expressions of ecclesiastical displeasure, such sharp penalties, should be of daily use? If they are rusty, because they have been

long without using, then have they ever been rusty. Is a Council a rusty tool, because none had been held, till 1870, since the sixteenth century? or because there have been but nineteen in 1900 years? How many times is it in the history of Christianity that the Pope has solemnly drawn and exercised his sword upon a king or an emperor? If an extraordinary weapon must be a rusty tool, I suppose Gregory VII.'s sword was not keen enough for the German Henry; and the seventh Pius too used a rusty tool in his excommunication of Napoleon. How could Mr Gladstone ever "fondly think that Rome had disused" her weapons, and that they had hung up as antiquities and curiosities in her celestial armoury,—or, in his own words, as "hideous mummies," p. 46,—when the passage of arms between the great Conqueror and the aged Pope was so close upon his memory! Would he like to see a mummy come to life again? That unexpected miracle actually took place in the first years of this century. Gregory was considered to have done an astounding deed in the middle ages, when he brought Henry, the German Emperor, to do penance and shiver in the snow at Canossa; but Napoleon had his snow-penance too, and that with an actual interposition of Providence in the infliction of it. I describe it in the words of Alison :—

"'What does the Pope mean,' said Napoleon to Eugene, in July, 1807, 'by the threat of excommunicating me? does he think the world has gone back a thousand years? does he suppose the arms will fall from the hands of my soldiers?' Within two years after these remarkable words were written, the Pope did excommunicate him, in return for the confiscation of his whole dominions, and in less than four years more, the arms did fall from the hands of his soldiers; and the hosts, apparently invincible, which he had collected were dispersed and ruined by the blasts of winter. 'The weapons of the soldiers,' says Segur, in describing the Russian retreat, 'appeared of an insupportable weight to their stiffened arms. During their frequent falls they fell from their hands, and destitute of the power of raising them from the ground, they were left in the snow. They did not throw them away: famine and cold tore them from their grasp.' 'The soldiers could no longer hold their weapons,' says Salgues, 'they fell from the hands even of the bravest and most robust. The muskets dropped from the frozen arms of those who bore them.'" (*Hist.* ch. lx. 9th ed.)

Alison adds: "There is something in these marvellous coincidences beyond the operations of chance, and which even a Protestant historian feels himself bound to mark for the observation of future ages. The world had not gone back a thousand years, but that Being existed with whom a thousand years are as one day, and one day as a thousand years." As He was with Gregory in 1077, so He was with Pius in 1812, and He will be with some future Pope again, when the necessity shall come.

5. In saying this, I am far from saying that Popes are never in the wrong, and are never to be resisted; or that their excommunications always avail. I am not bound to defend the policy or the acts of particular

Popes, whether before or after the great revolt from their authority in the 16th century. There is no reason that I should contend, and I do not contend, for instance, that they at all times have understood our own people, our natural character and resources, and our position in Europe; or that they have never suffered from bad counsellors or misinformation. I say this the more freely, because Urban VIII., about the year 1641 or 1642, seems to have blamed the policy of some Popes of the preceding century in their dealings with our country.[2]

But, whatever we are bound to allow to Mr. Gladstone on this head, that does not warrant the passionate invective against the Holy See and us individually, which he has carried on through sixty-four pages. What we have a manifest right to expect from him is lawyer-like exactness and logical consecutiveness in his impeachment of us. The heavier that is, the less does it need the exaggerations of a great orator. If the Pope's conduct towards us three centuries ago has righteously wiped out the memory of his earlier benefits, yet he should have a fair trial. The more intoxicating was his solitary greatness, when it was in the zenith, the greater

[2] " When he was urged to excommunicate the Kings of France and Sweden, he made answer, 'We may declare them excommunicate, as Pius V. declared Queen Elizabeth of England, and before him Clement VII. the King of England, Henry VIII. . . but with what success? The whole world can tell. We yet bewail it with tears of blood. Wisdom does not teach us to imitate Pius V. or Clement VII., but Paul V. who, in the beginning, being many times urged by the Spaniards to excommunicate James, King of England, never would consent to it.' " (State Paper Office, *Italy*, 1641—1662.) *Vide* Mr. Simpson's very able and careful life of Campion, 1867, p. 371.

consideration should be shown towards him in his present temporal humiliation, when concentration of ecclesiastical functions in one man, does but make him, in the presence of the haters of Catholicism, what a Roman Emperor contemplated, when he wished all his subjects had but one neck that he might destroy them by one blow. Surely, in the trial of so august a criminal, one might have hoped, at least, to have found gravity and measure in language, and calmness in tone—not a pamphlet written as if on impulse, in defence of an incidental parenthesis in a previous publication, and then, after being multiplied in 22,000 copies, appealing to the lower classes in the shape of a sixpenny tract, the lowness of the price indicating the width of the circulation. Surely Nana Sahib will have more justice done to him by the English people, than has been shown to the Father of European civilization.

6. I have been referring to the desolate state in which the Holy See has been cast during the last years, such that the Pope, humanly speaking, is at the mercy of his enemies, and morally a prisoner in his palace. That state of secular feebleness cannot last for ever; sooner or later there will be, in the divine mercy, a change for the better, and the Vicar of Christ will no longer be a mark for insult and indignity. But one thing, except by an almost miraculous interposition, cannot be; and that is, a return to the universal religious sentiment, the public opinion, of the medieval time. The Pope himself calls those centuries " the ages of faith." Such endemic faith may certainly be decreed for some future time; but, as far as we have the means of judging at present,

centuries must run out first. Even in the fourth century the ecclesiastical privileges, claimed on the one hand, granted on the other, came into effect more or less under two conditions, that they were recognized by public law, and that they had the consent of the Christian populations. Is there any chance whatever, except by miracles which were not granted then, that the public law and the inhabitants of Europe will allow the Pope that exercise of his rights, which they allowed him as a matter of course in the 11th and 12th centuries? If the whole world will at once answer No, it is surely inopportune to taunt us this day with the acts of medieval Popes towards certain princes and nobles, when the sentiment of Europe was radically Papal. How does the past bear upon the present in this matter? Yet Mr. Gladstone is in earnest alarm, earnest with the earnestness which distinguishes him as a statesman, at the harm which society may receive from the Pope, at a time when the Pope can do nothing. He grants (p. 46) that "the fears are visionary . . that either foreign foe or domestic treason can, at the bidding of the Court of Rome, disturb these peaceful shores;" he allows that "in the middle ages the Popes contended, not by direct action of fleets and armies," but mainly "by interdicts," p. 35. Yet, because men then believed in interdicts, though now they don't, therefore the civil Power is to be roused against the Pope. But his *animus* is bad; his *animus!* what can *animus* do without matter to work upon? Mere *animus*, like big words, breaks no bones.

As if to answer Mr. Gladstone by anticipation, and to

allay his fears, the Pope made a declaration three years
ago on the subject, which, strange to say, Mr. Gladstone
quotes without perceiving that it tells against the very
argument which he brings it to corroborate ;—that is except as the Pope's *animus* goes. Doubtless he would wish
to have the place in the political world which his predecessors had, because it was given to him by Providence,
and is conducive to the highest interests of mankind,
but he distinctly tells us in the declaration in question
that he has not got it, and cannot have it, till the time
comes, which we can speculate about as well as he,
and which we say cannot come at least for centuries.
He speaks of what is his highest political power, that
of interposing in the quarrel between a prince and his
subjects, and of declaring upon appeal made to him
from them, that the Prince had or had not forfeited
their allegiance. This power, most rarely exercised,
and on very extraordinary occasions, it is not necessary
for any Catholic to acknowledge ; and I suppose, comparatively speaking, few Catholics do acknowledge it ;
to be honest, I may say, I do ; that is, under the conditions which the Pope himself lays down in the declaration to which I have referred, his answer to the
address of the Academia. He speaks of his right "to
depose sovereigns, and release the people from the
obligation of loyalty, a right which had undoubtedly
sometimes been exercised in crucial circumstances," and
he says, " This right (*diritto*) in those ages of faith,—
(which discerned in the Pope, what he is, that is to say,
the Supreme Judge of Christianity, and recognized the
advantages of his tribunal in the great contests of

peoples and sovereigns)—was freely extended,—(aided indeed as a matter of duty by the public law (*diritto*) and by the common consent of peoples) —to the most important (*i piu gravi*) interest of states and their rulers." (*Guardian*, Nov. 11, 1874.)

Now let us observe how the Pope restrains the exercise of this right. He calls it his right—that is in the sense in which right in one party is correlative with duty in the other, so that, when the duty is not observed, the right cannot be brought into exercise; and this is precisely what he goes on to intimate; for he lays down the conditions of that exercise. First it can only be exercised in rare and critical circumstances (*supreme circonstanze, i più gravi interessi*). Next he refers to his being the supreme judge of Christendom and to his decision as coming from a tribunal; his prerogative then is not a mere arbitrary power, but must be exercised by a process of law and a formal examination of the case, and in the presence and the hearing of the two parties interested in it. Also in this limitation is implied that the Pope's definite sentence involves an appeal to the supreme standard of right and wrong, the moral law, as its basis and rule, and must contain the definite reasons on which it decides in favour of the one party or the other. Thirdly, the exercise of this right is limited to the ages of faith; ages which, on the one hand, inscribed it among the provisions of the *jus publicum*, and on the other so fully recognized the benefits it conferred, as to be able to enforce it by the common consent of the peoples. These last words should be dwelt on : it is no consent which is merely local, as of one country, of Ireland or of Belgium, if that were probable; but a united consent of various nations of Europe, for instance, as a common wealth, of which the Pope was the head. Thirty years ago we heard much of the Pope being made the head of an Italian confederation : no word came from England against such an arrangement. It was possible, because the members of it were all of one religion; and in like manner a European commonwealth would be reasonable, if Europe were of one religion. Lastly, the Pope declares with indignation that a Pope is not infallible in the exercise of this right; such a notion is an invention of the enemy; he calls it " malicious."

What is there in all this to arouse the patriotic anxieties of Mr. Gladstone?

§ 4. *Divided Allegiance.*

BUT one attribute the Church has, and the Pope as
head of the Church, whether he be in high estate, as this
world goes, or not, whether he has temporal possessions
or not, whether he is in honour or dishonour, whether he
is at home or driven about, whether those special claims
of which I have spoken are allowed or not,—and that is
Sovereignty. As God has sovereignty, though He may
be disobeyed or disowned, so has His Vicar upon earth;
and farther than this, since Catholic populations are
found everywhere, he ever will be in fact lord of a vast
empire; as large in numbers, as far spreading as the
British; and all his acts are sure to be such as are in
keeping with the position of one who is thus supremely
exalted.

I beg not to be interrupted here, as many a reader
will interrupt me in his thoughts, for I am using these
words, not at random, but as the commencement of a
long explanation, and, in a certain sense, limitation, of
what I have hitherto been saying concerning the Church's
and the Pope's power. To this task the remaining pages,
which I have to address to your Grace, will be directed;
and I trust that it will turn out, when I come to the end
of them, that, by first stating fully what the Pope's

claims are, I shall be able most clearly to show what he does not claim.

Now the main point of Mr. Gladstone's Pamphlet is this :—that, since the Pope claims infallibility in faith and morals, and since there are no "departments and functions of human life which do not and cannot fall within the domain of morals," p. 36, and since he claims also " the domain of all that concerns the government and discipline of the Church," and moreover, " claims the power of determining the limits of those domains," and "does not sever them, by any acknowledged or intelligible line from the domains of civil duty and allegiance," p. 45, therefore Catholics are moral and mental slaves, and "every convert and member of the Pope's Church places his loyalty and civil duty at the mercy of another," p. 45.

I admit Mr. Gladstone's premisses, but I reject his conclusion ; and now I am going to show why I reject it.

In doing this, I shall, with him, put aside for the present and at first the Pope's prerogative of infallibility in general enunciations, whether of faith or morals, and confine myself to the consideration of his authority (in respect to which he is not infallible) in matters of conduct, and of our duty of obedience to him. "There is something wider still," he says, (than the claim of infallibility,) "and that is the claim to an Absolute and entire Obedience," p. 37. "Little does it matter to me, whether my Superior claims infallibility, so long as he is entitled to demand and exact conformity," p. 39. He speaks of a third province being opened, "not indeed to the abstract assertion of Infallibility, but to the far more practical and decisive demand of Absolute Obedience," p. 41, "the Absolute Obedience, at the peril of salvation, of every member of his communion," p. 42.

Now, I proceed to examine this large, direct, religious, sovereignty of the Pope, both in its relation to his subjects, and to the Civil Power; but first, I beg to be allowed to say just one word on the principle of obedience itself, that is, by way of inquiring whether it is or is not now a religious duty.

Is there then such a duty at all as obedience to ecclesiastical authority now? or is it one of those obsolete ideas, which are swept away, as unsightly cobwebs, by the New Civilization? Scripture says, "Remember them which have the *rule* over you, who have spoken unto you the word of God, whose faith follow." And, "*Obey* them that have the *rule* over you, and *submit yourselves;* for they watch *for your souls,* as they that must give account, that they may do it with joy and not with grief; for that is unprofitable for you." The margin in the Protestant Version reads, "those who are your *guides;*" and the word may also be translated "leaders." Well, as rulers, or guides and leaders, whichever word be right, they are to be *obeyed.* Now Mr. Gladstone dislikes our way of fulfilling this precept, whether as regards our choice of ruler and leader, or our " Absolute Obedience " to him ; but he does not give us his own. Is there any liberalistic reading of the Scripture passage? Or are the words only for the benefit of the poor and ignorant, not for the *Schola* (as it may be called) of political and periodical writers, not for individual members

Q

of Parliament, not for statesmen and Cabinet ministers, and people of Progress? Which party then is the more "Scriptural," those who recognize and carry out in their conduct texts like these, or those who don't? May not we Catholics claim some mercy from Mr. Gladstone, though we be faulty in the object and the manner of our obedience, since in a lawless day an object and a manner of obedience we have? Can we be blamed, if, arguing from those texts which say that ecclesiastical authority comes from above, we obey it in that one form in which alone we find it on earth, in that one person who, of all the notabilities of this nineteenth century into which we have been born, alone claims it of us? The Pope has no rival in his claim upon us; nor is it our doing that his claim has been made and allowed for centuries upon centuries, and that it was he who made the Vatican decrees, and not they him. If we give him up, to whom shall we go? Can we dress up any civil functionary in the vestments of divine authority? Can I. for instance, follow the faith, can I put my soul into the hands, of our gracious Sovereign? or of the Archbishop of Canterbury? or of the Bishop of Lincoln, albeit he is not broad and low, but high? Catholics have "done what they could,"—all that any one could: and it should be Mr Gladstone's business, before telling us that we are slaves, because we obey the Pope, first of all to tear away those texts from the Bible.

With this preliminary remark, I proceed to consider whether the Pope's authority is either a slavery to his subjects, or a menace to the Civil Power; and first, as to his power over his flock.

1. Mr. Gladstone says that "the Pontiff declares to belong to him the *supreme direction* of Catholics in respect to all duty," p. 37. Supreme direction; true, but "supreme" is not "minute," nor does "direction" mean "supervision" or "management." Take the parallel of human law; the Law is *supreme*, and the Law *directs* our conduct under the manifold circumstances in which we have to act, and may and must be absolutely obeyed; but who therefore says that the Law has the "supreme direction" of us? The State, as well as the Church, has the power at its will of imposing laws upon us, laws bearing on our moral duties, our daily conduct, affecting our actions in various ways, and circumscribing our liberties; yet no one would say that the Law, after all, with all its power in the abstract and its executive vigour in fact, interferes either with our comfort or our conscience. There are numberless laws about property, landed and personal, titles, tenures, trusts, wills, covenants, contracts, partnerships, money transactions, life-insurances, taxes, trade, navigation, education, sanitary measures, trespasses, nuisances, all in addition to the criminal law. Law, to apply Mr. Gladstone's words, "is the shadow that cleaves to us, go where we will." Moreover, it varies year after year, and refuses to give any pledge of fixedness or finality. Nor can any one tell what restraint is to come next, perhaps painful personally to himself. Nor are its enactments easy of interpretation; for actual cases, with the opinions and speeches of counsel, and the decisions of judges, must prepare the raw material, as it proceeds from the Legislature, before it can be rightly

understood ; so that "the glorious uncertainty of the
Law" has become a proverb. And, after all, no one is
sure of escaping its penalties without the assistance of
lawyers, and that in such private and personal matters
that the lawyers are, as by an imperative duty, bound to
a secrecy which even courts of justice respect. And
then, besides the Statute Law, there is the common and
traditional ; and, below this, usage. Is not all this
enough to try the temper of a free-born Englishman, and
to make him cry out with Mr. Gladstone, "Three-
fourths of my life are handed over to the Law; I care
not to ask if there be dregs or tatters of human life,
such as can escape from the description and boundary
of Parliamentary tyranny?" Yet, though we may dislike it, though we may at times suffer from it ever so
much, who does not see that the thraldom and irk-
someness is nothing compared with the great blessings
which the Constitution and Legislature secure to us?

Such is the jurisdiction which the Law exercises over
us. What rule does the Pope claim which can be compared to its strong and its long arm? What interference with our liberty of judging and acting in our
daily work, in our course of life, comes to us from
him? Really, at first sight, I have not known where
to look for instances of his actual interposition in our
private affairs, for it is our routine of personal duties
about which I am now speaking. Let us see how we
stand in this matter.

We are guided in our ordinary duties by the books of
moral theology, which are drawn up by theologians of
authority and experience, as an instruction for our Con-

fessors. These books are based on the three Christian foundations of Faith, Hope, and Charity, on the Ten Commandments, and on the six Precepts of the Church, which relate to the observance of Sunday, of fast days, of confession and communion, and, in one shape or other, to paying tithes. A great number of possible cases are noted under these heads, and in difficult questions a variety of opinions are given, with plain directions, when it is that private Catholics are at liberty to choose for themselves whatever answer they like best, and when they are bound to follow some one of them in particular. Reducible as these directions in detail are to the few and simple heads which I have mentioned, they are little more than reflexions and memoranda of our moral sense, unlike the positive enactments of the Legislature; and, on the whole, present to us no difficulty—though now and then some critical question may arise, and some answer may be given (just as by the private conscience itself) which it is difficult to us or painful to accept. And again, cases may occur now and then, when our private judgment differs from what is set down in theological works, but even then it does not follow at once that our private judgment must give way, for those books are no utterance of Papal authority.

And this is the point to which I am coming. So little does the Pope come into this whole system of moral theology by which (as by our conscience) our lives are regulated, that the weight of his hand upon us, as private men, is absolutely unappreciable. I have had a difficulty where to find a measure or gauge of his interposition. At length I have looked through Busenbaum's " Me-

dulla," to ascertain what light such a book would throw
upon the question.   It is a book of casuistry for the use
of Confessors, running to 700 pages, and is a large
repository of answers made by various theologians on
points of conscience, and generally of duty.   It was first
published in 1645—my own edition is of 1844—and
in this latter are marked those propositions, bearing on
subjects treated in it, which have been condemned by
Popes in the intermediate 200 years.   On turning over
the pages I find they are in all between fifty and sixty.
This list includes matters sacramental, ritual, ecclesiastical, monastic, and disciplinarian, as well as moral,—
relating to the duties of ecclesiastics and regulars, of
parish priests, and of professional men, as well as of private Catholics.   And these condemnations relate for the
most part to mere occasional details of duty, and are in
reprobation of the lax or wild notions of speculative
casuists, so that they are rather restraints upon theologians than upon laymen.   For instance, the following
are some of the propositions condemned :—" The ecclesiastic, who on a certain day is hindered from saying
Matins and Lauds, is not bound to say, if he can, the
remaining hours ;" " Where there is good cause, it is
lawful to swear without the purpose of swearing, whether
the matter is of light or grave moment ;" " Domestics
may steal from their masters, in compensation for their
service, which they think greater than their wages ;"
" It is lawful for a public man to kill an opponent, who
tries to fasten a calumny upon him, if he cannot otherwise escape the ignominy."   I have taken these instances
at random.   It must be granted, I think, that in the

long course of 200 years the amount of the Pope's
authoritative enunciations has not been such as to press
heavily on the back of the private Catholic. He leaves
us surely far more than that "one fourth of the department of conduct," which Mr. Gladstone allows us. Indeed, if my account and specimens of his sway over us in
morals be correct, I do not see what he takes away at
all from our private consciences.

But here Mr. Gladstone will object, that the Pope
does really exercise a claim over the whole domain of
conduct, inasmuch as he refuses to draw any line across
it in limitation of his interference, and *therefore* it
is that we are his slaves:—let us see if another
illustration or parallel will not show this to be a *non-
sequitur.* Suppose a man, who is in the midst of various
and important lines of business, has a medical adviser, in
whom he has full confidence, as knowing well his constitution. This adviser keeps a careful and anxious eye
upon him; and, as an honest man, says to him, "You
must not go off on a journey to-day," or "You must
take some days' rest," or "You must attend to your
diet." Now, this is not a fair parallel to the Pope's
hold upon us; for the Pope does not speak to us personally, but to all, and, in speaking definitively on ethical
subjects, what he propounds must relate to things good
and bad in themselves, not to things accidental, change-
able, and of mere expedience; so that the argument
which I am drawing from the case of a medical adviser
is *à fortiori* in its character. However, I say that
though a medical man exercises a "supreme direction"
over those who put themselves under him, yet we do not

therefore say, even of him, that he interferes with our daily conduct, and that we are his slaves. He certainly does thwart many of our wishes and purposes; and in a true sense we are at his mercy: he may interfere any day, suddenly; he will not, he cannot, draw any intelligible line between the acts which he has a right to forbid us, and the acts which he has not. The same journey, the same press of business, the same indulgence at table, which he passes over one year, he sternly forbids the next. Therefore if Mr. Gladstone's argument is good, he has a finger in all the commercial transactions of the great trader or financier who has chosen him. But surely there is a simple fallacy here. Mr. Gladstone asks us whether our political and civil life is not at the Pope's mercy; every act, he says, of at least three-quarters of the day, is under his control. No, not *every*, but *any*, and this is all the difference—that is, we have no guarantee given us that there will never be a case, when the Pope's general utterances may come to have a bearing upon some personal act of ours. In the same way we are all of us in this age under the control of public opinion and the public prints; nay, much more intimately so. Journalism can be and is very personal; and, when it is in the right, more powerful just now than any Pope; yet we do not go into fits, as if we were slaves, because we are under a *surveillance* much more like tyranny than any sway, so indirect, so practically limited, so gentle, as his is.

But it seems the cardinal point of our slavery lies, not simply in the domain of morals, but in the Pope's general authority over us in all things whatsoever. This count in his indictment Mr. Gladstone founds on a passage in the third chapter of the *Pastor æternus*, in which the Pope, speaking of the Pontifical jurisdiction, says, —"Towards it (erga quam) pastors and people of whatsoever rite or dignity, each and all, are bound by the duty of hierarchical subordination and true obedience, not only in matters which pertain to faith and morals, but also in those which pertain to the *discipline* and the *regimen* of the Church spread throughout the world; so that, unity with the Roman Pontiff (both of communion and of profession of the same faith) being preserved, the Church of Christ may be one flock under one supreme Shepherd. This is the doctrine of Catholic truth, from which no one can deviate without loss of faith and salvation."

On Mr. Gladstone's use of this passage I observe first, that he leaves out a portion of it which has much to do with the due understanding of it (ita ut custoditâ, &c.) Next, he speaks of "*absolute* obedience" so often, that any reader, who had not the passage before him, would think that the word "absolute" was the Pope's word, not his. Thirdly, three times (at pp. 38, 41, and 42) does he make the Pope say that no one can *disobey* him without risking his salvation, whereas what the Pope does say is, that no one can *disbelieve* the *duty* of obedience and unity without such risk. And fourthly, in order to carry out this false sense, or rather to hinder its being evidently impossible, he mistranslates, p. 38, "doctrina" (Hæc est doctrina) by the word "rule."

But his chief attack is directed to the words "disciplina" and "regimen." "Thus," he says, "are swept

into the Papal net whole multitudes of facts, whole
systems of government, prevailing, though in different
degrees, in every country of the world," p. 41. That is,
disciplina and *regimen* are words of such lax, vague,
indeterminate meaning, that under them any matters can
be slipped in, which may be required for the Pope's purpose in this or that country, such as, to take Mr. Gladstone's instances, blasphemy, poor-relief, incorporation,
and mortmain; as if no definitions were contained in
our theological and ecclesiastical works of words in such
common use, and as if in consequence the Pope was at
liberty to give them any sense of his own. As to discipline, Fr. Perrone says, "Discipline comprises the
exterior worship of God, the liturgy, sacred rites,
psalmody, the administration of the sacraments, the
canonical form of sacred elections and the institution of
ministers, vows, feast-days, and the like;" all of them
(observe) matters internal to the Church, and without
any relation to the Civil Power and civil affairs. Perrone adds, "Ecclesiastical discipline is a practical and
external rule, prescribed by the Church, in order to
retain the faithful in their *faith,* and the more easily
lead them on to *eternal happiness," Præl. Theol.,* t. 2,
p. 381, 2nd ed., 1841. Thus discipline is in no sense a
political instrument, except as the profession of our faith
may accidentally become political. In the same sense
Zallinger: "The Roman Pontiff has by divine right the
power of passing universal laws pertaining to the *disci
pline* of the Church; for instance, to divine worship,
sacred rites, the ordination and manner of life of the
clergy, the order of the ecclesiastical regimen, and the

right administration of the temporal possessions of the church."—*Jur. Eccles.*, lib. i. t. 2, § 121.

So too the word "regimen" has a definite meaning, relating to a matter strictly internal to the Church : it means government, or the mode or form of government, or the course of government ; and, as, in the intercourse of nation with nation, the nature of a nation's government, whether monarchical or republican, does not come into question, so the constitution of the Church simply belongs to its nature, not to its external action. Certainly there are aspects of the Church which involve relations toward secular powers and to nations, as, for instance, its missionary office; but regimen has relation to one of its internal characteristics, viz., its form of government, whether we call it a pure monarchy or with others a monarchy tempered by aristocracy. Thus Tournely says, "Three kinds of regimen or government are set down by philosophers, monarchy, aristocracy, and democracy."—*Theol.*, t. 2, p. 100. Bellarmine says the same, *Rom. Pont.*, i. 2 ; and Perrone takes it for granted, *ibid.* pp. 70, 71.

Now, why does the Pope speak at this time of regimen and discipline? He tells us in that portion of the sentence, which, thinking it of no account, Mr. Gladstone has omitted. The Pope tells us that all Catholics should recollect their duty of obedience to him, not only in faith and morals, but in such matters of regimen and discipline as belong to the universal Church, "so that unity with the Roman Pontiff, both of communion and of profession of the same faith being preserved, the Church of Christ may be one flock under one supreme Shepherd." I consider this passage to be especially aimed at Nationalism : " Recollect," the Pope seems to say, " the Church is one, and that, not only in faith and morals, for schismatics may profess as much as this, but one, wherever it is, all over the world ; and not only one, but one and the same, bound together by its one regimen and diScipline and by the same regimen and discipline,—the same rites, the same sacraments, the same usages, and the same one Pastor ; and in these bad times it is necessary for all Catholics to recollect, that this doctrine of the Church's individuality and, as it were, personality, is not a mere received opinion or understanding, which may be entertained or not, ·· we please, but is a fundamental, necessary truth." This being, speaking under correction, the drift of the passage, I observe that the words " spread throughout the world " or " universal " are so far from turning " discipline and regimen " into what Mr. Gladstone calls a " net," that they contract the range of both of them, not including, as he would have it, " marriage," here, " blasphemy " there, and " poor-relief " in a third country, but noting and specifying that one and the same structure of laws, rites, rules of government, independency, everywhere, of which the Pope himself is the centre and life. And surely this is what every one of us will say as well as the Pope, who is not an Erastian, and who believes that the Gospel is no mere philosophy thrown upon the world at large, no mere quality of mind and thought, no mere beautiful and deep sentiment or subjective opinion, but a substantive message from above, guarded and preserved in a visible polity.

2. And now I am naturally led on to speak of the Pope's supreme authority, such as I have described it, in its bearing towards the Civil Power all over the world,—a power which as truly comes from God, as his own does, though diverse, as the Church is invariable.

That collisions can take place between the Holy See and national governments, the history of fifteen hundred years sufficiently teaches us; also, that on both sides there may occur grievous mistakes. But my question all along lies, not with "quicquid delirant reges," but with what, under the circumstance of such a collision, is the duty of those who are both children of the Pope and subjects of the Civil Power. As to the duty of the Civil Power, I have already intimated in my first section, that it should treat the Holy See as an independent sovereign, and if this rule had been observed, the difficulty to Catholics in a country not Catholic, would be most materially lightened. Great Britain recognizes and is recognized by the United States; the two powers have ministers at each other's court; here is one standing prevention of serious quarrels. Misunderstandings between the two co-ordinate powers may arise; but there follow explanations, removals of the causes of offence, acts of restitution. In actual collisions, there are conferences, compromises, arbitrations. Now the point to observe here is, that in such cases neither party gives up its abstract rights, but neither party practically insists on them. And each party thinks itself in the right in the particular case, protests against any other view, but still concedes. Neither party says, "I will not make it up with you, till you draw an intelligible line between your domain and mine." I suppose in the Geneva arbitration, though we gave way, we still thought that, in our conduct in the American civil war, we had acted within our rights. I say all this in answer to Mr. Gladstone's challenge to us to draw the line between the Pope's domain and the State's domain in civil or political questions. Many a private American, I suppose, lived in London and Liverpool, all through the correspondence between our Foreign Office and the government of the United States, and Mr. Gladstone never addressed any expostulation to them, or told them they had lost their moral freedom because they took part with their own government. The French, when their late war began, did sweep their German sojourners out of France, (the number, as I recollect, was very great,) but they were not considered to have done themselves much credit by such an act. When we went to war with Russia, the English in St. Petersburg made an address, I think to the Emperor, asking for his protection, and he gave it;—I don't suppose they pledged themselves to the Russian view of the war, nor would he have called them slaves instead of patriots, if they had refused to do so. Suppose England were to send her ironclads to support Italy against the Pope and his allies, English Catholics would be very indignant, they would take part with the Pope before the war began, they would use all constitutional means to hinder it; but who believes that, when they were once in the war, their action would be anything else than prayers and exertions for a termination of it? What reason is there for saying that they would commit themselves to any step of a treasonable nature, any more than loyal Germans, had they been allowed to remain in France? Yet, because those Germans would not relinquish their allegiance to their country, Mr. Gladstone, were he consistent, would at once send them adrift.

Of course it will be said that in these cases, there is no double allegiance, and again that the German government did not call upon Germans in France, as the Pope might call upon English Catholics, nay command them, to take a side; but my argument at least shows this, that till there comes to us a special, direct command from the Pope to oppose our country, we need not be said to have " placed our loyalty and civil duty at the mercy of another," p. 45. It is strange that a great statesman, versed in the new and true philosophy of compromise, instead of taking a practical view of the actual situation, should proceed against us, like a Professor in the schools, with the "parade" of his "relentless" (and may I add "rusty"?) "logic," p. 23.

I say, *till* the Pope told us to exert ourselves for his cause in a quarrel with this country, as in the time of the Armada, we need not attend to an abstract and hypothetical difficulty :—then and not till then. I add, as before, that, if the Holy See were frankly recognized by England, as other Sovereignties are, direct quarrels between the two powers would in this age of the world be rare indeed; and still rarer, their becoming so energetic and urgent as to descend into the hearts of the community, and to disturb the consciences and the family unity of private Catholics.

But now, lastly, let us suppose one of these extraordinary cases of direct and open hostility between the two

powers actually to occur;—here first, we must bring
before us the state of the case. Of course we must recollect, on the one hand, that Catholics are not only
bound by allegiance to the British Crown, but have
special privileges as citizens, can meet together, speak
and pass resolutions, can vote for members of Parliament,
and sit in Parliament, and can hold office, all which are
denied to foreigners sojourning among us; while on the
other hand there is the authority of the Pope, which,
though not "absolute" even in religious matters, as
Mr. Gladstone would have it to be, has a call, a supreme
call on our obedience. Certainly in the event of such a
collision of jurisdictions, there are cases in which we
should obey the Pope and disobey the State. Suppose,
for instance, an Act was passed in Parliament, bidding
Catholics to attend Protestant service every week, and
the Pope distinctly told us not to do so, for it was to
violate our duty to our faith :—I should obey the Pope
and not the Law. It will be said by Mr. Gladstone, that
such a case is impossible. I know it is; but why ask
me for what I should do in extreme and utterly impro-
bable cases such as this, if my answer cannot help bearing
the character of an axiom? It is not my fault that I
must deal in truisms. The circumferences of State
jurisdiction and of Papal are for the most part quite apart
from each other; there are just some few degrees out of
the 360 in which they intersect, and Mr. Gladstone,
instead of letting these cases of intersection alone, till
they occur actually, asks me what I should do, if I found
myself placed in the space intersected. If I must answer
then, I should say distinctly that did the State tell me in

a question of worship to do what the Pope told me not to do, I should obey the Pope, and should think it no sin, if I used all the power and the influence I possessed as a citizen to prevent such a Bill passing the Legislature, and to effect its repeal if it did.

But now, on the other hand, could the case ever occur, in which I should act with the Civil Power, and not with the Pope? Now, here again, when I begin to imagine instances, Catholics will cry out (as Mr. Gladstone, in the case I supposed, cried out in the interest of the other side), that instances never can occur. I know they cannot; I know the Pope never can do what I am going to suppose; but then, since it cannot possibly happen in fact, there is no harm in just saying what I should (hypothetically) do, if it did happen. I say then in certain (impossible) cases I should side, not with the Pope, but with the Civil Power. For instance, let us suppose members of Parliament, or of the Privy Council, took an oath that they would not acknowledge the right of succession of a Prince of Wales, if he became a Catholic: in that case I should not consider the Pope could release me from that oath, had I bound myself by it. Of course, I might exert myself to the utmost to get the act repealed which bound me; again, if I could not, I might retire from parliament or office, and so rid myself of the engagement I had made; but I should be clear that, though the Pope bade all Catholics to stand firm in one phalanx for the Catholic Succession, still, while I remained in office, or in my place in Parliament, I could not do as he bade me.

Again, were I actually a soldier or sailor in her Ma-

R

jesty's service, and sent to take part in a war which I could not in my conscience see to be unjust, and should the Pope suddenly bid all Catholic soldiers and sailors to retire from the service, here again, taking the advice of others, as best I could, I should not obey him.

What is the use of forming impossible cases? One can find plenty of them in books of casuistry, with the answers attached in respect to them. In an actual case, a Catholic would, of course, not act simply on his own judgment; at the same time, there are supposable cases in which he would be obliged to go by it solely—viz., when his conscience could not be reconciled to any of the courses of action proposed to him by others.

In support of what I have been saying, I refer to one or two weighty authorities :—

Cardinal Turrecremata says, "Although it clearly follows from the circumstance that the Pope can err at times, and command things which must not be done, that we are not to be simply obedient to him in all things, that does not show that he must not be obeyed by all when his commands are good. To know in what cases he is to be obeyed and in what not . . . it is said in the Acts of the Apostles, 'One ought to obey God rather than man :' therefore, were the Pope to command anything against Holy Scripture, or the articles of faith, or the truth of the Sacraments, or the commands of the natural or divine law, *he ought not to be obeyed*, but in such commands is to be passed over (despiciendus)." —*Summ. de Eccl.*, pp. 47, 48.

Bellarmine, speaking of resisting the Pope, says,

" In order to resist and defend oneself no authority is required. . . . Therefore, as it is lawful to resist the Pope, if he assaulted a man's person, so it is lawful to resist him, if he assaulted souls, or *troubled the state* (turbanti rempublicam), and much more if he strove to aestroy the Church. It is lawful, I say, to resist him, by not doing what he commands, and hindering the execution of his will."—*De Rom. Pont.*, ii. 29.

Archbishop Kenrick says, " His power was given for edification, not for destruction. If he uses it from the love of domination (quod absit) *scarcely will he meet with obedient populations.*"—*Theolog. Moral.*, t. i. p. 158.

When, then, Mr. Gladstone asks Catholics how they can obey the Queen and yet obey the Pope, since it may happen that the commands of the two authorities may clash, I answer, that it is my *rule*, both to obey the one and to obey the other, but that there is no rule in this world without exceptions, and if either the Pope or the Queen demanded of me an "Absolute Obedience," he or she would be transgressing the laws of human society. I give an absolute obedience to neither. Further, if ever this double allegiance pulled me in contrary ways, which in this age of the world I think it never will, then I should decide according to the particular case, which is beyond all rule, and must be decided on its own merits. I should look to see what theologians could do for me, what the Bishops and clergy around me, what my confessor; what friends whom I revered: and if, after all, I could not take their view of the matter, then I must rule myself by my own judgment and my own conscience. But all this is hypothetical and unreal.

Here, of course, it will be objected to me, that I am. after all, having recourse to the Protestant doctrine of Private Judgment; not so; it is the Protestant doctrine that Private Judgment is our *ordinary* guide in religious matters, but I use it, in the case in question, in very extraordinary and rare, nay, impossible emergencies. Do not the highest Tories thus defend the substitution of William for James II.? It is a great mistake to suppose our state in the Catholic Church is so entirely subjected to rule and system, that we are never thrown upon what is called by divines " the Providence of God." The teaching and assistance of the Church does not supply all conceivable needs, but those which are ordinary; thus, for instance, the sacraments are necessary for dying in the grace of God and hope of heaven, yet, when they cannot be got, acts of faith, hope, and contrition, with the desire for those aids which the dying man has not, will convey in substance what those aids ordinarily convey. And so a Catechumen, not yet baptized, may be saved by his purpose and preparation to receive the rite. And so, again, though " Out of the Church there is no salvation," this does not hold in the case of good men who are in invincible ignorance. And so it is also in the case of our ordinations; Chillingworth and Macaulay say that it is morally impossible that we should have kept up for 1800 years an Apostolical succession of ministers without some breaks in the chain; and we in answer say that, however true this may be humanly speaking, there has been a special Providence over the Church to secure it. Once more, how else could private Catholics save their souls when there was a Pope and Anti-popes, each severally claiming their allegiance?

§ 5. *Conscience.*

It seems, then, that there are extreme cases in which Conscience may come into collision with the word of a Pope, and is to be followed in spite of that word. Now I wish to place this proposition on a broader basis, acknowledged by all Catholics, and, in order to do this satisfactorily, as I began with the prophecies of Scripture and the primitive Church, when I spoke of the Pope's prerogatives, so now I must begin with the Creator and His creature, when I would draw out the prerogatives and the supreme authority of Conscience.

I say, then, that the Supreme Being is of a certain character, which, expressed in human language, we call ethical. He has the attributes of justice, truth, wisdom, sanctity, benevolence and mercy, as eternal characteristics in His nature, the very Law of His being, identical with Himself; and next, when He became Creator, He implanted this Law, which is Himself, in the intelligence of all His rational creatures. The Divine Law, then, is the rule of ethical truth, the standard of right and wrong, a sovereign, irreversible, absolute authority in the presence of men and Angels. "The eternal law," says St. Augustine, "is the Divine Reason or Will of God, commanding the observance, forbidding the disturbance, of the natural order of things." " The natural law," says St. Thomas, " is an impression of the Divine Light in us, a participation of the eternal law in the rational creature." (Gousset, *Theol. Moral.*, t. i. pp. 24, &c.) This law, as apprehended in the minds of individual men, is called " conscience;" and though it may suffer refraction in passing into the intellectual medium of each, it is not therefore so affected as to lose its character of being the Divine Law, but still has, as such, the prerogative of commanding obedience. " The Divine Law," says Cardinal Gousset, " is the supreme rule of actions; our thoughts, desires, words, acts, all that man is, is subject to the domain of the law of God; and this law is the rule of our conduct by means of our conscience. Hence it is never lawful to go against our conscience; as the fourth Lateran council says, ' Quidquid fit contra conscientiam, ædificat ad gehennam.' "

This view of conscience, I know, is very different from that ordinarily taken of it, both by the science and literature, and by the public opinion, of this day. It is founded on the doctrine that conscience is the voice of God, whereas it is fashionable on all hands now to consider it in one way or another a creation of man. Of course, there are great and broad exceptions to this statement. It is not true of many or most religious bodies of men; especially not of their teachers and ministers. When Anglicans, Wesleyans, the various Presbyterian sects in Scotland, and other denominations among us, speak of conscience, they mean what we mean, the voice of God in the nature and heart of man, as distinct from the voice of Revelation

They speak of a principle planted within us, before we
have had any training, although training and experience are necessary for its strength, growth, and due
formation.   They consider it a constituent element of
the mind, as our perception of other ideas may be, as
our powers of reasoning, as our sense of order and the
beautiful, and our other intellectual endowments.   They
consider it, as Catholics consider it, to be the internal
witness of both the existence and the law of God.   They
think it holds of God, and not of man, as an Angel
walking on the earth would be no citizen or dependent
of the Civil Power.   They would not allow, any more
than we do, that it could be resolved into any combination
of principles in our nature, more elementary than itself;
nay, though it may be called, and is, a law of the mind,
they would not grant that it was nothing more; I mean,
that it was not a dictate, nor conveyed the notion of
responsibility, of duty, of a threat and a promise, with a
vividness which discriminated it from all other constituents of our nature.

This, at least, is how I read the doctrine of Protestants
as well as of Catholics.   The rule and measure of duty
is not utility, nor expedience, nor the happiness of the
greatest number, nor State convenience, nor fitness,
order, and the *pulchrum*.   Conscience is not a long-
sighted selfishness, nor a desire to be consistent with
oneself; but it is a messenger from Him, who, both in
nature and in grace, speaks to us behind a veil, and
teaches and rules us by His representatives.   Conscience
is the aboriginal Vicar of Christ, a prophet in its informations, a monarch in its peremptoriness, a priest in its

blessings and anathemas, and, even though the eternal priesthood throughout the Church could cease to be, in it the sacerdotal principle would remain and would have a sway.

Words such as these are idle empty verbiage to the great world of philosophy now. All through my day there has been a resolute warfare, I had almost said conspiracy against the rights of conscience, as I have described it. Literature and science have been embodied in great institutions in order to put it down. Noble buildings have been reared as fortresses against that spiritual, invisible influence which is too subtle for science and too profound for literature. Chairs in Universities have been made the seats of an antagonist tradition. Public writers, day after day, have indoctrinated the minds of innumerable readers with theories subversive of its claims. As in Roman times, and in the middle age, its supremacy was assailed by the arm of physical force, so now the intellect is put in operation to sap the foundations of a power which the sword could not destroy. We are told that conscience is but a twist in primitive and untutored man; that its dictate is an imagination; that the very notion of guiltiness, which that dictate enforces, is simply irrational, for how can there possibly be freedom of will, how can there be con-sequent responsibility, in that infinite eternal network of cause and effect, in which we helplessly lie? and what retribution have we to fear, when we have had no real choice to do good or evil?

So much for philosophers; now let us see what is the notion of conscience in this day in the popular mind.

There, no more than in the intellectual world, does "conscience" retain the old, true, Catholic meaning of the word. There too the idea, the presence of a Moral Governor is far away from the use of it, frequent and emphatic as that use of it is. When men advocate the rights of conscience, they in no sense mean the rights of the Creator, nor the duty to Him, in thought and deed, of the creature; but the right of thinking, speaking, writing, and acting, according to their judgment or their humour, without any thought of God at all. They do not even pretend to go by any moral rule, but they demand, what they think is an Englishman's prerogative, for each to be his own master in all things, and to profess what he pleases, asking no one's leave, and accounting priest or preacher, speaker or writer, unutterably impertinent, who dares to say a word against his going to perdition, if he like it, in his own way. Conscience has rights because it has duties; but in this age, with a large portion of the public, it is the very right and freedom of conscience to dispense with conscience, to ignore a Lawgiver and Judge, to be independent of unseen obligations. It becomes a licence to take up any or no religion, to take up this or that and let it go again, to go to church, to go to chapel, to boast of being above all religions and to be an impartial critic of each of them. Conscience is a stern monitor, but in this century it has been superseded by a counterfeit, which the eighteen centuries prior to it never heard of, and could not have mistaken for it, if they had. It is the right of self-will.

And now I shall turn aside for a moment to show

how it is that the Popes of our century have been misunderstood by the English people, as if they really were speaking against conscience in the true sense of the word, when in fact they were speaking against it in the various false senses, philosophical or popular, which in this day are put upon the word. The present Pope, in his Encyclical of 1864, *Quantâ curâ,* speaks (as will come before us in the next section) against " liberty of conscience," and he refers to his predecessor, Gregory XVI., who, in his *Mirari vos,* calls it a " deliramentum." It is a rule in formal ecclesiastical proceedings, as I shall have occasion to notice lower down, when books or authors are condemned, to use the very words of the book or author, and to condemn the words in that particular sense which they have in their context and their drift, not in the literal, not in the religious sense, such as the Pope might recognize, were they in another book or author. To take a familiar parallel, among many which occur daily. Protestants speak of the " Blessed Reformation;" Catholics too talk of " the Reformation," though they do not call it blessed. Yet every " reformation " ought, from the very meaning of the word, to be good, not bad ; so that Catholics seem to be implying a eulogy on an event which, at the same time, they consider a surpassing evil. Here then they are taking the word and using it in the popular sense of it, not in the Catholic. They would say, if they expressed their full meaning, " the *so-called* reformation." In like manner, if the Pope condemned " the Reformation," it would be utterly sophistical to say in consequence that he had declared himself against all reforms; yet this is how Mr. Gladstone treats him, when he speaks of (so-called) liberty of conscience. To make this distinction clear, viz., between the Catholic sense of the word "conscience," and that sense in which the Pope condemns it, we find in the *Recueil des Allocutions*, &c., the words accompanied with quotation-marks, both in Pope Gregory's and Pope Pius's Encyclicals, thus:—Gregory's, "Ex hoc putidissimo 'indifferentismi' fonte," (mind, "indifferentismi" is under quotation-marks, because the Pope will not make himself answerable for so unclassical a word) "absurda illa fluit ac erronea sententia, seu potius deliramentum, asserendam esse ac vindicandam cuilibet 'libertatem conscientiæ.'" And that of Pius, "Haud timent erroneam illam fovere opinionem a Gregorio XVI. deliramentum appellatam, nimirum 'libertatem conscientiæ' esse proprium cujuscunque hominis jus." Both Popes certainly scoff at the so-called "liberty of conscience," but there is no scoffing of any Pope, in formal documents addressed to the faithful at large, at that most serious doctrine, the right and the duty of following that Divine Authority, the voice of conscience, on which in truth the Church herself is built.

So indeed it is ; did the Pope speak against Conscience in the true sense of the word, he would commit a suicidal act. He would be cutting the ground from under his feet. His very mission is to proclaim the moral law, and to protect and strengthen that "Light which enlighteneth every man that cometh into the world." On the law of conscience and its sacredness are founded both his authority in theory and his power in fact. Whether this or that particular Pope in this bad world always kept this great truth in view in all he did, it is for history to tell. I am considering here the Papacy in its office and its duties, and in reference to those who acknowledge its claims. They are not bound by the Pope's personal character or private acts, but by his formal teaching. Thus viewing his position, we shall find that it is by the universal sense of right and wrong, the consciousness of transgression, the pangs of guilt, and the dread of retribution, as first principles deeply lodged in the hearts of men, it is thus and only thus, that he has gained his footing in the world and achieved his success. It is his claim to come from the Divine Lawgiver, in order to elicit, protect, and enforce those truths which the Lawgiver has sown in our very nature, it is this and this only that is the explanation of his length of life more than antediluvian. The championship of the Moral Law and of conscience is his *raison d'être*. The fact of his mission is the answer to the complaints of those who feel the insufficiency of the natural light; and the insufficiency of that light is the justification of his mission.

All sciences, except the science of Religion, have their certainty in themselves; as far as they are sciences, they consist of necessary conclusions from undeniable premises, or of phenomena manipulated into general truths by an irresistible induction. But the sense of right and wrong, which is the first element in religion, is so delicate, so fitful, so easily puzzled, obscured, perverted, so subtle in its argumentative methods, so impressible by education, so biassed by pride and passion, so unsteady in its course, that, in the struggle for existence amid the various exercises and triumphs of the human intellect this sense is at once the highest of all teachers, yet the least luminous; and the Church, the Pope, the Hierarchy are, in the Divine purpose, the supply of an urgent demand. Natural Religion, certain as are its grounds and its doctrines as addressed to thoughtful, serious minds, needs, in order that it may speak to mankind with effect and subdue the world, to be sustained and completed by Revelation.

In saying all this, of course I must not be supposed to be limiting the Revelation of which the Church is the keeper to a mere republication of the Natural Law; but still it is true, that, though Revelation is so distinct from the teaching of nature and beyond it, yet it is not independent of it, nor without relations towards it, but is its complement, reassertion, issue, embodiment, and interpretation. The Pope, who comes of Revelation, has no jurisdiction over Nature. If, under the plea of his revealed prerogatives, he neglected his mission of preaching truth, justice, mercy, and peace, much more if he trampled on the consciences of his subjects,—if he had done so all along, as Protestants say, then he could not have lasted all these many centuries till now, so as to supply a mark for their reprobation. Dean Milman has told us above, how faithful he was to his duty in the medieval time, and how successful. Afterwards, for a while the Papal chair was filled by men who gave themselves up to luxury, security, and a Pagan kind of Christianity; and we all know what a moral earthquake was the consequence, and how the Church lost, thereby, and has lost to this day, one-half of Europe. The Popes could not have recovered from so terrible a catastrophe, as they have done, had they not returned to their first and better ways, and the grave lesson of the past is in itself the guarantee of the future.

Such is the relation of the ecclesiastical power to the human conscience:—however, a contrary view may be taken of it. It may be said that no one doubts that the Pope's power rests on those weaknesses of human nature, that religious sense, which in ancient days Lucretius noted as the cause of the worst ills of our race; that he uses it dexterously, forming under shelter of it a false code of morals for his own aggrandisement and tyranny; and that thus conscience becomes his creature and his slave, doing, as if on a divine sanction, his will; so that in the abstract indeed and in idea it is free, but never free in fact, never able to take a flight of its own, independent of him, any more than birds whose wings are clipped;—moreover, that, if it were able to exert a will of its own, then there would ensue a collision more unmanageable than that between the Church and the State, as being in one and the same subject-matter—viz., religion; for what would become of the Pope's "absolute authority," as Mr. Gladstone calls it, if the private conscience had an absolute authority also?

I wish to answer this important objection distinctly.

1. First, I am using the word "conscience" in the high sense in which I have already explained it,—not as a fancy or an opinion, but as a dutiful obedience to what claims to be a divine voice, speaking within us; and that this is the view properly to be taken of it, I shall not attempt to prove here, but shall assume it as a first principle.

2. Secondly, I observe that conscience is not a judgment upon any speculative truth, any abstract doctrine, but bears immediately on conduct, on something to be done or not done. "Conscience," says St. Thomas, "is the practical judgment or dictate of reason, by which we judge what *hic et nunc* is to be done as being good, or to be avoided as evil." Hence conscience cannot come into direct collision with the Church's or the Pope's infallibility; which is engaged on general propositions, and in the condemnation of particular and given errors.

3. Next, I observe that, conscience being a practical dictate, a collision is possible between it and the Pope's authority only when the Pope legislates, or gives particular orders, and the like. But a Pope is not infallible in his laws, nor in his commands, nor in his acts of state, nor in his administration, nor in his public policy. Let it be observed that the Vatican Council has left him just as it found him here. Mr. Gladstone's language on this point is to me quite unintelligible. Why, instead of using vague terms, does he not point out precisely the very words by which the Council has made the Pope in his acts infallible? Instead of so doing, he assumes a conclusion which is altogether false. He says, p. 34, "First comes the Pope's infallibility:" then in the next page he insinuates that, under his infallibility, come acts of excommunication, as if the Pope could not make mistakes in this field of action. He says, p. 35, "It may be sought to plead that the Pope does not propose to invade the country, to seize Woolwich, or burn Portsmouth. He will only, at the worst, excommunicate

opponents. . . . Is this a good answer? After all, even
in the Middle Ages, it was not by the direct action of
fleets and armies of their own that the Popes contended
with kings who were refractory; it was mainly by interdicts," &c. What have excommunication and interdict
to do with Infallibility? Was St. Peter infallible on
that occasion at Antioch when St. Paul withstood him?
was St. Victor infallible when he separated from his
communion the Asiatic Churches? or Liberius when in
like manner he excommunicated Athanasius? And, to
come to later times, was Gregory XIII., when he had
a medal struck in honour of the Bartholomew massacre?
or Paul IV. in his conduct towards Elizabeth? or
Sextus V. when he blessed the Armada? or Urban VIII.
when he persecuted Galileo? No Catholic ever pretends
that these Popes were infallible in these acts. Since
then infallibility alone could block the exercise of conscience, and the Pope is not infallible in that subject-
matter in which conscience is of supreme authority, no
dead-lock, such as is implied in the objection which I
am answering, can take place between conscience and
the Pope.

4. But, of course, I have to say again, lest I should be
misunderstood, that when I speak of Conscience, I mean
conscience truly so called. When it has the right of
opposing the supreme, though not infallible Authority
of the Pope, it must be something more than that miserable counterfeit which, as I have said above, now goes
by the name. If in a particular case it is to be taken as
a sacred and sovereign monitor, its dictate, in order to
prevail against the voice of the Pope, must follow upon

s

serious thought, prayer, and all available means of arriving at a right judgment on the matter in question. And further, obedience to the Pope is what is called " in possession ; " that is, the *onus probandi* of establishing a case against him lies, as in all cases of exception, on the side of conscience. Unless a man is able to say to himself, as in the Presence of God, that he must not, and dare not, act upon the Papal injunction, he is bound to obey it, and would commit a great sin in disobeying it. *Primâ facie* it is his bounden duty, even from a sentiment of loyalty, to believe the Pope right and to act accordingly. He must vanquish that mean, ungenerous, selfish, vulgar spirit of his nature, which, at the very first rumour of a command, places itself in opposition to the Superior who gives it, asks itself whether he is not exceeding his right, and rejoices, in a moral and practical matter to commence with scepticism. He must have no wilful determination to exercise a right of thinking, saying, doing just what he pleases, the question of truth and falsehood, right and wrong, the duty if possible of obedience, the love of speaking as his Head speaks, and of standing in all cases on his Head's side, being simply discarded. If this necessary rule were observed, collisions between the Pope's authority and the authority of conscience would be very rare. On the other hand, in the fact that, after all, in extraordinary cases, the conscience of each individual is free, we have a safeguard and security, were security necessary (which is a most gratuitous supposition), that no Pope ever will be able, as the objection supposes, to create a false conscience for his own ends.

Now, I shall end this part of the subject, for I have not done with it altogether, by appealing to various of our theologians in evidence that, in what I have been saying, I have not misrepresented Catholic doctrine on these important points.

That is, on the duty of obeying our conscience at all hazards.

I have already quoted the words which Cardinal Gousset has adduced from the Fourth Lateran ; that " He who acts against his conscience loses his soul." This *dictum* is brought out with singular fulness and force in the moral treatises of theologians. The celebrated school, known as the Salmanticenses, or Carmelites of Salamanca, lays down the broad proposition, that conscience is ever to be obeyed whether it tells truly or erroneously, and that, whether the error is the fault of the person thus erring or not.[1] They say that this opinion is certain, and refer, as agreeing with them, to St Thomas, St. Bonaventura, Caietan, Vasquez, Durandus, Navarrus, Corduba, Layman, Escobar, and fourteen others. Two of them even say this opinion is *de fide*. Of course, if a man is culpable in being in error, which he might have escaped, had he been more in earnest, for that error he is answerable to God, but still he must act according to that error, while he is in it, because he in full sincerity thinks the error to be truth.

---

[1] " Aliqui opinantur quod conscientia erronea non obligat ; Secundam sententiam, et certam, asserentem esse peccatum discordare à conscientiâ erroneâ, invincibili aut vincibili, tenet D. Thomas ; quem sequuntur omnes Scholastici."—*Theol. Moral.*, t. v. p. 12, ed. 1728.

Thus, if the Pope told the English Bishops to order their priests to stir themselves energetically in favour of teetotalism, and a particular priest was fully persuaded that abstinence from wine, &c., was practically a Gnostic error, and therefore felt he could not so exert himself without sin ; or suppose there was a Papal order to hold lotteries in each mission for some religious object, and a priest could say in God's sight that he believed lotteries to be morally wrong, that priest in either of these cases would commit a sin *hic et nunc* if he obeyed the Pope, whether he was right or wrong in his opinion, and, if wrong, although he had not taken proper pains to get at the truth of the matter.

Busenbaum, of the Society of Jesus, whose work I have already had occasion to notice, writes thus :—" A heretic, as long as he judges his sect to be more or equally deserving of belief, has no obligation to believe [in the Church]." And he continues, " When men who have been brought up in heresy, are persuaded from boyhood that we impugn and attack the word of God, that we are idolators, pestilent deceivers, and therefore are to be shunned as pests, they cannot, while this persuasion lasts, with a safe conscience, hear us."—t. l, p. 54.

Antonio Corduba, a Spanish Franciscan, states the doctrine with still more point, because he makes mention of Superiors. " In no manner is it lawful to act against conscience, even though a Law, or a Superior commands it."—*De Conscient.*, p. 138.

And the French Dominican, Natalis Alexander :— " If, in the judgment of conscience, through a mistaken conscience, a man is persuaded that what his Superior commands is displeasing to God, he is bound not to obey."—*Theol.* t. 2, p. 32.

The word "Superior" certainly includes the Pope; Cardinal Jacobatius brings out this point clearly in his authoritative work on Councils, which is contained in Labbe's Collection, introducing the Pope by name: —"If it were doubtful," he says, "whether a precept [of the Pope] be a sin or not, we must determine thus:—that, if he to whom the precept is addressed has a conscientious sense that it is a sin and injustice, first it is duty to put off that sense; but, if he cannot, nor conform himself to the judgment of the Pope, in that case it is his duty to follow his own private conscience, and patiently to bear it, if the Pope punishes him."— lib. iv. p. 241.

Would it not be well for Mr. Gladstone to bring passages from our recognized authors as confirmatory of his view of our teaching, as those which I have quoted are destructive of it? and they must be passages declaring, not only that the Pope is ever to be obeyed, but that there are no exceptions to the rule, for exceptions there must be in all concrete matters.

I add one remark. Certainly, if I am obliged to bring religion into after-dinner toasts, (which indeed does not seem quite the thing) I shall drink —to the Pope, if you please,—still, to Conscience first, and to the Pope afterwards.

§ 6. *The Encyclical of* 1864.

THE subject of Conscience leads us to the Encyclical,
which is one of the special objects of Mr. Gladstone's
attack; and to do justice to it, I must, as in other
sections, begin from an earlier date than 1864.

Modern Rome then is not the only place where the
traditions of the old Empire, its principles, provisions,
and practices, have been held in honour; they have been
retained, they have been maintained in substance, as the
basis of European civilization down to this day, and
notably among ourselves. In the Anglican establishment the king took the place of the Pope; but the
Pope's principles kept possession. When the Pope was
ignored, the relations between Pope and king were
ignored too, and therefore we had nothing to do any
more with the old Imperial laws which shaped those
relations; but the old idea of a Christian Polity was
still in force. It was a first principle with England
that there was one true religion, that it was inherited
from an earlier time, that it came of direct Revelation,
that it was to be supported to the disadvantage, to say
the least, of other religions, of private judgment, of personal conscience. The Puritans held these principles as
firmly as the school of Laud. As to the Scotch Presby

terians, we read enough about them in the pages of
Mr. Buckle. The Stuarts went, but still their principles
suffered no dethronement : their action was restrained,
but they were still in force, when this century opened.

It is curious to see how strikingly in this matter the
proverb has been fulfilled, " Out of sight, out of mind."
Men of the present generation, born in the new civilization, are shocked to witness in the abiding Papal system
the words, ways, and works of their grandfathers.   In
my own lifetime has that old world been alive, and has
gone its way.   Who will say that the plea of conscience
was as effectual, sixty years ago, as it is now in England,
for the toleration of every sort of fancy religion ?   Had
the Press always that wonderful elbow-room which it has
now ?   Might public gatherings be held, and speeches
made, and republicanism avowed in the time of the
Regency, as is now possible ?   Were the thoroughfares
open to monster processions at that date, and the squares
and parks at the mercy of Sunday manifestations?
Could *savants* in that day insinuate in scientific assemblies
what their hearers mistook for atheism, and artisans
practise it in the centres of political action ?   Could
public prints day after day, or week after week, carry
on a war against religion, natural and revealed, as now
is the case ?   No ; law or public opinion would not
suffer it ; we may be wiser or better now, but we were
then in the wake of the Holy Roman Church, and had
been so from the time of the Reformation.   We were
faithful to the tradition of fifteen hundred years.   All
this was called Toryism, and men gloried in the name ;
now it is called Popery and reviled.

When I was young the State had a conscience, and the Chief Justice of the day pronounced, not as a point of obsolete law, but as an energetic, living truth, that Christianity was the law of the land. And by Christianity was meant pretty much what Bentham calls Church-of-Englandism, its cry being the dinner toast, "Church and king." Blackstone, though he wrote a hundred years ago, was held, I believe, as an authority on the state of the law in this matter, up to the beginning of this century. On the supremacy of Religion he writes as follows, that is, as I have abridged him for my purpose.

"The belief of a future state of rewards and punishments, &c., &c., . . . these are the grand foundation of all judicial oaths. All moral evidence, all confidence in human veracity, must be weakened by irreligion, and overthrown by infidelity. Wherefore all affronts to Christianity, or endeavours to depreciate its efficacy, are highly deserving of human punishment. It was enacted by the statute of William III. that if any person *educated in*, and *having made profession of*, the Christian religion, shall by writing, printing, teaching, or advised speaking, deny the Christian religion to be true, or the Holy Scriptures to be of divine authority," or again in like manner, "if any person *educated* in the Christian religion shall by writing, &c., deny any one of the Persons of the Holy Trinity to be God, or maintain that there are more gods than one, he shall on the first offence be rendered incapable to hold any office or place of trust; and for the second, be rendered incapable of bringing any action, being guardian, executor, legatee, or purchaser of lands, and shall suffer three years' imprisonment without bail. To give room, however, for repentance, if, within four months after the first conviction, the delinquent will in open court publicly renounce his error, he is discharged for that once from all disabilities."

Again : " those who absent themselves from the divine worship in the established Church, through total irreligion, and attend the service of no other persuasion, forfeit one shilling to the poor every Lord's day they so absent themselves, and £20 to the king, if they continue such a default for a month together.   And if they keep any inmate, thus irreligiously disposed, in their houses, they forfeit £10 per month."

Further, he lays down that " reviling the ordinances of the Church is a crime of a much grosser nature than the other of non-conformity ; since it carries with it the utmost indecency, arrogance, and ingratitude ;— indecency, by setting up private judgment in opposition to public ; arrogance, by treating with contempt and rudeness what has at least a better chance to be right than the singular notions of any particular man ; and ingratitude, by denying that indulgence and liberty of conscience to the members of the national Church, which the retainers to every petty conventicle enjoy."

Once more : "In order to secure the established Church against perils from non-conformists of all denominations, infidels, Turks, Jews, heretics, papists, and sectaries, there are two bulwarks erected, called the Corporation and Test Acts ; by the former, no person can be legally elected to any office relating to the Government of any city or corporation, unless, within a twelvemonth before,

he has received the sacrament of the Lord's Supper
according to the rites of the Church of England ; . . .
the other, called the Test Act, directs all officers, civil
and military, to make the declaration against transub-
stantiation within six months after their admission,
and also within the same time to receive the sacrament
according to the usage of the Church of England."
The same test being undergone by all persons who
desired to be naturalized, the Jews also were excluded
from the privileges of Protestant churchmen.

Laws, such as these, of course gave a tone to society,
to all classes, high and low, and to the publications,
periodical or other, which represented public opinion.
Dr. Watson, who was the liberal prelate of his day, in
his answer to Paine, calls him (unless my memory betrays
me) " a child of the devil and an enemy of all righteousness."   Cumberland, a man of the world, (here again I
must trust to the memory of many past years) reproaches a
Jewish writer with ingratitude for assailing, as he seems
to have done, a tolerant religious establishment; and
Gibbon, an unbeliever, feels himself at liberty, in his
posthumous Autobiography, to look down on Priestly,
whose " Socinian shield," he says, " has been repeatedly
pierced by the mighty spear of Horsley, and whose
trumpet of sedition may at length awake the magistrates
of a free country."

Such was the position of free opinion and dissenting
worship in England till quite a recent date, when one
after another the various di abilities which I have been
recounting, and many others besides, melted away, like
snow at spring-tide; and we all wonder how they

could ever have been in force. The cause of this
great revolution is obvious, and its effect inevitable
Though I profess to be an admirer of the principles now
superseded in themselves, mixed up as they were with
the imperfections and evils incident to everything human,
nevertheless I say frankly I do not see how they could
possibly be maintained in the ascendant. When the
intellect is cultivated, it is as certain that it will develope
into a thousand various shapes, as that infinite hues and
tints and shades of colour will be reflected from the earth's
surface, when the sun-light touches it; and in matters
of religion the more, by reason of the extreme subtlety
and abstruseness of the mental action by which they are
determined. During the last seventy years, first one
class of the community, then another, has awakened up
to thought and opinion. Their multiform views on
sacred subjects necessarily affected and found expression
in the governing order. The State in past time had a
conscience; George the Third had a conscience; but
there were other men at the head of affairs besides him
with consciences, and they spoke for others besides
themselves, and what was to be done, if he could not
work without them, and they could not work with him,
as far as religious questions came up at the Council-
board? This brought on a dead-lock in the time of his
successor. The ministry of the day could not agree
together in the policy or justice of keeping up the state
of things which Blackstone describes. The State ought
to have a conscience; but what if it happened to have
half-a-dozen, or a score, or a hundred, in religious matters,
each different from each? I think Mr. Gladstone has

brought out the difficulties of the situation himself in his Autobiography. No government could be formed, if religious unanimity was a *sine qua non*. What then was to be done? As a necessary consequence, the whole theory of Toryism, hitherto acted on, came to pieces and went the way of all flesh. This was in the nature of things. Not a hundred Popes could have hindered it, unless Providence interposed by an effusion of divine grace on the hearts of men, which would amount to a miracle, and perhaps would interfere with human responsibility. The Pope has denounced the sentiment that he ought to come to terms with "progress, liberalism, and the new civilization." I have no thought at all of disputing his words. I leave the great problem to the future. God will guide other Popes to act when Pius goes, as He has guided him. No one can dislike the democratic principle more than I do. No one mourns, for instance, more than I, over the state of Oxford, given up, alas! to "liberalism and progress," to the forfeiture of her great medieval motto, "Dominus illuminatio mea," and with a consequent call on her to go to Parliament or the Heralds' College for a new one; but what can we do? All I know is, that Toryism, that is, loyalty to persons, "springs immortal in the human breast"; that religion is a spiritual loyalty; and that Catholicity is the only divine form of religion. And thus, in centuries to come, there may be found out some way of uniting what is free in the new structure of society with what is authoritative in the old, without any base compromise with "Progress" and "Liberalism."

But to return :—I have noticed the great revolution in

the state of the Law which has taken place since 1828 for this reason :—to suggest that Englishmen, who within fifty years kept up the Pope's system, are not exactly the parties to throw stones at the Pope for keeping it up still.

But I go further :—in fact the Pope has not said on this subject of conscience (for that is the main subject in question) what Mr. Gladstone makes him say. On this point I desiderate that fairness in his Pamphlet which we have a right to expect from him ; and in truth his unfairness is wonderful. He says, pp. 15, 16, that the Holy See has "condemned" the maintainers of "the Liberty of the Press, of conscience, and of worship." Again, that the "Pontiff has condemned free speech, free writing, a free press, toleration of non-conformity, liberty of conscience," p. 42. Now, is not this accusation of a very wholesale character? Who would not understand it to mean that the Pope had pronounced a universal anathema against *all* these liberties *in toto*, and that English law, on the contrary, allowed those liberties *in toto*, which the Pope had condemned? But the Pope has done no such thing. The real question is, in what respect, in what measure, has he spoken against liberty : the grant of liberty admits of degrees. Blackstone is careful to show how much more liberty the law allowed to the subject in his day, how much less severe it was in its safeguards against abuse, than it had used to be ; but he never pretends that it is conceivable that liberty should have no boundary at all. The very idea of political society is based upon the principle that each member of it gives up a portion of his natural liberty for advantages which are greater than that liberty; and the question is, whether the Pope, in any act of his which touches us Catholics, in any ecclesiastical or theological statement of his, has propounded any principle, doctrine, or view, which is not carried out in fact at this time in British courts of law, and would not be conceded by Blackstone. I repeat, the very notion of human society is a relinquishment, to a certain point, of the liberty of its members individually, for the sake of a common security. Would it be fair on that account to say that the British Constitution condemns *all* liberty of conscience in word and in deed?

We Catholics, on our part, are denied liberty of our religion by English law in various ways, but we do not complain, because a limit must be put to even innocent liberties, and we acquiesce in it for the social compensations which we gain on the whole. Our school boys cannot play cricket on Sunday, not even in country places, for fear of being taken before a magistrate and fined. In Scotland we cannot play music on Sundays. Here we cannot sound a bell for church. I have had before now a lawyer's authority for saying that a religious procession is illegal even within our own premises. Till the last year or two we could not call our Bishops by the titles which our Religion gave them. A mandate from the Home Secretary obliged us to put off our cassocks when we went out of doors. We are forced to pay rates for the establishment of secular schools which we cannot use, and then we have to find means over again for building schools of our own. Why is not all this as much

an outrage on our conscience as the prohibition upon
Protestants at Rome, Naples, and Malaga, before the
late political changes—(*not,* to hold their services in a
private house, or in the ambassador's, or outside the
walls),—but to flaunt them in public and thereby to
irritate the natives? Mr. Gladstone seems to think it
is monstrous for the Holy See to sanction such a prohibition. If so, may we not call upon him to gain for
us in Birmingham "the free exercise of our religion,"
in making a circuit of the streets in our vestments, and
chanting the "Pange Lingua," and the protection of the
police against the mob which would be sure to gather
round us—particularly since we are English born, whereas the Protestants at Malaga or Naples were foreigners.[1]
But we have the good sense neither to feel such disabilities
a hardship, nor to protest against them as a grievance.

But now for the present state of English Law :—I
say seriously Mr. Gladstone's accusation of us avails
quite as much against Blackstone's four volumes, against
laws in general, against the social contract, as against
the Pope. What the Pope has said, I will show presently : first let us see what the statute book has to tell
us about the present state of English liberty of speech,
of the press, and of worship.

First, as to public speaking and meetings:—do we
allow of seditious language, or of insult to the sovereign,
or his representatives? Blackstone says, that a misprision
is committed against him by speaking or writing against

---

[1] "Hominibus illuc immigrantibus." These words Mr. Gladstone
omits ; also he translates "publicum" "free," pp. 17, 18, as if worship
could not be free without being public.

him, cursing or wishing him ill, giving out scandalous
stories concerning him, or doing anything that may tend
to lessen him in the esteem of his subjects, may weaken
his government, or may raise jealousies between him
and his people. Also he says, that "threatening and
reproachful words to any judge sitting in the Courts"
involve "a high misprision, and have been punished
with large fines, imprisonment, and corporal punishment." And we may recollect quite lately the judges
of the Queen's Bench prohibited public meetings and
speeches which had for their object the issue of a case
then proceeding in Court.

Then, again, as to the Press, there are two modes of
bridling it, one before the printed matter is published,
the other after. The former is the method of censorship,
the latter that of the law of libel. Each is a restriction
on the liberty of the Press. We prefer the latter. I
never heard it said that the law of libel was of a mild
character; and I never heard that the Pope, in any
Brief or Rescript, had insisted on a censorship.

Lastly, liberty of worship: as to the English restriction of it, we have had a notable example of it in the
last session of Parliament, and we shall have still
more edifying illustrations of it in the next, though
certainly not from Mr. Gladstone. The ritualistic
party, in the free exercise of their rights, under the
shelter of the Anglican rubrics, of certain of the Anglican offices, of the teaching of their great divines, and of
their conscientious interpretation of the Thirty-nine
Articles have, at their own expense, built churches for
worship after their own way; and, on the other hand,

Parliament and the newspapers are attempting to put
them down, not so much because they are acting against
the tradition and the law of the Establishment, but because of the national dislike and dread of the principles
and doctrines which their worship embodies.

When Mr. Gladstone has a right to say broadly, by
reason of these restrictions, that British law and the
British people condemn the maintainers of liberty of
conscience, of the press, and of worship, *in toto*, then
may he say so of the Encyclical, on account of those
words which to him have so frightful a meaning.

But now let us see, on the other hand, what the proposition really is, the condemnation of which leads him
to say, that the Pope has unrestrictedly " condemned
those who maintain *the* liberty of the Press, *the* liberty
of conscience and of worship, and *the* liberty of speech,"
p. 16,—has " condemned free speech, free writing, and
a free press," p. 42. The condemned proposition speaks
as follows :—

" Liberty of conscience and worship, is the *inherent
right* of all men.   2. It ought to be proclaimed in *every*
rightly constituted society.   3. It is a right to *all sorts
of liberty* (omnimodam libertatem) such, that it ought
not to be restrained by any authority, ecclesiastical *or
civil*, as far as public speaking, printing, or any other
public manifestation of opinions is concerned."

Now, is there any government on earth that could
stand the strain of such a doctrine as this ?   It starts
by taking for granted that there are certain Rights of
man ; Mr. Gladstone so considers, I believe ; but other
deep thinkers of the day are quite of another opinion ;

T

however, if the doctrine of the proposition is true, then
the right of conscience, of which it speaks, being inherent in man, is of universal force— that is, all over
the world—also, says the proposition, it is a right
which must be recognised by all rightly constituted
governments. Lastly, what is the right of conscience
thus inherent in our nature, thus necessary for all
states ? The proposition tells us. It is the liberty of
every one to give *public* utterance, in *every* possible shape,
by *every* possible channel, without *any* let or hindrance
from God or man, to *all* his notions *whatsoever*.[2]

Which of the two in this matter is peremptory and
sweeping in his utterance, the author of this thesis himself, or the Pope who has condemned what the other has
uttered ? Which of the two is it who would force upon
the world a universal ? All that the Pope has done is to
deny a universal, and what a universal! a universal liberty
to all men to say out whatever doctrines they may hold by
preaching, or by the press, uncurbed by church or civil
power. Does not this bear out what I said in the foregoing section of the sense in which Pope Gregory denied
a "liberty of conscience" ? It is a liberty of self-will.
What if a man's conscience embraces the duty of regi-
cide? or infanticide? or free love ? You may say that
in England the good sense of the nation would stifle and
extinguish such atrocities. True, but the proposition
says that it is the very right of every one, by nature, in

---

[2] " Jus civibus *inesse* ad *omnimodam* libertatem, *nullâ* vel eccle-
siasticâ vel civili auctoritate coarctandam, quo suos conceptus *quos-
cunque* sive voce, sive typis, sive aliâ ratione, *palam publiceque* mani-
festare ac declarare valeant."

every well constituted society. If so, why have we
gagged the Press in Ireland on the ground of its being
seditious? Why is not India brought within the British
constitution? It seems a light epithet for the Pope to
use, when he calls such a doctrine of conscience *deliramentum:* of all conceivable absurdities it is the wildest
and most stupid. Has Mr. Gladstone really no better
complaint to make against the Pope's condemnations
than this?

Perhaps he will say, Why should the Pope take the
trouble to condemn what is so wild?[3] But he does:
and to say that he condemns something which he does
not condemn, and then to inveigh against him on the
ground of that something else, is neither just nor
logical.

[3] This question is directly answered, in the Postscript on this Section, infr. pp. 362 – 364.

§ 7. *The Syllabus.*

Now I come to the Syllabus of " Errors," the publication of which has been exclaimed against in England as such a singular enormity, and especially by Mr. Gladstone.   The condemnation of theological statements which militate against the Catholic Faith is of long usage in the Church.   Such was the condemnation of the heresies of Wickliffe in the Council of Constance ; such those of Huss, of Luther, of Baius, of Jansenius ; such the condemnations which were published by Sextus IV., Innocent XI., Clement XI., Benedict XIV., and other Popes.   Such condemnations are no invention of Pius IX.   The Syllabus is a collection of such erroneous propositions as he has noted during his Pontificate ; there are eighty of them.

What does the word "Syllabus" mean ?   A collection ; the French translation calls it a " *Resumé ;*"—a Collection of what ?   I have already said, of propositions,—propositions which the Pope in his various Allocutions, Encyclicals, and like documents, since he has been Pope, has pronounced to be Errors.   Who gathered the propositions out of these Papal documents, and put them together in one ?   We do not know ; all we know is that, by the Pope's command, this Collection of Errors was sent by his Foreign Minister to the Bishops.   He,

Cardinal Antonelli, sent to them at the same time the Encyclical of December, 1864, which is a document of dogmatic authority. The Cardinal says, in his circular to them, that the Pope ordered him to do so. The Pope thought, he says, that perhaps the Bishops had not seen some of his Allocutions, and other authoritative letters and speeches of past years; in consequence the Pope had had the Errors which, at one time or other he had therein noted, brought together into one, and that for the use of the Bishops.

Such is the Syllabus and its object. There is not a word in it of the Pope's own writing; there is nothing in it at all but the Erroneous Propositions themselves— that is, except the heading " A Syllabus, containing the principal Errors of our times, which are noted in the Consistorial Allocutions, in the Encyclicals, and in other Apostolical Letters of our most Holy Lord, Pope Pius IX." There is one other addition—viz., after each Error a reference is given to the Allocution, Encyclical, or other document in which it is proscribed.

The Syllabus, then, is to be received with profound submission, as having been sent by the Pope's authority to the Bishops of the world. It certainly comes to them with his indirect extrinsic sanction; but intrinsically, and viewed in itself, it is nothing more than a digest of certain Errors made by an anonymous writer. There would be nothing on the face of it, to show that the Pope had ever seen it, page by page, unless the " Imprimatur " implied in the Cardinal's letter had been an evidence of this. It has no mark or seal put upon it which gives it a direct relation to the Pope.

Who is its author? Some select theologian or high official doubtless; can it be Cardinal Antonelli himself? No surely: anyhow it is not the Pope, and I do not see my way to accept it for what it is not. I do not speak as if I had any difficulty in recognizing and condemning the Errors which it catalogues, did the Pope himself bid me; but he has not as yet done so, and he cannot delegate his *Magisterium* to another. I wish with St. Jerome to "speak with the Successor of the Fisherman and the Disciple of the Cross." I assent to that which the Pope propounds in faith and morals, but it must be he speaking officially, personally, and immediately, and not any one else, who has a hold over me. The Syllabus is not an official act, because it is not signed, for instance, with "Datum Romæ, Pius P. P. IX.," or "sub annulo Piscatoris," or in some other way; it is not a personal, for he does not address his "Venerabiles Fratres," or "Dilecto Filio," or speak as "Pius Episcopus;" it is not an immediate, for it comes to the Bishops only through the Cardinal Minister of State.

If, indeed, the Pope should ever make that anonymous compilation directly his own, then of course I should bow to it and accept it as strictly his. He might have done so; he might do so still; again, he might issue a fresh list of Propositions in addition, and pronounce them to be Errors, and I should take that condemnation to be of dogmatic authority, because I believe him appointed by his Divine Master to determine in the detail of faith and morals what is true and what is false. But such an act of his he would formally authenticate; he would speak in his own name, as Leo X. or Innocent XI. did, by Bull or Letter Apostolic. Or, if he wished to speak less authoritatively, he would speak through a Sacred Congregation; but the Syllabus makes no claim to be acknowledged as the word of the Pope. Moreover, if the Pope drew up that catalogue, as it may be called, he would have pronounced in it some definite judgment on the propositions themselves. What gives cogency to this remark is, that a certain number of Bishops and theologians, when a Syllabus was in contemplation, did wish for such a formal act on the part of the Pope, and in consequence they drew up for his consideration the sort of document on which, if he so willed, he might suitably stamp his infallible sanction; but he did not accede to their prayer. This composition is contained in the "*Recueil des Allocutions*," &c., and is far more than a mere "collection of errors." It is headed, "Theses ad Apostolicam Sedem delatæ *cum censuris*," &c., and each error from first to last has the ground of its condemnation marked upon it. There are sixty-one of them. The first is "impia, injuriosa religioni," &c.; the second is "complexivè sumptu, falsa," &c.; the third the same; the fourth, "hæretica," and so on, the epithets affixed having a distinct meaning, and denoting various degrees of error. Such a document, unlike the Syllabus, has a substantive character.

Here I am led to interpose a remark;—it is plain, then, that there are those near, or with access, to the Holy Father, who would, if they could, go much further in the way of assertion and command, than the divine *Assistentia*, which overshadows him, wills or permits: so that his acts and his words on doctrinal subjects must be carefully scrutinized and weighed, before we can be sure what really he has said. Utterances which must be received as coming from an Infallible Voice are not made every day, indeed they are very rare; and those which are by some persons affirmed or assumed to be such, do not always turn out what they are said to be; nay, even such as are really dogmatic must be read by definite rules and by traditional principles of interpretation, which are as cogent and unchangeable as the Pope's own decisions themselves. What I have to say presently will illustrate this truth; meanwhile I use the circumstance which has led to my mentioning it, for another purpose here. When intelligence which we receive from Rome startles and pains us from its seemingly harsh or extreme character, let us learn to have some little faith and patience, and not take for granted that all that is reported is the truth. There are those who wish and try to carry measures, and declare they have carried, when they have not carried them. How many strong things, for instance, have been reported with a sort of triumph on one side and with irritation and despondency on the other, of what the Vatican Council has done; whereas the very next year after it, Bishop Fessler, the Secretary General of the Council, brings out his work on "True and False Infallibility," reducing what was said to be so monstrous to its true dimensions. When I see all this going on, those grand lines in the Greek Tragedy always rise on my lips—

Οὔποτε τὰν Διὸς ἁρμονίαν

θνατῶν παρεξίασι βουλαί,—

and still more the consolation given us by a Divine Speaker that, though the swelling sea is so threatening to look at, yet there is One who rules it and says, " Hitherto shalt thou come and no further, and here shall thy proud waves be stayed ! "

But to return :—the Syllabus then has no dogmatic force ; it addresses us, not in its separate portions, but as a whole, and is to be received from the Pope by an act of obedience, not of faith, that obedience being shown by having recourse to the original and authoritative documents, (Allocutions and the like,) to which it pointedly refers. Moreover, when we turn to those documents, which *are* authoritative, we find the Syllabus cannot even be called an echo of the Apostolic Voice ; for, in matters in which wording is so important, it is not an exact transcript of the words of the Pope, in its account of the errors condemned,—just as is natural in what is professedly an index for reference.

Mr. Gladstone indeed wishes to unite the Syllabus to that Encyclical which so moved him in December, 1864, and says that the Errors noted in the Syllabus are all brought under the infallible judgment pronounced on certain errors specified in the Encyclical. This is an untenable assertion. He says of the Pope and of the Syllabus, p. 20 : " These are not mere opinions of the Pope himself, nor even are they opinions which he might paternally recommend to the pious consideration of the faithful. With the promulgation of his opinions is unhappily combined, in the Encyclical Letter *which virtually, though not expressly, includes the whole,* a *command* to all his spiritual children (from which command we, the disobedient children, are in no way excluded) *to hold them*," and Mr. Gladstone appeals in proof of this to the language of the Encyclical; but let us see what that language is. The Pope speaks thus, as Mr. Gladstone himself quotes him: "All and each of the wrong opinions and doctrines, *mentioned one by one in this Encyclical* (*hisce litteris*), by our Apostolical authority, we reprobate, &c." He says then, as plainly as words can speak, that the wrong opinions which in this passage he condemns, are specified *in* the Encyclical, not outside of it; and, when we look into the earlier part of it, there they are, about ten of them; there is not a single word in the Encyclical to show that the Pope in it was alluding to the Syllabus. The Syllabus does not exist, as far as the language of the Encyclical is concerned. This gratuitous assumption seems to me marvellously unfair.

The only connexion between the Syllabus and the Encyclical is one external to them both, the connexion of time and organ; Cardinal Antonelli sending them both to the Bishops with the introduction of one and the same letter. In that letter he speaks to the Bishops thus, as I paraphrase his words: [1]—" The Holy Father sends you

---

[1] His actual words (abridged) are these :—" Notre T.S.S. Pius IX., n'a jamais cessé de proscrire les principales erreurs de notre très-malheureuse époque, par ses Encycliques, et par ses Allocutions, &c. Mais comme il peut arriver que tous les actes pontificaux ne per-viennent pas à chacun des Ordinaires, le même Souverain Pontife a voulu que l'on rédigeât un Syllabus de ces mêmes erreurs, destiné à être envoyé à tous les Evêques, &c. Il m'a ensuite ordonné de veiller à ce que ce Syllabus imprimé fût envoyé à V.E.R. dans ce temps où le même Souverain Pontife a jugé à propos d'écrire un autre Lettre Encyclique. Ainsi, je m'empresse d'envoyer à V.E. ce Syllabus avec ces Lettres "

by me a list, which he has caused to be drawn up and
printed, of the errors which he has in various formal
documents, in the course of the last eighteen years,
noted. With that list of errors, he is also sending
you a new Encyclical, which he has judged it *apropos*
to write to the Catholic Bishops ;—so I send you both at
once."

The Syllabus, then, is a list, or rather an index, of the
Pope's Encyclical or Allocutional "proscriptions," an
index *raisonné*,—(not alphabetical, as is found, for instance, in Bellarmine's or Lambertini's works,)—drawn
up by the Pope's orders, out of his paternal care for the
flock of Christ, and conveyed to the Bishops through his
Minister of State. But we can no more accept it as *de
fide*, as a dogmatic document, than any other index or
table of contents. Take a parallel case, *mutatis mutandis :*
Counsel's opinion being asked on a point of law, he goes
to his law books, writes down his answer, and, as authority, refers his client to 23 George III., c. 5, s. 11 ;
11 Victoria, c. 12, s. 19, and to Thomas *v.* Smith, Att.
Gen. *v.* Roberts, and Jones *v.* Owen. Who would say
that that sheet of foolscap has force of law, when it was
nothing more than a list of references to the Statutes
of the Realm, or Judges' decisions, in which the Law's
voice really was found?

The value of the Syllabus, then, lies in its references ;
but of these Mr. Gladstone has certainly availed himself
very little. Yet, in order to see the nature and extent
of the blame cast on any proposition of the Syllabus, it
is absolutely necessary to turn out the passage of the
Allocution, Encyclical, or other document, in which the

error is noted; for the wording of the errors which the Syllabus contains is to be interpreted by its references. Instead of this Mr. Gladstone uses forms of speech about the Syllabus which only excite in me fresh wonder. Indeed, he speaks upon these ecclesiastical subjects generally in a style in which priests and parsons are accused by their enemies of speaking concerning geology. For instance, the Syllabus, as we have seen, is a list or index; but he calls it "extraordinary declarations," p. 21. How can a list of errors be a series of Pontifical "Declarations"?

However, perhaps he would say that, in speaking of "Declarations," he was referring to the authoritative allocutions, &c., which I have accused him of neglecting. With all my heart; but then let us see how the statements in these allocutions fulfil the character he gives of them. He calls them "Extraordinary declarations on personal and private duty," p. 21, and "stringent condemnations," p. 19. Now, I certainly must grant that some are stringent, but only some. One of the most severe that I have found among them is that in the Apostolic Letter of June 10, 1851, against some heretic priest out at Lima, whose elaborate work in six volumes against the Curia Romana, is pronounced to be in its various statements "scandalous, rash, false, schismatical, injurious to the Roman Pontiffs and Ecumenical Councils, impious and heretical." It well deserved to be called by these names, which are not terms of abuse, but each with its definite meaning; and, if Mr. Gladstone, in speaking of the condemnations, had confined his epithet "stringent" to it, no one would have complained of him. And another severe condemnation is that of the works of Professor Nuytz. But let us turn to some other of the so-called condemnations, in order to ascertain whether they answer to his general description of them.

1. For instance, take his own 16th (the 77th of the "erroneous Propositions"), that, "It is no longer expedient that the Catholic Religion should be established to the exclusion of all others." When we turn to the Allocution, which is the ground of its being put into the Syllabus, what do we find there? First, that the Pope was speaking, not of States universally, but of one particular State, Spain, definitely Spain; secondly, that he was not noting the erroneous proposition directly, or categorically, but was protesting against the breach in many ways of the Concordat on the part of the Spanish government; further, that he was not referring to any work containing the said proposition, nor contemplating any proposition at all; nor, on the other hand, using any word of condemnation whatever, nor using any harsher terms of the Government in question than an expression of "his wonder and distress." And again, taking the Pope's remonstrance as it stands, is it any great cause of complaint to Englishmen, who so lately were severe in their legislation upon Unitarians, Catholics, unbelievers, and others, that the Pope merely does *not* think it expedient for *every* state *from this time forth* to tolerate *every* sort of religion on its territory, and to disestablish the Church at once? for this is all that he denies. As in the instance in the foregoing section, he does but deny a universal, which the "erroneous proposition" asserts without any explanation.

2. Another of Mr. Gladstone's "stringent Condemnations" (his 18th) is the Pope's denial of the proposition that "the Roman Pontiff can and ought to come to terms with Progress, Liberalism, and the New Civilization." I turn to the Allocution of March 18, 1861, and find there no formal condemnation of this Proposition at all. The Allocution is a long *argument* to the effect that the moving parties in that Progress, Liberalism, and New Civilization, make use of it so seriously to the injury of the Faith and the Church, that it is both out of the power, and contrary to the duty, of the Pope to come to terms with them. Nor would those prime movers themselves differ from him here; certainly in this country it is the common cry that Liberalism is and will be the Pope's destruction, and they wish and mean it so to be. This Allocution on the subject is at once beautiful, dignified, and touching: and I cannot conceive how Mr. Gladstone should make stringency his one characteristic of these condemnations, especially when after all there is here no condemnation at all.

3. Take, again, Mr. Gladstone's 15th—"That the abolition of Temporal Power of the Popedom would be highly advantageous to the Church." Neither can I find in the Pope's Allocution any formal condemnation whatever of this proposition, much less a "stringent" one. Even the Syllabus does no more in the case of any one of the eighty, than to call it an "error;" and what the Pope himself says of this particular error is only this:—"We cannot but in particular *warn* and *reprove* (monere et redarguere) those who applaud the decree by which the Roman Pontiff has been despoiled of all the

honour and dignity of his civil rule, and assert that the said decree, more than anything else, conduces to the liberty and prosperity of the Church itself."—*Alloc.*, April 20, 1849.

4. Take another of his instances, the 17th, the "error" that "in countries called Catholic the public exercise of other religions may laudably be allowed." I have had occasion to mention already his mode of handling the Latin text of this proposition—viz., that whereas the men who were forbidden the public exercise of their religion were foreigners, who had no right to be in a country not their own at all, and might fairly have conditions imposed upon them during their stay there, nevertheless Mr. Gladstone (apparently through haste) has left out the word "hominibus illuc immigrantibus," on which so much turns. Next, as I have observed above, it was only the sufferance of their *public* worship, and again of all worships whatsoever, however many and various, which the Pope blamed; and further, the Pope's words do not apply to all States, but specially, and, as far as the Allocution goes, definitely, to New Granada.

However, the point I wish to insist upon here is, that there was in this case no condemned proposition at all, but it was merely, as in the case of Spain, an act of the Government which the Pope protested against. The Pope merely told that Government that that act, and other acts which they had committed, gave him very great pain; that he had expected better things of them; that the way they went on was all of a piece; and they had his best prayers. Somehow, it seems to me strange, for any one to call an expostulation like this one of a set of "extraordinary declarations" "stringent condemnations."

I am convinced that the more the propositions and the references contained in the Syllabus are examined, the more signally will the charge break down, brought against the Pope on occasion of it: as to those Propositions which Mr. Gladstone specially selects, some of them I have already taken in hand, and but few of them present any difficulty.

5. As to those on Marriage, I cannot follow Mr. Gladstone's meaning here, which seems to me very confused, and it would be going out of the line of remark which I have traced out for myself, (and which already is more extended than I could wish), were I to treat of them.[2]

6. His fourth Error, (taken from the Encyclical) that "Papal judgments and decrees may, without sin, be disobeyed or differed from," is a denial of the principle of Hooker's celebrated work on Ecclesiastical Polity, and would be condemned by him as well as by the Pope. And it is plain to common sense that no society can stand if its rules are disobeyed. What club or union would not expel members who refused so to be bound?

7. And the 5th,[3] 8th, and 9th propositions are neces-

---

[2] I have observed on them in Postscript on § 7, infr. pp. 368—370.

[3] Father Coleridge, in his Sermon on "The Abomination of Desolation," observes that, whereas Proposition 5th speaks of "jura," Mr. Gladstone translates "*civil* jura." Vid. also the "Month" for December, but above all Mgr. Dupanloup's works on the general subject.

sarily errors, if the Sketch of Church Polity drawn out in my former Sections is true, and are necessarily considered to be such by those, as the Pope, who maintain that Polity.

8. The 10th Error, as others which I have noticed above, is a *universal* (that " in the conflict of laws, civil and ecclesiastical, the civil law should prevail"), and the Pope does but deny a universal.

9. Mr. Gladstone's 11th, which I do not quite understand in his wording of it, runs thus :—" Catholics can approve of that system of education for youth which is separated from the Catholic faith and the Church's power, and which regards the science only of physical things, and the outlines (fines) of earthly social life alone or at least primarily." How is this not an " Error"? Surely there are Englishmen enough who protest against the elimination of religion from our schools; is such a protest so dire an offence to Mr. Gladstone?

10. And the 12th Error is this :—That " the science of philosophy and of morals, also the laws of the State, can and should keep clear of divine and ecclesiastical authority." This too will not be anything short of an error in the judgment of great numbers of our own people. Is Benthamism so absolutely the Truth, that the Pope is to be denounced because he has not yet become a convert to it?

11. There are only two of the condemnations which really require a word of explanation; I have already referred to them. One is that of Mr. Gladstone's sixth Proposition, " Roman Pontiffs and Ecumenical Councils, have departed from the limits of their power, have

U

usurped the rights of Princes, and even in defining matters of faith and morals have erred." These words are taken from the Lima Priest's book. We have to see then what *he* means by "the Rights of Princes," for the proposition is condemned in *his* sense of the word. It is a rule of the Church in the condemnation of a book to state the proposition condemned in the words of the book itself, without the Church being answerable for those words as employed.[4] I have already referred to this rule in my 5th Section. Now this priest includes among the rights of Catholic princes that of deposing Bishops from their sacred Ministry, of determining the impediments to marriage, of forming Episcopal sees, and of being free from episcopal authority in spiritual matters. When, then, the Proposition is condemned "that Popes had usurped the rights of Princes;" what is meant is, "the so-called rights of Princes," which were really the rights of the Church, in assuming which there was no usurpation at all.

12. The other proposition, Mr. Gladstone's seventh, the condemnation of which requires a remark, is this: "The Church has not the power to employ force (vis inferendæ) nor any temporal power direct or indirect.'

---

[4] Propositiones, de quibus Ecclesia judicium suum pronunciat, duobus præsertim modis spectari possunt, vel absolutè ac in se ipsis, vel relativè ad sensum libri et auctoris. In censurâ propositionis alicujus auctoris vel libri, Ecclesia attendit ad sensum ab eo intentum, qui quidem ex verbis, ex totâ doctrinæ ipsius serie, libri textura et confirmatione, consilio, institutoque elicitur. Propositio libri vel auctoris *æquivoca* esse potest, duplicemque habere sensum, rectum unum et alterum malum. *Ubi contingit Ecclesiam propositiones hujusmodi æquivocas absque prævia distinctione sensuum configere, censura unicè cadit in sensum perversum libri vel auctoris.*—Tournely t. 2, p. 170, ed. 1752.

This is one of a series of Propositions found in the
work of Professor Nuytz, entitled, "Juris Ecclesiastici
Institutiones," all of which are condemned in the
Pope's Apostolic Letter of August 22, 1851. Now
here "employing force" is not the Pope's phrase but
Professor Nuytz's, and the condemnation is meant to
run thus, "It is an error to say, with Professor Nuytz,
that what *he* calls 'employing force' is not allowable to
the Church." That this is the right interpretation of
the "error" depends of course on a knowledge of the
Professor's work, which I have never had an opportunity of seeing ; but here I will set down what the received doctrine of the Church is on ecclesiastical punishments, as stated in a work of the highest authority,
since it comes to us with letters of approval from
Gregory XVI. and Pius IX.

"The opinion," says Cardinal Soglia, "that the
coercive power divinely bestowed upon the Church consists in the infliction of spiritual punishments alone,
and not in corporal or temporal, seems more in har-
mony with the gentleness of the Church. Accordingly
I follow their judgment, who withdraw from the Church
the corporal sword, by which the body is destroyed or
blood is shed. Pope Nicholas thus writes : ' The Church
has no sword but the spiritual. She does not kill, but
gives life, hence that well-known saying, 'Ecclesia
abhorret a sanguine.' But the lighter punishments,
though temporal and corporal, such as shutting up in a
monastery, prison, flogging, and others of the same
kind, short of effusion of blood, the Church *jure suo* can
inflict."—(Institut. Jur., pp. 167-8, Paris.)

And the Cardinal quotes the words of Fleury, "The Church has enjoined on penitent sinners almsgivings, fastings, and other corporal inflictions. . . . Augustine speaks of beating with sticks, as practised by the Bishops, after the manner of masters in the case of servants, parents in the case of children and school-masters in that of scholars. Abbots flogged monks in the way of paternal and domestic chastisement. . . . Imprisonment for a set time or for life is mentioned among canonical penances; priests and other clerics, who had been deposed for their crimes, being committed to prison in order that they might pass the time to come in penance for their crime, which thereby was withdrawn from the memory of the public."

But now I have to answer one question. If what I have said is substantially the right explanation to give to the drift and contents of the Syllabus, have not I to account for its making so much noise, and giving such deep and wide offence on its appearance? It has already been reprobated by the voice of the world. Is there not, then, some reason at the bottom of the aversion felt by educated Europe towards it, which I have not mentioned? This is a very large question to entertain, too large for this place; but I will say one word upon it.

Doubtless one of the reasons of the excitement and displeasure which the Syllabus caused and causes so widely, is the number and variety of the propositions marked as errors, and the systematic arrangement to which they were subjected. So large and elaborate a work struck the public mind as a new law, moral, social, and ecclesiastical, which was to be the foundation of a European code, and the beginning of a new world, in opposition to the social principles of the 19th century ; and there certainly were persons in high station who encouraged this idea. When this belief was once received, it became the interpretation of the whole Collection through the eighty Propositions, of which it recorded the erroneousness ; as if it had for its object in all its portions one great scheme of aggression. Then, when the public mind was definitively directed to the examination of these erroneous *Theses*, they were sure to be misunderstood, from their being read apart from the context, occasion, and drift of each. They had been noted as errors in the Pope's Encyclicals and Allocutions in the course of the preceding eighteen years, and no one had taken any notice of them ; but now, when they were brought all together, they made a great sensation. Why were they brought together, except for some purpose sinister and hostile to society? and if they themselves were hard to understand, still more so, and doubly so was their proscription.

Another circumstance, which I am not theologian enough to account for, is this,—that the wording of many of the erroneous propositions, as they are drawn up in the Syllabus, gives an apparent breadth to the matter condemned which is not found in the Pope's own words in his Allocutions and Encyclicals. Not that really there is any difference between the Pope's words and Cardinal Antonelli's, for (as I have shown in various instances) what the former says in the concrete, the latter does but repeat in the abstract. Or, to speak logically, when the Pope enunciates as true the particular affirmative, "Spain ought to keep up the establishment of the Catholic Religion," then (since its contradictory is necessarily false) the Cardinal declares, "To say that no State should keep up the establishment of the Catholic Religion is an error." But there is a dignity and beauty in the Pope's own language which the Cardinal's abstract Syllabus cannot have, and this gave to opponents an opportunity to declaim against the Pope, which opportunity was in no sense afforded by what he said himself.

Then, again, it must be recollected, in connexion with what I have said, that theology is a science, and a science of a special kind; its reasoning, its method, its modes of expression, and its language are all its own. Every science must be in the hands of a comparatively few persons—that is, of those who have made it a study. The courts of law have a great number of rules in good measure traditional; so has the House of Commons, and, judging by what one reads in the public prints, men must have a noviceship there before they can be at perfect ease in their position. In like manner young theologians, and still more those who are none, are sure to mistake in matters of detail; indeed a really first-rate theologian is rarely to be found. At Rome the rules of interpreting authoritative documents are known with a perfection which at this time is scarcely to be found elsewhere. Some of these rules, indeed, are known to all priests; but even this general knowledge is not possessed by laymen, much less by Protestants, however able and experienced in their own several lines of study or profession. One of those rules I have had several times occasion to mention. In the censure of books, which offend against doctrine or discipline, it is a common rule to take sentences out of them in the author's own words, whether those are words in themselves good or bad, and to affix some note of condemnation to them in the sense in which they occur in the book in question. Thus it may happen that even what seems at first sight a true statement, is condemned for being made the shelter of an error; for instance: " Faith justifies when it works," or "There is no religion where there is no charity," may be taken in a good sense; but each proposition is condemned in Quesnell, because it is false as he uses it.

A further illustration of the necessity of a scientific education in order to understand the value of Proposi-tions, is afforded by a controversy which has lately gone on among us as to the validity of Abyssinian Orders. In reply to a document urged on one side of the question, it was allowed on the other, that, " if that document was to be read in the same way as we should read any ordinary judgment, the interpretation which had been given to it was the most obvious and natural." " But it was well known," it was said, "to those who are familiar with the practical working of such decisions, that they are only interpreted with safety in the light of certain rules, which arise out of what is called the *stylus curiæ.*" And then some of these rules were given; first, " that to understand the real meaning of a decision, no matter how clearly set forth, we should know the nature of the difficulty or *dubium,* as it was understood by the tribunal that had to decide upon it. Next, nothing but the direct proposition, in its nudest and severest sense, as distinguished from indirect propositions, the grounds of the decision, or implied statements, is ruled by the judgment. Also, if there is anything in the wording of a decision which appears inconsistent with the teaching of an approved body of theologians, &c., the decision is to be interpreted so as to leave such teaching intact;" and so on.[5] It is plain that the view thus opened upon us has further bearings than that for which I make use of it here.

These remarks on scientific theology apply also of course to its language. I have employed myself in illustration in framing a sentence, which would be plain enough to any priest, but I think would perplex any Protestant. I hope it is not of too light a character to introduce here. We will suppose then a theologian to write as follows :—" Holding, as we do, that there is only *material* sin in those who, being *invincibly* ignorant, reject the truth, therefore in charity we hope that they have the future portion of *formal* believers, as considering that by *virtue* of their good faith, though not of the *body* of the faithful, they *implicitly* and *interpretatively* believe what they seem to deny." Now let us consider what sense would this statement convey to the mind of a member of some Reformation Society or Protestant League? He would read it as follows, and consider it all the more insidious and dangerous for its being so very unintelligible :—" Holding, as we do, that there is

----

[5] Month, Nov. and Dec., 1873.

only a very considerable sin in those who reject the truth out of contumacious ignorance, therefore in charity we hope that they have the future portion of nominal Christians, as considering, that by the excellence of their living faith, though not in the number of believers, they believe without any hesitation, as interpreters [of Scripture ?] what they seem to deny."

Now, considering that the Syllabus was intended for the Bishops, who would be the interpreters of it, as the need arose, to their people, and it got bodily into English newspapers even before it was received at many an episcopal residence, we shall not be surprised at the commotion which accompanied its publication.

I have spoken of the causes intrinsic to the Syllabus, which have led to misunderstandings about it. As to external, I can be no judge myself as to what Catholics who have means of knowing are very decided in declaring, the tremendous power of the Secret Societies. It is enough to have suggested here, how a widespread organization like theirs might malign and frustrate the most beneficial acts of the Pope. One matter I had information of myself from Rome at the time when the Syllabus had just been published, before there was yet time to ascertain how it would be taken by the world at large. Now, the Rock of St. Peter on its summit enjoys a pure and serene atmosphere, but there is a great deal of Roman *malaria* at the foot of it. While the Holy Father was in great earnestness and charity addressing the Catholic world by his Cardinal Minister, there were circles of light-minded men in his city who were laying bets with each other whether the Syllabus would "make a row in Europe" or not. Of course it was the interest of those who betted on the affirmative side to represent the Pope's act to the greatest disadvantage; and it was very easy to kindle a flame in the mass of English and other visitors at Rome which with a very little nursing was soon strong enough to take care of itself.

§ 8. *The Vatican Council.*

IN beginning to speak of the Vatican Council, I am obliged from circumstances to begin by speaking of myself. The most unfounded and erroneous assertions have publicly been made about my sentiments towards it, and as confidently as they are unfounded. Only a few weeks ago it was stated categorically by some anonymous correspondent of a Liverpool paper, with reference to the prospect of my undertaking the task on which I am now employed, that it was, " in fact understood that at one time Dr. Newman was on the point of uniting with Dr. Dollinger and his party, and that it required the earnest persuasion of several members of the Roman Catholic Episcopate to prevent him from taking that step,"—an unmitigated and most ridiculous untruth in every word of it, nor would it be worth while to notice it here, except for its connexion with the subject on which I am entering.

But the explanation of such reports about me is easy. They arise from forgetfulness on the part of those who spread them, that there are two sides of ecclesiastical acts, that right ends are often prosecuted by very unworthy means, and that in consequence those who, like myself, oppose a line of action, are not necessarily opposed to the issue for which it has been adopted.

Jacob gained by wrong means his destined blessing. "All are not Israelites, who are of Israel," and there are partisans of Rome who have not the sanctity and wisdom of Rome herself.

I am not referring to anything which took place within the walls of the Council chambers; of that of course we know nothing; but even though things occurred there which it is not pleasant to dwell upon, that would not at all affect, not by an hair's breadth, the validity of the resulting definition, as I shall presently show. What I felt deeply, and ever shall feel, while life lasts, is the violence and cruelty of journals and other publications, which, taking as they professed to do the Catholic side, employed themselves by their rash language (though, of course, they did not mean it so), in unsettling the weak in faith, throwing back inquirers, and shocking the Protestant mind. Nor do I speak of publications only; a feeling was too prevalent in many places that no one could be true to God and His Church, who had any pity on troubled souls, or any scruple of "scandalizing those little ones who believe in" Christ, and of "despising and destroying him for whom He died."

It was this most keen feeling, which made me say, as I did continually, "I will not believe that the Pope's Infallibility will be defined, till defined it is."

Moreover, a private letter of mine became public property. That letter, to which Mr. Gladstone has referred with a compliment to me which I have not merited, was one of the most confidential I ever wrote in my life. I wrote it to my own Bishop, under a deep sense of the responsibility I should incur, were I not to speak out to him my whole mind. I put the matter from me when I had said my say, and kept no proper copy of the letter. To my dismay I saw it in the public prints : to this day I do not know, nor suspect, how it got there; certainly from no want of caution in the quarter to which it was addressed. I cannot withdraw it, for I never put it forward, so it will remain on the columns of newspapers whether I will or not ; but I withdraw it as far as I can, by declaring that it was never meant for the public eye.

1. So much as to my posture of mind before the Definition : now I will set down how I felt after it. On July 24, 1870, I wrote as follows :—

"I saw the new Definition yesterday, and am pleased at its moderation—that is, if the doctrine in question is to be defined at all. The terms are vague and comprehensive ; and, personally, I have no difficulty in admitting it. The question is, does it come to me with the authority of an Ecumenical Council ?

" Now the *primâ facie* argument is in favour of its having that authority. The Council was legitimately called ; it was more largely attended than any Council before it ; and innumerable prayers from the whole of Christendom, have preceded and attended it, and merited a happy issue of its proceedings.

" Were it not then for certain circumstances, under which the Council made the definition, I should receive that definition at once. Even as it is, if I were called upon to profess it, I should be unable, considering it came from the Holy Father and the competent local authorities, at once to refuse to do so. On the other hand, it cannot be denied that there are reasons for a Catholic, till better informed, to suspend his judgment on its validity.

"We all know that ever since the opening of the Council, there has been a strenuous opposition to the definition of the doctrine ; and that, at the time when it was actually passed, more than eighty Fathers absented themselves from the Council, and would have nothing to do with its act. But, if the fact be so, that the Fathers were not unanimous, is the definition valid ? This depends on the question whether unanimity, at least moral, is or is not necessary for its validity ? As at present advised I think it is ; certainly Pius IV. lays great stress on the unanimity of the Fathers in the Council of Trent. 'Quibus rebus perfectis,' he says in his Bull of Promulgation, ' concilium tantâ *omnium qui illi interfuerunt* concordiâ peractum fuit, ut consensum plane *a Domino* effectum esse constiterit ; idque in nostris atque omnium oculis valdè mirabile fuerit."

"Far different has been the case now,—though the Council is not yet finished. But, if I must now at once decide what to think of it, I should consider that all turned on what the dissentient Bishops now do.

"If they separate and go home without acting as a body, if they act only individually, or as individuals, and each in his own way, then I should not recognize in their opposition to the majority that force, firmness, and unity of view, which creates a real case of want of moral unanimity in the Council.

"Again, if the Council continues to sit, if the dissen-

tient Bishops more or less take part in it, and concur in
its acts; if there is a new Pope, and he continues the
policy of the present; and if the Council terminates
without any reversal or modification of the definition, or
any effective movement against it on the part of the
dissentients, then again there will be good reason for
saying that the want of a moral unanimity has not been
made out.

" And further, if the definition is consistently received
by the whole body of the faithful, as valid, or as the
expression of a truth, then too it will claim our assent
by the force of the great dictum, ' Securus judicat orbis
terrarum.'

"This indeed is a broad principle by which all acts
of the rulers of the Church are ratified. But for it, we
might reasonably question some of the past Councils or
their acts."

Also I wrote as follows to a friend, who was troubled
at the way in which the dogma was passed, in order to
place before him in various points of view the duty of
receiving it :—

July 27, 1870.

" I have been thinking over the subject which just
now gives you and me with thousands of others, who
care for religion, so much concern.

" First, till better advised, nothing shall make me say
that a mere majority in a Council, as opposed to a moral
unanimity, in itself creates an obligation to receive its
dogmatic decrees. This is a point of history and precedent, and of course on further examination I may find
myself wrong in the view which I take of history and

precedent; but I do not, cannot see, that a majority in the present Council can of itself *rule* its own sufficiency, without such external testimony.

"But there are other means by which I can be brought under the obligation of receiving a doctrine as a dogma. If I am clear that there is a primitive and uninterrupted tradition, as of the divinity of our Lord; or where a high probability drawn from Scripture or Tradition is partially or probably confirmed by the Church. Thus a particular Catholic might be so nearly sure that the promise to Peter in Scripture proves that the infallibility of Peter is a necessary dogma, as only to be kept from holding it as such by the absence of any judgment on the part of the Church, so that the present unanimity of the Pope and 500 Bishops, even though not sufficient to constitute a formal Synodal act, would at once put him in the position, and lay him under the obligation, of receiving the doctrine as a dogma, that is, to receive it with its anathema.

"Or again, if nothing definitely sufficient from Scripture or Tradition can be brought to contradict a definition, the fact of a legitimate Superior having defined it, may be an obligation in conscience to receive it with an internal assent. For myself, ever since I was a Catholic, I have held the Pope's infallibility as a matter of theological opinion; at least, I see nothing in the Definition which necessarily contradicts Scripture, Tradition, or History; and the "Doctor Ecclesiæ" (as the Pope is styled by the Council of Florence) bids me accept it. In this case, I do not receive it on the word of the Council, but on the Pope's self-assertion.

" And I confess, the fact that all along for so many centuries the Head of the Church and Teacher of the faithful and Vicar of Christ has been allowed by God to assert virtually his own infallibility, is a great argument in favour of the validity of his claim.

" Another ground for receiving the dogma, still not upon the direct authority of the Council, or with acceptance of the validity of its act *per se*, is the consideration that our Merciful Lord would not care so little for His elect people, the multitude of the faithful, as to allow their visible Head, and such a large number of Bishops to lead them into error, and an error so serious, if an error it be. This consideration leads me to accept the doctrine as a dogma, indirectly indeed from the Council, but not so much from a Council, as from the Pope and a very large number of Bishops. The question is not whether they had a right to impose, or even were right in imposing the dogma on the faithful; but whether, having done so, I have not an obligation to accept it, according to the maxim, 'Fieri non debuit, factum valet.'"

This letter, written before the minority had melted away, insists on this principle, that a Council's definition would have a virtual claim on our reception, even though it were not passed *conciliariter*, but in some indirect way; the great object of a Council being in some way or other to declare the judgment of the Church. I think the Third Ecumenical will furnish an instance of what I mean. There the question in dispute was settled and defined, even before certain constituent portions of the Episcopal body had made their appearance; and this, with a protest of sixty-eight of the Bishops then present

against the opening of the Council.   When the expected
party arrived, these did more than protest against the
definition which had been carried ; they actually anathematized the Fathers who carried it, and in this state of
disunion the Council ended.   How then was its definition valid ?   In consequence of after events, which I
suppose must be considered complements, and integral
portions of the Council.   The heads of the various
parties entered into correspondence with each other, and
at the end of two years their differences with each other
were arranged.   There are those who have no belief in
the authority of Councils at all, and feel no call upon
them to discriminate between one Council and another ;
but Anglicans, who are so fierce against the Vatican, and
so respectful towards the Ephesine, should consider
what good reason they have for swallowing the third
Council, while they strain out the nineteenth.

The Council of Ephesus furnishes us with another
remark, bearing upon the Vatican.   It was natural for
men who were in the minority at Ephesus to think that
the faith of the Church had been brought into the utmost
peril by the definition of the Council which they had
unsuccessfully opposed.   They had opposed it on the
conviction that the definition gave great encouragement
to religious errors in the opposite extreme to those which
it condemned ; and, in fact, I think that, humanly speaking, the peril was extreme.   The event proved it to be so,
when twenty years afterwards another Council was held
under the successors of t a majority at Ephesus and carried
triumphantly those very errors whose eventual success
had been predicted by the minority.   But Providence is

never wanting to His Church. St. Leo, the Pope of the day, interfered with this heretical Council, and the innovating party was stopped in its career. Its acts were cancelled at the great Council of Chalcedon, the Fourth Ecumenical, which was held under the Pope's guidance, and which, without of course touching the definition of the Third, which had been settled once for all, trimmed the balance of doctrine by completing it, and excluded for ever from the Church those errors which seemed to have received some sanction at Ephesus. There is nothing of course that can be reversed in the definitions of the Vatican Council; but the series of its acts was cut short by the great war, and, should the need arise (which is not likely) to set right a false interpretation, another Leo will be given us for the occasion ; " in monte Dominus videbit."

In this remark, made for the benefit of those who need it, as I do not myself. I shelter myself under the following passage of Molina, which a friend has pointed out to me :—" Though the Holy Ghost has always been present to the Church, to hinder error in her definitions, and in consequence they are all most true and consistent, yet it is not therefore to be denied, that God, when any matters have to be defined, requires of the Church a co-operation and investigation of those matters, and that, in proportion to the quality of the men who meet together in Councils, to the investigation and diligence which is applied, and the greater or less experience and knowledge which is possessed more at one time than at other times, definitions more or less perspicuous are drawn up and matters are defined more exactly and completely at one

time than at other times. . . . And, whereas by disputa-
tions, persevering reading, meditation, and investigation
of matters, there is wont to be increased in course of time
the knowledge and understanding of the same, and the
Fathers of the later Councils are assisted by the investigation and definitions of the former, hence it arises that
the definitions of later Councils are wont to be more
luminous, fuller, more accurate and exact than those of
the earlier.   Moreover, it belongs to the later Councils
to interpret and to define more exactly and fully what
in earlier Councils have been defined less clearly, fully
and exactly." (*De Concord. Lib. Arbit.*, &c., xiii. 15,
p. 59.)   So much on the circumstances under which the
Vatican Council passed its definition.

2. The other main objection made to the Council is
founded upon its supposed neglect of history in the
decision which its Definition embodies.   This objection
is touched upon by Mr. Gladstone in the beginning of
his Pamphlet, where he speaks of its "repudiation of
ancient history," and I have an opportunity given me of
noticing it here.

He asserts that, during the last forty years, "more
and more have the assertions of continuous uniformity of
doctrine " in the Catholic Church "receded into scarcely
penetrable shadow.   More and more have another series
of assertions, of a living authority, ever ready to open,
adopt, and shape Christian doctrine according to the
times, taken their place."   Accordingly, he considers
that a dangerous opening has been made in the authoritative teaching of the Church for the repudiation of
ancient truth and the rejection of new.   However, as

I understand him, he withdraws this charge from the
controversy he has initiated (though not from his
Pamphlet) as far as it is aimed at the pure theology
of the Church. So far it "belongs," he says, "to the
theological domain," and "is a matter unfit for him to
discuss, as it is a question of divinity." It has been,
then, no duty of mine to consider it, except as it relates
to matters ecclesiastical; but I am unwilling, when a
charge has been made against our theology, unsup-
ported indeed, yet unretracted, to leave it altogether
without reply; and that the more, because, after renouncing "questions of divinity" at p. 14, nevertheless
Mr. Gladstone brings them forward again at p. 15,
speaking, as he does, of the "deadly blows of 1854 and
1870 at the old, historic, scientific, and moderate school"
by the definitions of the Immaculate Conception and
Papal Infallibility.

Mr. Gladstone then insists on the duty of "maintaining
the truth and authority of history, and the inestimable
value of the historic spirit;" and so far of course I have
the pleasure of heartily agreeing with him. As the
Church is a sacred and divine creation, so in like manner
her history, with its wonderful evolution of events, the
throng of great actors who have a part in it, and its
multiform literature, stained though its annals are with
human sin and error, and recorded on no system, and by
uninspired authors, still is a sacred work also; and those
who make light of it, or distrust its lessons, incur a grave
responsibility. But it is not every one that can read its
pages rightly; and certainly I cannot follow Mr. Gladstone's reading of it. He is too well informed indeed,

too large in his knowledge, too acute and comprehensive in his views, not to have an acquaintance with
history, far beyond the run of even highly educated
men ; still when he accuses us of deficient attention
to history, one cannot help asking, whether he does
not, as a matter of course, take for granted as true the
principles for using it familiar with Protestant divines,
and denied by our own, and in consequence whether his
impeachment of us does not resolve itself into the fact
that he is Protestant and we are Catholics.   Nay, has it
occurred to him that perhaps it is the fact, that we have
views on the relation of History to Dogma different from
those which Protestants maintain ?   And is he so certain
of the facts of History in detail, of their relevancy, and
of their drift, as to have a right, I do not say to have an
opinion of his own, but to publish to the world, on his
own warrant, that we have "repudiated ancient history"?
He publicly charges us, not merely with having "neglected" it, or "garbled" its evidence, or with having
contradicted certain ancient usages or doctrines to which
it bears witness, but he says "repudiated."   He could
not have used a stronger term, supposing the Vatican
Council had, by a formal act, cut itself off from early
times, instead of professing, as it does (hypocritically, if
you will, but still professing) to speak, "supported by
Holy Scripture and the decrees both of preceding Popes
and General Councils," and "faithfully adhering to the
aboriginal tradition of the Church."   Ought any one
but an *oculatus testis*, a man whose profession was to
acquaint himself with the details of history, to claim to
himself the right of bringing, on his own authority, so

extreme a charge against so august a power, so inflexible and rooted in its traditions through the long past, as Mr. Gladstone would admit the Roman Church to be?

Of course I shall be reminded that, though Mr. Gladstone cannot be expected to speak on so large a department of knowledge with the confidence decorous in one who has made a personal study of it, there are others who have a right to do so; and that by those others he is corroborated and sanctioned. There are authors, it may be said, of so commanding an authority from their learning and their honesty, that, for the purposes of discussion or of controversy, what they say may be said by any one else without presumption or risk, of confutation. I will never say a word of my own against those learned and distinguished men to whom I refer. No: their present whereabout, wherever it is, is to me a thought full of melancholy. It is a tragical event, both for them and for us, that they have left us. It robs us of a great *prestige;* they have left none to take their place. I think them utterly wrong in what they have done and are doing; and, moreover, I agree as little in their view of history as in their acts. Extensive as may be their historical knowledge, I have no reason to think that they, more than Mr. Gladstone, would accept the position which History holds among the *Loci Theologici*, as Catholic theologians determine it; and I am denying not their report of facts, but their use of the facts they report, and that, because of that special stand-point from which they view the relations existing between the records of History and the enunciations of Popes and Councils. They seem to me to expect from History more than

History can furnish, and to have too little confidence in the Divine Promise and Providence as guiding and determining those enunciations.

Why should Ecclesiastical History, any more than the text of Scripture, contain·in it "the whole counsel of God"? Why should private judgment be unlawful in interpreting Scripture against the voice of authority, and yet be lawful in the interpretation of history? There are those who make short work of questions such as these by denying authoritative interpretation altogether; that is their private concern, and no one has a right to inquire into their reason for so doing; but the case would be different were one of them to come forward publicly, and to arraign others, without first confuting their theological *præambula*, for repudiating history, or for repudiating the Bible.

For myself, I would simply confess that no doctrine of the Church can be rigorously proved by historical evidence : but at the same time that no doctrine can be simply disproved by it. Historical evidence reaches a certain way, more or less, towards a proof of the Catholic doctrines; often nearly the whole way; sometimes it goes only as far as to point in their direction; sometimes there is only an absence of evidence for a conclusion contrary to them; nay, sometimes there is an apparent leaning of the evidence to a contrary conclusion, which has to be explained;—in all cases there is a margin left for the exercise of faith in the word of the Church. He who believes the dogmas of the Church only because he has reasoned them out of History, is scarcely a Catholic. It is the Church's dogmatic use of History in which the Catholic believes; and she uses other informants also,

Scripture, tradition, the ecclesiastical sense or φρόνημα, and a subtle ratiocinative power, which in its origin is a divine gift. There is nothing of bondage or "renunciation of mental freedom" in this view, any more than in the converts of the Apostles believing what the Apostles might preach to them or teach them out of Scripture.

What has been said of History in relation to the formal Definitions of the Church, applies also to the exercise of Ratiocination. Our logical powers, too, being a gift from God, may claim to have their informations respected; and Protestants sometimes accuse our theologians, for instance, the medieval schoolmen, of having used them in divine matters a little too freely. Still it has ever been our teaching and our protest that, as there are doctrines which lie beyond the direct evidence of history, so there are doctrines which transcend the discoveries of reason; and, after all, whether they are more or less recommended to us by the one informant or the other, in all cases the immediate motive in the mind of a Catholic for his reception of them is, not that they are proved to him by Reason or by History, but because Revelation has declared them by means of that high ecclesiastical *Magisterium* which is their legitimate exponent.

What has been said applies also to those other truths, with which Ratiocination has more to do than History, which are sometimes called developments of Christian doctrine, truths which are not upon the surface of the Apostolic *depositum*—that is, the legacy of Revelation,—but which from time to time are brought into form by theologians, and sometimes have been proposed to the

faithful by the Church, as direct objects of faith. No
Catholic would hold that they ought to be logically
deduced in their fulness and exactness from the belief of
the first centuries, but only this,—that, on the assumption
of the Infallibility of the Church (which will overcome
every objection except a contradiction in thought), there
is nothing greatly to try the reason in such difficulties
as occur in reconciling those evolved doctrines with the
teaching of the ancient Fathers; such development being
evidently the new form, explanation, transformation, or
carrying out of what in substance was held from the
first, what the Apostles said, but have not recorded in
writing, or would necessarily have said under our circumstances, or if they had been asked, or in view of
certain uprisings of error, and in that sense being really
portions of the legacy of truth, of which the Church, in
all her members, but especially in her hierarchy, is the
divinely appointed trustee.

Such an evolution of doctrine has been, as I would
maintain, a law of the Church's teaching from the earliest
times, and in nothing is her title of " semper eadem "
more remarkably illustrated than in the correspondence
of her ancient and modern exhibition of it. As to the
ecclesiastical Acts of 1854 and 1870, I think with Mr.
Gladstone that the principle of doctrinal development,
and that of authority, have never in the proceedings of
the Church been so freely and largely used as in the
Definitions then promulgated to the faithful; but I deny
that at either time the testimony of history was repudiated or perverted. The utmost that can be fairly said
by an opponent against the theological decisions of those

years is, that antecedently to the event, it might appear that there were no sufficient historical grounds in behalf of either of them—I do not mean for a personal belief in either, but—for the purpose of converting a doctrine long existing in the Church into a dogma, and making it a portion of the Catholic Creed. This adverse anticipation was proved to be a mistake by the fact of the definition being made.

3. I will not pass from this question of History without a word about Pope Honorius, whose condemnation by anathema in the Sixth Ecumenical Council, is certainly a strong *primâ facie* argument against the Pope's doctrinal infallibility. His case is this:—Sergius, Patriarch of Constantinople, favoured, or rather did not condemn, a doctrine concerning our Lord's Person which afterwards the Sixth Council pronounced to be heresy. He consulted Pope Honorius upon the subject, who in two formal letters declared his entire concurrence with Sergius's opinion. Honorius died in peace, but, more than forty years after him, the Sixth Ecumenical Council was held, which condemned him as a heretic on the score of those two letters. The simple question is, whether the heretical documents proceeded from him as an infallible authority or as a private Bishop.

Now I observe that, whereas the Vatican Council has determined that the Pope is infallible only when he speaks *ex cathedrâ*, and that, in order to speak *ex cathedrâ*, he must at least speak " as exercising the office of Pastor and Doctor of all Christians, defining, by virtue of his Apostolical authority, a doctrine whether of faith or of morals for the acceptance of the universal Church " (though Mr. Gladstone strangely says, p. 34, " There is *no* established or accepted definition of the phrase *ex cathedrâ*"), from this Pontifical and dogmatic explanation of the phrase it follows, that, whatever Honorius said in answer to Sergius, and whatever he held, his words were not *ex cathedrâ,* and therefore did not proceed from his infallibility.

I say so first, because he could not fulfil the above conditions of an *ex cathedrâ* utterance, if he did not actually *mean* to fulfil them. The question is unlike the question about the Sacraments; external and positive acts, whether material actions or formal words, speak for themselves. Teaching on the other hand has no sacramental visible signs; it is an *opus operantis,* and mainly a question of intention. Who would say that the architriclinus at the wedding-feast who said, " Thou hast kept the good wine until now," was teaching the Christian world, though the words have a great ethical and evangelical sense? What is the worth of a signature, if a man does not consider he is signing? The Pope cannot address his people East and West, North and South, without meaning it, as if his very voice, the sounds from his lips, could literally be heard from pole to pole ; nor can he exert his " Apostolical authority" without knowing he is doing so; nor can he draw up a form of words and use care and make an effort in doing so accurately, without intention to do so ; and, therefore, no words of Honorius proceeded from his prerogative of infallible teaching, which were not accompanied with the intention of exercising that prerogative ; and who will dream of saying, be he Anglican, Protestant, unbeliever, or on the other hand Catholic, that Honorius on the occasion in question did actually intend to exert that infallible teaching voice which is heard so distinctly in the *Quantâ curâ* and the *Pastor Æternus?*

What resemblance do these letters of his, written almost as private instructions, bear to the "Pius Episcopus, Servus Servorum Dei, Sacro approbante Concilio, ad *perpetuam rei memoriam*," or with the "Si quis huic nostræ definitioni contradicere (quod Deus avertat), præsumpserit, *anathema* sit" of the *Pastor Æternus?* what to the "Venerabilibus fratribus, Patriarchis primatibus, Archiepiscopis, et Episcopis *universis*, &c., with the "reprobamus, proscribimus, atque damnamus," and the date and signature, "Datum Romæ apud Sanctum Petrum, Die 8 Dec. anno 1864, &c., Pius P.P. IX." of the *Quantâ curâ?*

Secondly, it is no part of our doctrine, as I shall say in my next section, that the discussions previous to a Council's definition, or to an *ex cathedrâ* utterance of a Pope, are infallible, and these letters of Honorius on their very face are nothing more than portions of a discussion with a view to some final decision.

For these two reasons the condemnation of Honorius by the Council in no sense compromises the doctrine of Papal Infallibility. At the utmost it only decides that Honorius in his own person was a heretic, which is inconsistent with no Catholic doctrine; but we may rather hope and believe that the anathema fell, not upon him, but upon his letters in their objective sense, he not intending personally what his letters legitimately expressed.

4. And I have one remark to make upon the argumentative method by which the Vatican Council was carried on to its definition. The *Pastor Æternus* refers to various, witnesses as contributing their evidence towards the determination of the contents of the *depositum*, such as Tradition, the Fathers and Councils, History, but especially Scripture. For instance, the Bull, speaks of the Gospel ("juxta Evangelii testimonia," c. 1) and of Scripture ("manifesta S.S. Scripturarum doctrina," c. 1: "apertis S.S. Literarum testimoniis," c. 3. "S S. Scripturis consentanea," c. 4.) And it lays an especial stress on three passages of Scripture in particular—viz., "Thou art Peter," &c., Matthew xvi. 16—19; "I have prayed for thee," &c., Luke xxii. 32, and "Feed My sheep," &c., John xxi. 15—17. Now I wish all objectors to this method of ours, viz. of reasoning from Scripture, would view it in the light of the following passage in the great philosophical work of Butler, Bishop of Durham.

He writes as follows:—"As it is owned the whole scheme of Scripture is not yet understood, so, if it ever comes to be understood, before the 'restitution of all things,' and without miraculous interpositions, it must be in the same way as natural knowledge is come at, by the continuance and progress of learning and of liberty, and by particular persons attending to, comparing, and pursuing intimations scattered up and down it, which are overlooked and disregarded by the generality of the world. For this is the way in which all improvements are made by thoughtful men tracing on obscure hints, as it were, dropped us by nature accidentally, or which seem to come into our minds by chance. Nor is it at all incredible that a book, which has been so long in the possession of mankind, should contain many truths as yet undiscovered. For all the same phenomena, and the same faculties of investigation, from which such great discoveries in natural knowledge have been made in the present and last age, were equally in the possession of mankind several thousand years before. And possibly it might be intended that events, as they come to pass, should open and ascertain the meaning of several parts of Scripture," ii 3, *vide* also ii. 4, fin.

What has the long history of the contest for and against the Pope's infallibility been, but a growing insight through centuries into the meaning of those three texts, to which I just now referred, ending at length by the Church's definitive recognition of the doctrine thus gradually manifested to her?

§ 9. *The Vatican Definition.*

Now I am to speak of the Vatican definition, by which
the doctrine of the Pope's infallibility has become *de fide*,
that is, a truth necessary to be believed, as being included
in the original divine revelation, for those terms, revelation, *depositum*, dogma, and *de fide*, are correlatives ; and
I begin with a remark which suggests the drift of all I
have to say about it.   It is this :—that so difficult a
virtue is faith, even with the special grace of God, in
proportion as the reason is exercised, so difficult is it to
assent inwardly to propositions, verified to us neither by
reason nor experience, but depending for their reception
on the word of the Church as God's oracle, that she has
ever shown the utmost care to contract, as far as possible,
the range of truths and the sense of propositions, of which
she demands this absolute reception.   " The Church,"
says Pallavicini, " as far as may be, has ever abstained
from imposing upon the minds of men that command-
ment, the most arduous of the Christian Law—viz., to believe obscure matters without doubting."[1]   To co-operate
in this charitable duty has been one special work of her
theologians, and rules are laid down by herself, by

[1] Quoted by Father Ryder (to whom I am indebted for other of my
references), in his " Idealism in Theology," p. 25.

tradition, and by custom, to assist them in the task. She only speaks when it is necessary to speak; but hardly has she spoken out magisterially some great general principle, when she sets her theologians to work to explain her meaning in the concrete, by strict interpretation of its wording, by the illustration of its circumstances, and by the recognition of exceptions, in order to make it as tolerable as possible, and the least of a temptation, to self-willed, independent, or wrongly educated minds. A few years ago it was the fashion among us to call writers, who conformed to this rule of the Church, by the name of " Minimizers;" that day of tyrannous *ipse-dixits,* I trust, is over : Bishop Fessler, a man of high authority, for he was Secretary General of the Vatican Council, and of higher authority still in his work, for it has the approbation of the Sovereign Pontiff, clearly proves to us that a moderation of doctrine, dictated by charity, is not inconsistent with soundness in the faith. Such a sanction, I suppose, will be considered sufficient for the character of the remarks which I am about to make upon definitions in general, and upon the Vatican in particular.

The Vatican definition, which comes to us in the shape of the Pope's Encyclical Bull called the *Pastor Æternus,* declares that " the Pope has that same infallibility which the Church has": [2] to determine therefore what is meant by the infallibility of the Pope we must turn first to consider the infallibility of the Church. And again, to

[2] Romanum Pontificem eâ infallibilitate pollere, quâ divinus Redemptor Ecclesiam suam in definiendâ doctrinâ de fide vel moribus instructam esse voluit.

determine the character of the Church's infallibility, we
must consider what is the characteristic of Christianity,
considered as a revelation of God's will.

Our Divine Master might have communicated to us
heavenly truths without telling us that they came from
Him, as it is commonly thought He has done in the case
of heathen nations; but He willed the Gospel to be a
revelation acknowledged and authenticated, to be public,
fixed, and permanent; and accordingly, as Catholics
hold, He framed a Society of men to be its home, its
instrument, and its guarantee.   The rulers of that
Association are the legal trustees, so to say, of the sacred
truths which He spoke to the Apostles by word of mouth.
As He was leaving them, He gave them their great
commission, and bade them "teach" their converts
all over the earth, "to observe all things whatever
He had commanded them;" and then He added,
"Lo, I am with you always, even to the end of the
world."

Here, first, He told them to "teach" His revealed
Truth; next, "to the consummation of all things;"
thirdly, for their encouragement, He said that He would
be with them "all days," all along, on every emergency
or occasion, until that consummation.   They had a duty
put upon them of teaching their Master's words, a duty
which they could not fulfil in the perfection which
fidelity required, without His help; therefore came His
promise to be with them in their performance of it.
Nor did that promise of supernatural help end with the
Apostles personally, for He adds, "to the consummation
of the world," implying that the Apostles would have

successors, and engaging that He would be with those successors as He had been with them.

The same safeguard of the Revelation—viz. an authoritative, permanent tradition of teaching, is insisted on by an informant of equal authority with St. Matthew, but altogether independent of him, I mean St. Paul. He calls the Church "the pillar and ground of the Truth;" and he bids his convert Timothy, when he had become a ruler in that Church, to "take heed unto his doctrine," to "keep the deposit" of the faith, and to "commit" the things which he had heard from himself "to faithful men who should be fit to teach others."

This is how Catholics understand the Scripture record, nor does it appear how it can otherwise be understood; but, when we have got as far as this, and look back, we find that we have by implication made profession of a further doctrine. For, if the Church, initiated in the Apostles and continued in their successors, has been set up for the direct object of protecting, preserving, and declaring the Revelation, and that, by means of the Guardianship and Providence of its Divine Author, we are led on to perceive that, in asserting this, we are in other words asserting, that, so far as the message entrusted to it is concerned, the Church is infallible; for what is meant by infallibility in teaching but that the teacher in his teaching is secured from error? and how can fallible man be thus secured except by a supernatural infallible guidance? And what can have been the object of the words, "I am with you all along to the end," but to give thereby an answer by anticipation to the spontaneous, silent alarm of the feeble company of fishermen and labourers, to whom they were addressed, on their finding themselves laden with superhuman duties and responsibilities?

Such then being, in its simple outline, the infallibility of the Church, such too will be the Pope's infallibility, as the Vatican Fathers hàve defined it. And if we find that by means of this outline we are able to fill out in all important respects the idea of a Council's infallibility, we shall thereby be ascertaining in detail what has been defined in 1870 about the infallibility of the Pope. With an attempt to do this I shall conclude.

1. The Church has the office of teaching, and the matter of that teaching is the body of doctrine, which the Apostles left behind them as her perpetual possession. If a question arises as to what the Apostolic doctrine is on a particular point, she has infallibility promised to her to enable her to answer correctly. And, as by the teaching of the Church is understood, not the teaching of this or that Bishop, but their united voice, and a Council is the form the Church must take, in order that all men may recognize that in fact she is teaching on any point in dispute, so in like manner the Pope must come before us in some special form or posture, if he is to be understood to be exercising his teaching office, and that form is called _ex cathedrâ._ This term is most appropriate, as being on one occasion used by our Lord Himself. When the Jewish doctors taught, they placed themselves in Moses' seat, and spoke _ex cathedrâ_; and then, as He tells us, they were to be obeyed by their people, and that, whatever were their private lives or characters. "The

Scribes and Pharisees," He says, "are seated on the chair of Moses: all things therefore whatsoever they shall say to you, observe and do; but according to their works do you not, for they say and do not."

2. The forms, by which a General Council is identified as representing the Church herself, are too clear to need drawing out; but what is to be that moral *cathedra*, or teaching chair, in which the Pope sits, when he is to be recognized as in the exercise of his infallible teaching? the new definition answers this question. He speaks *ex cathedrâ*, or infallibly, when he speaks, first, as the Universal Teacher; secondly, in the name and with the authority of the Apostles; thirdly, on a point of faith or morals; fourthly, with the purpose of binding every member of the Church to accept and believe his decision.

3. These conditions of course contract the range of his infallibility most materially. Hence Billuart speaking of the Pope says, " Neither in conversation, nor in discussion, nor in interpreting Scripture or the Fathers, nor in consulting, nor in giving his reasons for the point which he has defined, nor in answering letters, nor in private deliberations, supposing he is setting forth his own opinion, is the Pope infallible," t. ii. p. 110. [3] And for this simple reason, because on these various occasions of speaking his mind, he is not in the chair of the universal doctor.

4. Nor is this all; the greater part of Billuart's nega-

[3] And so the Swiss Bishops: " The Pope is not infallible as a man, or a theologian, or a priest, or a bishop, or a temporal prince, or a judge, or a legislator, or in his political views, or even in his government of the Church. "—*Vid.* Fessler, French Transl., p. iv.

tives refer to the Pope's utterances when he is out of the
Cathedra Petri, but even, when he is in it, his words do
not necessarily proceed from his infallibility. He has
no wider prerogative than a Council, and of a Council
Perrone says, " Councils are not infallible in the reasons
by which they are led, or on which they rely, in making
their definition, nor in matters which relate to persons,
nor to physical matters which have no necessary connexion with dogma." *Præl. Theol.* t. 2, p. 492. Thus, if
a Council has condemned a work of Origen or Theodoret,
it did not in so condemning go beyond the work itself;
it did not touch the persons of either. Since this holds of
a Council, it also holds in the case of the Pope ; therefore,
supposing a Pope has quoted the so-called works of the
Areopagite as if really genuine, there is no call on us
to believe him ; nor again, if he condemned Galileo's
Copernicanism, unless the earth's immobility has a
"necessary connexion with some dogmatic truth," which
the present bearing of the Holy See towards that philosophy virtually denies.

5. Nor is a Council infallible, even in the prefaces and
introductions to its definitions. There are theologians
of name, as Tournely and Amort,[4] who contend that
even those most instructive *capitula* passed in the Tridentine Council, from which the Canons with anathemas
are drawn up, are not portions of the Church's infallible
teaching ; and the parallel introductions prefixed to the
Vatican anathemas have an authority not greater nor
less than that of those capitula.

[4] *Vid.* Amort. Dem. Cr., pp. 205-6. This applies to the Unam
Sanctam, *vid.* Fessler, Engl. Trans., p. 67.

6. Such passages, however, as these are too closely connected with the definitions themselves, not to be what is sometimes called, by a *catachresis*, " proximum fidei ;" still, on the other hand, it is true also that, in those circumstances and surroundings of formal definitions, which I have been speaking of, whether on the part of a Council or a Pope, there may be not only no exercise of an infallible voice, but actual error. Thus, in the Third Council, a passage of an heretical author was quoted in defence of the doctrine defined, under the belief he was Pope Julius, and narratives, not trustworthy, are introduced into the Seventh.

This remark and several before it will become intelligible if we consider that neither Pope nor Council are on a level with the Apostles. To the Apostles the whole revelation was given, by the Church it is transmitted ; no simply new truth has been given to us since St. John's death ; the one office of the Church is to guard " that noble deposit " of truth, as St. Paul speaks to Timothy, which the Apostles bequeathed to her, in its fulness and integrity. Hence the infallibility of the Apostles was of a far more positive and wide character than that needed by and granted to the Church. We call it, in the case of the Apostles, inspiration ; in the case of the Church, *assistentia.*

Of course there is a sense of the word "inspiration" in which it is common to all members of the Church, and therefore especially to its Bishops, and still more directly to those rulers, when solemnly called together in Council, after much prayer throughout Christendom, and in a frame of mind especially serious and earnest by reason of the work they have in hand. The Paraclete certainly is ever with them, and more effectively in a Council, as being " in Spiritu Sancto congregata;" but I speak of the special and promised aid necessary for their fidelity to Apostolic teaching; and, in order to secure this fidelity, no inward gift of infallibility is needed, such as the Apostles had, no direct suggestion of divine truth, but simply an external guardianship, keeping them off from error (as a man's good Angel, without at all enabling him to walk, might, on a night journey, keep him from pitfalls in his way), a guardianship, saving them, as far as their ultimate decisions are concerned, from the effects of their inherent infirmities, from any chance of extravagance, of confusion of thought, of collision with former decisions or with Scripture, which in seasons of excitement might reasonably be feared.

"Never," says Perrone, "have Catholics taught that the gift of infallibility is given by God to the Church after the manner of inspiration."—t. 2, p. 253. Again: "[Human] media of arriving at the truth are excluded neither by a Council's nor by a Pope's infallibility, for God has promised it, not by way of an infused " or habitual "gift, but by the way of *assistentia*."—*ibid* p. 541.

But since the process of defining truth is human, it is open to the chance of error; what Providence has guaranteed is only this, that there should be no error in the final step, in the resulting definition or dogma.

7. Accordingly, all that a Council, and all that the Pope, is infallible in, is the direct answer to the

special question which he happens to be considering; his prerogative does not extend beyond a power, when in his *Cathedra*, of giving that very answer truly. "Nothing," says Perrone, "but the *objects* of dogmatic definitions of Councils are immutable, for in these are Councils infallible, not in their *reasons*," &c.—*ibid*.

8. This rule is so strictly to be observed that, though dogmatic statements are found from time to time in a Pope's Apostolic Letters, &c., yet they are not accounted to be exercises of his infallibility if they are said only *obiter*—by the way, and without direct intention to define. A striking instance of this *sine qua non* condition is afforded by Nicholas I., who, in a letter to the Bulgarians, spoke as if baptism were valid, when administered simply in our Lord's Name, without distinct mention of the Three Persons; but he is not teaching and speaking *ex cathedrâ*, because no question on this matter was in any sense the occasion of his writing. The question asked of him was concerning the *minister* of baptism—viz., whether a Jew or Pagan could validly baptize; in answering in the affirmative, he added *obiter*, as a private doctor, says Bellarmine, "that the baptism was valid, whether adminstered in the name of the three Persons or in the name of Christ only." (*De Rom. Pont.*, iv. 12.)

9. Another limitation is given in Pope Pius's own conditions, set down in the *Pastor Æternus*, for the exercise of infallibility : viz., the proposition defined will be without any claim to be considered binding on the belief of Catholics, unless it is referable to the Apostolic *depositum*, through the channel either of Scripture or

Tradition ; and, though the Pope is the judge whether it is so referable or not, yet the necessity of his professing to abide by this reference is in itself a certain limitation of his dogmatic action. A Protestant will object indeed that, after his distinctly asserting that the Immaculate Conception and the Papal Infallibility are in Scripture and Tradition, this safeguard against erroneous definitions is not worth much, nor do I say that it is one of the most effective : but anyhow, in consequence of it, no Pope any more than a counsel, could, for instance, introduce Ignatius's Epistles into the Canon of Scripture ;—and, as to his dogmatic condemnation of particular books, which, of course, are foreign to the *depositum*, I would say, that, as to their false doctrine there can be no difficulty in condemning that, by means of that Apostolic deposit ; nor surely in his condemning the very wording, in which they convey it, when the subject is carefully considered. For the Pope's condemning the language, for instance, of Jansenius is a parallel act to the Church's sanctioning the word "Consubstantial," and if a Council and the Pope were not infallible so far in their judgment of language, neither Pope nor Council could draw up a dogmatic definition at all, for the right exercise of words is involved in the right exercise of thought.

10. And in like manner, as regards the precepts concerning moral duties, it is not in every such precept that the Pope is infallible.[5] As a definition of faith must be

---

[5] It is observable that the *Pastor Æternus* does not speak of "præcepta" at all in its definition of the Pope's Infallibility, only of his "defining doctrine," and of his "definitions."

drawn from the Apostolic *depositum* of doctrine, in order that it may be considered an exercise of infallibility, whether in the Pope or a Council, so too a precept of morals, if it is to be accepted as from an infallible voice, must be drawn from the Moral law, that primary revelation to us from God.

That is, in the first place, it must relate to things in themselves good or evil. If the Pope prescribed lying or revenge, his command would simply go for nothing, as if he had not issued it, because he has no power over the Moral Law. If he forbade his flock to eat any but vegetable food, or to dress in a particular fashion (questions of decency and modesty not coming into the question), he would also be going beyond the province of faith, because such a rule does not relate to a matter in itself good or bad. But if he gave a precept all over the world for the adoption of lotteries instead of tithes or offerings, certainly it would be very hard to prove that he was contradicting the Moral Law, or ruling a practice to be in itself good which was in itself evil; and there are few persons but would allow that it is at least doubtful whether lotteries are abstractedly evil, and in a doubtful matter the Pope is to be believed and obeyed.

However, there are other conditions besides this, necessary for the exercise of Papal infallibility, in moral subjects :—for instance, his definition must relate to things necessary for salvation. No one would so speak of lotteries, nor of a particular dress, nor of a particular kind of food ;—such precepts, then, did he make them, would be simply external to the range of his prerogative.

And again, his infallibility in consequence is not called into exercise, unless he speaks to the whole world; for, if his precepts, in order to be dogmatic, must enjoin what is necessary to salvation, they must be necessary for all men. Accordingly orders which issue from him for the observance of particular countries, or political or religious classes, have no claim to be the utterances of his infallibility. If he enjoins upon the hierarchy of Ireland to withstand mixed education, this is no exercise of his infallibility.

It may be added that the field of morals contains so little that is unknown and unexplored, in contrast with revelation and doctrinal fact, which form the domain of faith, that it is difficult to say what portions of moral teaching in the course of 1800 years actually have proceeded from the Pope, or from the Church, or where to look for such. Nearly all that either oracle has done in this respect, has been to condemn such propositions as in a moral point of view are false, or dangerous or rash; and these condemnations, besides being such as in fact will be found to command the assent of most men, as soon as heard, do not necessarily go so far as to present any positive statements for universal acceptance.

11. With the mention of condemned propositions I am brought to another and large consideration, which is one of the best illustrations that I can give of that principle of minimizing so necessary, as I think, for a wise and cautious theology: at the same time I cannot insist upon it in the connexion into which I am going to introduce it, without submitting myself to the cor-

rection of divines more learned than I can pretend to be
myself.

The infallibility, whether of the Church or of the
Pope, acts principally or solely in two channels, in direct
statements of truth, and in the condemnation of error.
The former takes the shape of doctrinal definitions, the
latter stigmatizes propositions as heretical, next to heresy,
erroneous, and the like. In each case the Church, as
guided by her Divine Master, has made provision for
weighing as lightly as possible on the faith and conscience of her children.

As to the condemnation of propositions all she tells us
is, that the thesis condemned when taken as a whole, or,
again, when viewed in its context, is heretical, or blas-
phemous, or impious, or whatever like epithet she affixes
to it. We have only to trust her so far as to allow ourselves to be warned against the thesis, or the work containing it. Theologians employ themselves in determining what precisely it is that is condemned in that thesis
or treatise; and doubtless in most cases they do so with
success; but that determination is not *de fide*; all that
is of faith is that there is in that thesis itself, which
is noted, heresy or error, or other like peccant matter,
as the case may be, such, that the censure is a peremptory command to theologians, preachers, students, and
all other whom it concerns, to keep clear of it. But so
light is this obligation, that instances frequently occur,
when it is successfully maintained by some new writer,
that the Pope's act does not imply what it has seemed to
imply, and questions which seemed to be closed, are after
a course of years re-opened. In discussions such as

these, there is a real exercise of private judgment and an allowable one; the act of faith, which cannot be superseded or trifled with, being, I repeat, the unreserved acceptance that the thesis in question is heretical, or the like, as the Pope or the Church has spoken of it.[6]

In these cases which in a true sense may be called the Pope's *negative* enunciations, the opportunity of a legitimate minimizing lies in the intensely concrete character of the matters condemned; in his affirmative enunciations a like opportunity is afforded by their being more or less abstract. Indeed, excepting such as relate to persons, that is, to the Trinity in Unity, the Blessed Virgin, the Saints, and the like, all the dogmas of Pope or of Council are but general, and so far, in consequence, admit of exceptions in their actual application,—these exceptions being determined either by other authoritative utterances, or by the scrutinizing vigilance, acuteness, and subtlety of the *Schola Theologorum.*

One of the most remarkable instances of what I am insisting on is found in a dogma, which no Catholic can ever think of disputing, viz., that "Out of the Church, and out of the faith, is no salvation." Not to go to Scripture, it is the doctrine of St. Ignatius, St. Irenæus, St. Cyprian in the first three centuries, as of St. Augustine and his contemporaries in the fourth and fifth. It can never be other than an elementary truth of Christianity; and the present Pope has proclaimed it as all Popes, doctors, and bishops before him. But that truth has two aspects, according as the force of the negative

---

[6] Fessler seems to confine the exercise of infallibility to the *Note* "heretical," p. 11, Engl. Transl.

falls upon the " Church " or upon the " salvation." The main sense is, that there is no other communion or so-called Church, but the Catholic, in which are stored the promises, the sacraments, and other means of salvation ; the other and derived sense is, that no one can be saved who is not *in* that one and only Church. But it does not follow, because there is no Church but one, which has the Evangelical gifts and privileges to bestow, that therefore no one can be saved without the intervention of that one Church. Anglicans quite understand this distinction ; for, on the one hand, their Article says, " They are to be had accursed (anathematizandi) that presume to say, that every man shall be saved *by* (in) the law or sect which he professeth, so that he be dili-gent to frame his life according to that law and the light of nature ;" while on the other hand they speak of and hold the doctrine of the " uncovenanted mercies of God." The latter doctrine in its Catholic form is the doctrine of invincible ignorance—or, that it is possible to belong to the soul of the Church without belonging to the body ; and, at the end of 1800 years, it has been formally and authoritatively put forward by the present Pope (the first Pope, I suppose, who has done so), on the very same occasion on which he has repeated the fundamental principle of exclusive salvation itself. It is to the pur-pose here to quote his words ; they occur in the course of his Encyclical, addressed to the Bishops of Italy, under date of August 10, 1863.

" *We and you know*, that those who lie under invin-cible ignorance as regards our most Holy Religion, and who, diligently observing the natural law and its precepts, which are engraven by God on the hearts of all, and prepared to obey God, lead a good and upright life, are able, by the operation of the power of divine light and grace, to obtain eternal life." [7]

Who would at first sight gather from the wording of so forcible a universal, that an exception to its operation, such as this, so distinct, and, for what we know, so very wide, was consistent with holding it?

Another instance of a similar kind is suggested by the general acceptance in the Latin Church, since the time of St. Augustine, of the doctrine of absolute predestination, as instanced in the teaching of other great saints besides him, such as St. Fulgentius, St. Prosper, St. Gregory, St. Thomas, and St. Buonaventure. Yet in the last centuries a great explanation and modification of this doctrine has been effected by the efforts of the Jesuit School, which have issued in the reception of a distinction between predestination to grace and predestination to glory; and a consequent admission of the principle that, though our own works do not avail for bringing us under the action of grace here, that does not hinder their availing, when we are in a state of grace, for our attainment of eternal glory hereafter. Two saints of late centuries, St. Francis de Sales and St. Alfonso, seemed to have professed this less rigid opinion, which is now the more common doctrine of the day.

---

[7] The Pope speaks more forcibly still in an earlier Allocution. After mentioning invincible ignorance he adds:—" Quis tantum sibi arroget, ut hujusmodi ignorantiæ designare limites queat, juxta populorum, regionum, ingeniorum, aliarumque rerum tam multarum rationem et varietatem?"—*Dec.* 9, 1854.

Another instance is supplied by the Papal decisions concerning Usury. Pope Clement V., in the Council of Vienne, declares, " If any one shall have fallen into the error of pertinaciously presuming to affirm that usury is no sin, we determine that he is to be punished as a heretic." However, in the year 1831 the Sacred *Pœnitentiaria* answered an inquiry on the subject, to the effect that the Holy See suspended its decision on the point, and that a confessor who allowed of usury was not to be disturbed, " non esse inquietandum." Here again a double aspect seems to have been realized of the idea intended by the word *usury.*

To show how natural this process of partial and gradually developed teaching is, we may refer to the apparent contradiction of Bellarmine, who says " the Pope, whether he can err or not, is to be obeyed by all the faithful " (*Rom. Pont.* iv. 2), yet, as I have quoted him above, p. 52—53, sets down (ii. 29) cases in which he is not to be obeyed. An illustration may be given in political history from the discussions which took place years ago as to the force of the Sovereign's Coronation Oath to uphold the Established Church. The words were large and general, and seemed to preclude any act on his part to the prejudice of the Establishment; but lawyers succeeded at length in making a distinction between the legislative and executive action of the Crown, which is now generally accepted.

These instances out of many similar are sufficient to show what caution is to be observed, on the part of private and unauthorized persons, in imposing upon the consciences of others any interpretation of dogmatic

z

enunciations which is beyond the legitimate sense of the words, inconsistent with the principle that all general rules have exceptions, and unrecognized by the Theological *Schola.*

12. From these various considerations it follows, that Papal and Synodal definitions, obligatory on our faith, are of rare occurrence; and this is confessed by all sober theologians. Father O'Reilly, for instance, of Dublin, one of the first theologians of the day, says:—

"The Papal Infallibility is comparatively seldom brought into action. I am very far from denying that the Vicar of Christ is largely assisted by God in the fulfilment of his sublime office, that he receives great light and strength to do well the great work entrusted to him and imposed on him, that he is continually guided from above in the government of the Catholic Church. But this is not the meaning of Infallibility. . . . What is the use of dragging in the Infallibility in connexion with Papal acts with which it has nothing to do,—papal acts, which are very good and very holy, and entitled to all respect and obedience, acts in which the Pontiff is commonly not mistaken, but in which he could be mistaken and still remain infallible in the only sense in which he has been declared to be so?" (The *Irish Monthly*, Vol. ii. No. 10, 1874.)[3]

This great authority goes on to disclaim any desire to minimize, but there is, I hope, no real difference between us here. He, I am sure, would sanction me in my repugnance to impose upon the faith of others more than what the Church distinctly claims of them: and I

[3] *Vid.* Fessler also; and I believe Father Perrone says the same.

should follow him in thinking it a more scriptural, Christian, dutiful, happy frame of mind, to be easy, than to be difficult, of belief. I have already spoken of that uncatholic spirit, which starts with a grudging faith in the word of the Church, and determines to hold nothing but what it is, as if by demonstration, compelled to believe. To be a true Catholic a man must have a generous loyalty towards ecclesiastical authority, and accept what is taught him with what is called the *pietas fidei*, and only such a tone of mind has a claim, and it certainly has a claim, to be met and to be handled with a wise and gentle *minimism*. Still the fact remains, that there has been of late years a fierce and intolerant temper abroad, which scorns and virtually tramples on the little ones of Christ.

I end with an extract from the Pastoral of the Swiss Bishops, a Pastoral which has received the Pope's approbation.

" It in no way depends upon the caprice of the Pope, or upon his good pleasure, to make such and such a doctrine, the object of a dogmatic definition. He is tied up and limited to the divine revelation, and to the truths which that revelation contains. He is tied up and limited by the Creeds, already in existence, and by the preceding definitions of the Church. He is tied up and limited by the divine law, and by the constitution of the Church. Lastly, he is tied up and limited by that doctrine, divinely revealed, which affirms that alongside religious society there is civil society, that alongside the

Ecclesiastical Hierarchy there is the power of temporal Magistrates, invested in their own domain with a full sovereignty, and to whom we owe in conscience obedience and respect in all things morally permitted, and belonging to the domain of civil society."

§ 10. *Conclusion.*

I have now said all that I consider necessary in order to fulfil the task which I have undertaken, a task very painful to me and ungracious. I account it a great misfortune, that my last words, as they are likely to be, should be devoted to a controversy with one whom I have always so much respected and admired. But I should not have been satisfied with myself, if I had not responded to the call made upon me from such various quarters, to the opportunity at last given me of breaking a long silence on subjects deeply interesting to me, and to the demands of my own honour.

The main point of Mr. Gladstone's charge against us is that in 1870, after a series of preparatory acts, a great change and irreversible was effected in the political attitude of the Church by the third and fourth chapters of the Vatican *Pastor Æternus*, a change which no state or statesman can afford to pass over. Of this cardinal assertion I consider he has given no proof at all; and my object throughout the foregoing pages has been to make this clear. The Pope's infallibility indeed and his supreme authority have in the Vatican *capita* been declared matters of faith; but his prerogative of infallibility lies in matters speculative, and his prerogative of authority is no infallibility in laws, commands, or measures. His infallibility bears upon the domain of thought, not directly of action, and while it may fairly exercise the theologian, philosopher, or man of science, it scarcely concerns the politician. Moreover, whether the recognition of his infallibility in doctrine will increase his actual power over the faith of Catholics, remains to be seen, and must be determined by the event; for there are gifts too large and too fearful to be handled freely. Mr. Gladstone seems to feel this, and therefore insists upon the increase made by the Vatican definition in the Pope's authority. But there is no real increase; he has for centuries upon centuries had and used that authority, which the Definition now declares ever to have belonged to him. Before the Council there was the rule of obedience and there were exceptions to the rule; and since the Council the rule remains, and with it the possibility of exceptions.

It may be objected that a representation such as this, is negatived by the universal sentiment, which testifies to the formidable effectiveness of the Vatican decrees, and to the Pope's intention that they should be effective; that it is the boast of some Catholics and the reproach levelled against us by all Protestants, that the Catholic Church has now become beyond mistake a despotic aggressive Papacy, in which freedom of thought and action is utterly extinguished. But I do not allow that this alleged unanimous testimony exists. Of course Prince Bismarck [9] and other statesmen such as Mr. Gladstone,

[9] Let me, from this accidental mention of Prince Bismarck, make for myself an opportunity, which my subject has not given me, of expressing my deep sympathy with the suffering Catholics of Germany. Who can doubt that, in their present resolute disobedience to that statesman's measures, they are only fulfilling their duty to God and His Church? Who can but pray that, were English Catholics in a similar trial, they might have grace to act as bravely in the cause of religion?

rest their opposition to Pope Pius on the political ground; but the Old-Catholic movement is based, not upon politics, but upon theology, and Dr. Dollinger has more than once, I believe, declared his disapprobation of the Prussian acts against the Pope, while Father Hyacinth has quarrelled with the anti-Catholic politics of Geneva. The French indeed have shown their sense of the political support which the Holy Father's name and influence would bring to their country; but does any one suppose that they expect to derive support definitely from the Vatican decrees, and not rather from the *prestige* of that venerable Authority, which those decrees have rather lowered than otherwise in the eyes of the world? So again the Legitimists and Carlists in France and Spain doubtless wish to associate themselves with Rome; but where and how have they signified that they can turn to profit the special dogma of the Pope's infallibility, and would not have been better pleased to be rid of the controversy which it has occasioned? In fact, instead of there being a universal impression that the proclamation of his infallibility and supreme authority has strengthened the Pope's secular position in Europe, there is room for suspecting that some of the politicians of the day, (I do not mean Mr. Gladstone) were not sorry that the Ultramontane party was successful at the Council in their prosecution of an object which those politicians considered to be favourable to the interests of the Civil Power. There is certainly some plausibility in the view, that it is not the "Curia Romana," as Mr. Gladstone considers, or the "Jesuits," who are the 'astute" party, but that rather they

themselves have fallen into a trap, and are victims of
the astuteness of secular statesmen.

The recognition, which I am here implying, of the
existence of parties in the Church reminds me of what,
while I have been writing these pages, I have all along
felt would be at once the *primâ facie* and also the most
telling criticism upon me. It will be said that there
are very considerable differences in argument and opinion
between me and others who have replied to Mr. Gladstone, and I shall be taunted with the evident break-
down, thereby made manifest, of that topic of glorifica-
tion so commonly in the mouths of Catholics, that they
are all of one way of thinking, while Protestant bodies
are all at variance with each other, and by reason of
that very variation of opinion can have no ground of
certainty severally in their own.

This is a showy and serviceable retort in controversy;
but it is nothing more. First, as regards the arguments
which Catholics use, it has to be considered whether these
are really incompatible with each other; if they are not,
then surely it is generally granted by Protestants as well
as Catholics, that two distinct arguments for the same
conclusion, instead of invalidating that conclusion, actually strengthen it. And next, supposing the difference
to be one of conclusions themselves, then it must be
considered whether the difference relates to a matter of
faith or to a matter of opinion. If a matter of faith is in
question I grant there ought to be absolute agreement,
or rather I maintain that there is; I mean to say that
only one out of the statements put forth can be true, and
that the other statements will be at once withdrawn by

their authors, by virtue of their being Catholics, as soon as they learn on good authority that they are erroneous. But if the differences which I have supposed are only in theological opinion, they do but show that after all private judgment is not so utterly unknown among Catholics and in Catholic Schools, as Protestants are desirous to establish.

I have written on this subject at some length in Lectures which I published many years ago, but, it would appear, with little practical effect upon those for whom they were intended. " Left to himself," I say, " each Catholic likes and would maintain his own opinion and his private judgment just as much as a Protestant ; and he has it and he maintains it, just so far as the Church does not, by the authority of Revelation, supersede it. The very moment the Church ceases to speak, at the very point at which she, that is, God who speaks by her, circumscribes her range of teaching, then private judgment of necessity starts up ; there is nothing to hinder it. . . . . A Catholic sacrifices his opinion to the Word of God, declared through His Church ; but from the nature of the case, there is nothing to hinder him having his own opinion and expressing it, whenever, and so far as, the Church, the oracle of Revelation, does not speak." [1]

In saying this, it must not be supposed that I am denying what is called the *pietas fidei*, that is, a sense of the great probability of the truth of enunciations made by the Church, which are not formally and actually to be considered as the " Word of God." Doubtless it is our

[1] *Vide* " Difficulties felt by Anglicans," Lecture X.

duty to check many a speculation, or at least many an utterance, even though we are not bound to condemn it as contrary to religious truth. But, after all, the field of religious thought which the duty of faith occupies, is small indeed compared with that which is open to our free, though of course to our reverent and conscientious, speculation.

I draw from these remarks two conclusions; first as regards Protestants,—Mr. Gladstone should not on the one hand declaim against us as having " no mental freedom," if the periodical press on the other hand is to mock us as admitting a liberty of private judgment, purely Protestant. We surely are not open to contradictory imputations. Every note of triumph over the differences which mark our answers to Mr. Gladstone is a distinct admission that we do not deserve his injurious reproach that we are captives and slaves of the Pope.

Secondly, for the benefit of some Catholics, I would observe that, while I acknowledge one Pope, *jure divino*, I acknowledge no other, and that I think it a usurpation, too wicked to be comfortably dwelt upon, when individuals use their own private judgment, in the discussion of religious questions, not simply "abundare in suo sensu," but for the purpose of anathematizing the private judgment of others.

I say there is only one Oracle of God, the Holy Catholic Church and the Pope as her head. To her teaching I have ever desired all my thoughts, all my words to be conformed; to her judgment I submit what I have now written, what I have ever written, not only

as regards its truth, but as to its prudence, its suitable-
ness, and its expedience. I think I have not pursued
any end of my own in anything that I have published,
but I know well, that, in matters not of faith, I may
have spoken, when I ought to have been silent.

And now, my dear Duke, I release you from this
long discussion, and, in concluding, beg you to accept
the best Christmas wishes and prayers for your present
and future from

Your affectionate Friend and Servant,

JOHN HENRY NEWMAN.

THE ORATORY.
Dec. 27, 1874.

POSTSCRIPT.

February 26, 1875. Mr. Gladstone's new Pamphlet, which has just appeared, is only partially directed against the foregoing Letter, and, when he remarks on what I have written, he does so with a gentleness which may be thought to be unfair to his argument. Moreover he, commences with some pages about me personally of so special a character, that, did I dare dwell upon them in their direct import, they would of course gratify me exceedingly. But I cannot do so, because I believe that, with that seriousness which is characteristic of him, he has wished to say what he felt to be true, not what was complimentary ; and because, looking on beyond his words to what they imply, I see in them, though he did not mean it so himself, a grave, or almost severe question addressed to me, which effectually keeps me from taking pleasure in them, however great is the honour they do me.

It is indeed a stern question which his words suggest, whether, now that I have come to the end of my days, I have used aright whatever talents God has given me, and as He would have had me use them, in building up religious truth, and not in pulling down, breaking up, and scattering abroad. All I can say in answer to it, is, that from the day I became a Catholic to this day, now close upon thirty years, I have never had a moment's

misgiving that the communion of Rome is that Church
which the Apostles set up at Pentecost, which alone has
" the adoption of sons, and the glory, and the covenants,
and the revealed law, and the service of God, and the
promises," and in which the Anglican communion, whatever its merits and demerits, whatever the great excellence
of individuals in it, has, as such, no part. Nor have I
ever, since 1845, for a moment hesitated in my conviction
that it was my clear duty to join, as I did then join, that
Catholic Church, which in my own conscience I felt to
be divine. Persons and places, incidents and circumstances of life, which belong to my first forty-four years,
are deeply lodged in my memory and my affections ;
moreover, I have had more to try and afflict me in various
ways as a Catholic than as an Anglican ; but never for a
moment have I wished myself back ; never have I ceased
to thank my Maker for His mercy in enabling me to
make the great change, and never has He let me feel for-
saken by Him, or in distress, or any kind of religious
trouble. I do not know how to avoid thus meeting Mr.
Gladstone's language about me : but I can say no more.
The judgment must be left to a day to come.

In the remarks that follow I shall take the order of my
Sections.

§ 1.

My first reason for writing in answer to Mr. Gladstone's Expostulation was his charge against us, " that
Catholics, if they act consistently with their principles,
cannot be loyal subjects," *supr.* p. 180. And he withdraws
this in his new Pamphlet (*Vaticanism,* p. 14), though not

in very gracious language, "The immediate purpose of my appeal," he says, "has been attained, in so far that the loyalty of our Roman Catholic fellow-subjects in the mass remains evidently untainted and secure."

My second reason was to protest against " his attack upon our moral uprightness," *supr. ibid.* Here again he seems to grant that, if what I say can be received as genuine Catholic teaching, I have succeeded in my purpose. He has a doubt, however, whether it does not "smack of Protestantism," *Vat.* p. 69. He does not give any distinct reason for this doubt; and, though I shall notice it in its place, *infr.* § 5, I think it but fair to maintain as a plain principle of controversy, that it is the accuser who has to prove his point, and that he must not content himself with professing that the accused parties have not succeeded to his satisfaction in disproving it.

Lastly, as springing out of these two charges and illustrating them, was his exaggerated notion of the force, drift, and range of the Vatican definition of the Pope's infallibility and supremacy. Here again I consider he leaves my interpretation of it without reply, though apparently it does not content him. Some of the objections to what I have said, which he throws out *obiter,* as well as some made by others, shall now be noticed.

Supr. pp. 190, 191. I have said, apropos of the prospect of a definition of the Pope's Infallibility in the times of Pitt and Peel, " If [the government] wanted to obtain some real information about the probabilities of the future, why did they not go to head-quarters? why not go to Rome? . . . It is impossible that they could have entered into formal negotiations with the Pope, without its becoming perfectly clear that Rome could never be a party to such a pledge as England wanted, and that no pledge from Catholics was of value to which Rome was not a party." To my astonishment Mr. Gladstone seems to consider this a fatal admission. He cries out, "Statesmen of the future, recollect the words ! . . . The lesson received is this: although pledges were given, although their validity was formally and even passionately asserted, although the subject-matter was one of civil allegiance, 'no pledge from Catholics was of any value, to which Rome was not a party,'" p. 39.

I deny that the question of infallibility was one of civil allegiance, but let that pass ; as to the main principle involved in what I have said, it certainly does perplex and confuse me that a statesman with Mr. Gladstone's experience should make light of credentials, and should not recognize the difference between party opinion and formal decisions and pledges. What is the use of accredited ministers and an official intercourse between foreign powers, if the acts of mere classes or interests will do instead of them ? At a congress, I believe the first act of plenipotentiaries is to show to each other their credentials. What minister of foreign affairs would go to the Cesarowitch, who happened to be staying among us, for an explanation of an expedition of Russia in upper Asia, instead of having recourse to the Russian ambassador ?

The common saying, that " Whigs are Tories out of place" illustrates again what is in itself so axiomatic Successive ministries of opposite views show in history, for the most part, as one consistent national government, and, when a foreign power mistakes the objections which public men in opposition make to the details, circumstances, or seasonableness of certain ministerial measures, for deliberate judgments in its favour, it is likely, as in the case of the great Napoleon, to incur eventually, when the opposition comes into office, great disappointment, and has no one to blame but itself. So again, the Czar Nicholas seems to have mistaken the deputation of the peace party before the Crimean war for the voice of the English nation. It is not a business-like way of acting to assume the assurances of partisans, however sincerely made, for conditions of a contract. There is nothing indeed to show that the Holy See in 1793 or 1829 had any notion that the infallibility of the Pope, even if ever made a dogma, would be so made within such limits of time as could affect the *bonâ fide* character of the prospects which English and Irish Catholics opened upon Mr. Pitt or Mr. Peel. The events in Europe of the foregoing half century had given no encouragement to the Papal cause. Nor did Catholics alone avow anticipations which helped to encourage the latter statesman in the course, into which the political condition of Ireland, not any kindness to the Irish religion, primarily turned him. There were Anglican ecclesiastics, whom he deservedly trusted, who gave it to him as their settled opinion, as regards the Protestantism of England, that, if the emancipation of Catholics could but be passed in the night, there would be no excitement about it next morning. Did such an influential judgment, thus offered to Mr. Peel, involve a breach of a pledge, because it was not fulfilled?

It was notorious all over the world that the North of Catholic Christendom took a different view of Papal infallibility from the South. A long controversy had gone on; able writers were to be found on either side; each side was positive in the truth of its own cause; each hoped to prevail. The Gallican party, towards which England and Ireland inclined, thought the other simply extravagant; but with the Ultramontane stood Rome itself. Ministers do not commonly believe all the representations of deputations who come to them with the advocacy of particular measures, though those deputations may be perfectly sincere in what they aver. The Catholics of England and Ireland in 1826 were almost as one man in thinking lightly of the question, but even then there were those who spoke out in a different sense, and warned the government that there was a contrary opinion, and one strong both in its pretensions and its prospects. I am not bound to go into this subject at length, for I have allowed that the dominant feeling among our Catholics at that day was against the prudence or likelihood of a definition of Papal infallibility; but I will instance one or two writers of name who had spoken in a different sense.

I cannot find that Mr. Gladstone deals with my reference to Archbishop Troy, whose pastoral bears the date (1793) of the very year in which as Mr. Gladstone tells us, *Vat.*, p. 48, a Relief Act was granted to Ireland. The Archbishop, as I have quoted him (*supr.*, p. 188), says, "*Many* Catholics contend that the Pope . . . is infallible. . . . others deny this. . . . *Until* the Church shall *decide* . . . either opinion may be adopted." This is a very significant, as well as an authoritative passage.

Again: Father Mumford's *Catholic Scripturist* is a popular Address to Protestants, in the vernacular, which has gone through various editions in the 17th, 18th, and 19th centuries. The edition from which I quote is that of 1863. He says, p. 39, " Whether the definition of a council alone, defining without their chief pastor, or the definition of the chief pastor alone, defining without a council, be infallible or no, there be several opinions amongst us, in which we do and may vary without any prejudice to our faith, which is not built upon what is *yet* under opinion, but upon that which is delivered as infallible."

Again, Bishop Hay is one of the most conspicuous Prelates and authoritative writers amongst us of the 18th century. In his "*Sincere Christian*," published between 1770 and 1780, he treats of the infallibility of the Pope at considerable length, and in its favour. He says, p. 188 (*ed.* 1871) that that doctrine " is not proposed to us as an article of divine faith, nor has the Church ever made any decision concerning it. Great numbers of the most learned divines are of opinion that, in such a case, the Head of the Church is infallible in what he teaches, but there are others who are of a contrary opinion." He proceeds, "On what grounds do those divines found their opinion, who believe that the Pope himself, when he speaks to the faithful as head of the Church, is infallible in what he teaches ? " and he answers, " On very strong reasons both from Scripture, tradition, and reason." These he goes through *seriatim;* then he adds, p. 194,

" What proof do the others bring for their opinion, that the Head of the Church is not infallible? They bring not a single text of Scripture, nor almost one argument from tradition to prove it."

I might add that the chief instrument in rousing and rallying the Protestant sentiment against Catholic emancipation was from first to last the episcopate and clergy of the Church Established ; now, if there was any body of men who were perfectly aware of the division of sentiment among Catholics as to the seat of infallibility, it was they. Their standard divines, writing in the vernacular, discharge it, as one of their most effective taunts, against their opponents, that, whilst the latter hold the doctrine of infallibility, they differ among themselves whether it is lodged in an Ecumenical Council or in the Roman See. It never can be said then that this opinion, which has now become a dogma, was not perfectly well known to be living and energetic in the Catholic communion, though it was not an article of faith, and was not spoken of as such by Catholics in this part of the world during the centuries of persecution.

Mr. Gladstone, as his mildest conclusion against us, is inclined to grant that it was not an act of duplicity in us, that in 1826 our Prelates spoke against the Pope's infallibility, though in 1870 they took part in defining it; but then he maintains it to be at least a proof that the Church has changed its doctrine, and thereby forfeited its claim to be " semper eadem." But it is no change surely to decide between two prevalent opinions ; however, if it is to be so regarded, then change has been the characteristic of the Church from the earliest times, as, for instance, in the third century, on the point of the validity of baptism by heretics. And hence such change as has taken place (which I should prefer to call doctrinal development), is in itself a positive argument in favour of the Church's identity from first to last; for a growth in its creed is a law of its life. I have already insisted upon this, *supra*, p. 314; also in former volumes, as in my *Apologia*, and *Difficulties of Anglicans*.

§. 3.

Supr. p. 195. As Mr. Gladstone denied that the Papal prerogatives were consistent with ancient history, I said in answer that that history on the contrary was the clearest witness in their favour, as showing how the promises made to St. Peter were providentially fulfilled by political, &c., changes, external to the Pope, which worked for him. I did not mean to deny that those prerogatives were his from the beginning, but merely that they were gradually brought into full exercise by a course of events, which history records. Thus it was a mistake to say that Catholics could not appeal in favour of the Papal power to history. To make my meaning quite clear, as I hoped, I distinctly said I was not speaking theologically, but historically, nay, looking at the state of things with "non-Catholic eyes." However, as the following passage from the *Etudes Religieuses* shows, it seems that I have been misunderstood, though the writer himself, Père Ramière, does me the justice and the favour to defend me, and I here adopt his words as my defence. He says,—

"Pour exprimer cette concentration providentielle,

dans les mains du Pape, du pouvoir ecclesiastique partagé
autrefois dans une plus large mesure par l'episcopat, le
P. Newman se sert d'un terme légal qu'il ne faut pas
prendre à la lettre. Il dit que le Pape est *héritier par
défaut* de la hierarchie écuménique du ive siècle. Le
savant directeur de la *Voce della Verità* blâme cette expression, qui impliquerait, selon lui, qui le Pape tient son
pouvoir de la hierarchie : mais le P. Newman exclut
cette interpretation, puis qu'il fait deriver le plenitude
du pouvoir pontifical de la promesse faite par Jésus-
Christ à Saint Pierre," p. 256, 7, note.

§ 4.

Supr., p. 242. I here say that "were I actually a
soldier or sailor in her Majesty's service in a just war,
and should the Pope suddenly bid all Catholic soldiers
and sailors to retire from her service, taking the advice,
&c., . . . I should not obey him." Here I avail myself
of a passage in Canon Neville's recent pamphlet ("A
few Comments, &c.," *Pickering*), in which he speaks with
the authority belonging to a late theological Professor of
Maynooth : —

"In the impossible hypothesis of the Pope being
engaged in a war with England, how would the allegiance of English Catholics be affected ? . . how would
it be, if they were soldiers or sailors ? . . . . Some one
will urge, the Pope may issue a mandate enforced by an
annexed excommunication, forbidding all Catholics to
engage in the war against him. . . . The supposed action
of the Pope does not change the question materially. . .
The soldiers and sailors would not incur it, because

'*grace fears*' excuse from censure [excommunication], censures being directed against the contumacious, not against those who act through fear or coercion. . . . It is a trite principle, that mere ecclesiastical laws do not bind, when there would be a very grave inconvenience in their observance; and it denies as a rule to any human legislator (*e.g.*, the Pope) the power of making laws or precepts, binding men to the performance of actions, which, from the danger and difficulty attendant on their fulfilment, are esteemed heroic," pp. 101, 2.

§ 5.

Supr., p. 254. I have said, "The Pope, who comes of Revelation, has no jurisdiction over Nature," *i.e.* the natural Law. Mr. Gladstone on the other hand says, "Idle it is to tell us, finally, that the Pope is bound by the moral and divine law, by the commandments of God, by the rules of the Gospel: . . . for of these, one and all, the Pope himself, by himself, is the judge without appeal," p. 102. That is, Mr. Gladstone thinks that the Pope may deny and anathematize the proposition, "There is one God:" and may proceed to circulate by Cardinal Antonelli a whole Syllabus of kindred "erroneous theses" for the instruction of the Bishops. Catholics think this impossible, as believing in a Divine Providence ever exercised over the Church. But let us grant, for argument-sake, that a Pope could commit so insane a violation of the Natural and the Revealed Law:—we know what would be the consequence to such a Pope. Cardinal Turrecremata teaches, as I have quoted him, that "were the Pope to command anything against Holy Scripture, or the articles of faith, or the truth of the Sacraments, or the commands of the natural or divine law, he ought not to be obeyed, but in such commands to be ignored." *Supr.*, p. 242. Other, and they the highest Ultramontane theologians, hold that a Pope who teaches heresy *ipso facto* ceases to be Pope.

Supr., p. 261. Here, after stating that there are cases in which the Pope's commands are to be resisted by individual Catholics, I challenge Mr. Gladstone to bring passages from our authoritative writers to the contrary : and I add, " they must be passages declaring not only that the Pope is ever to be obeyed, but that there are no exceptions to this rule, for exceptions ever must be in all concrete matters." Instead of doing so, Mr. Gladstone contents himself with enunciating the contradictory to what I have said. " Dr. Newman says there are exceptions to this precept of obedience. But this is just what the Council has not said. The Church by the Council imposes Aye. The private conscience reserves to itself the title to say No. I must confess that in this apology there is to me a strong, undeniable smack of Protestantism," p. 69.

Mr. Gladstone says " there is to me ;" yes, certainly to him and other Protestants, because they do not know our doctrine. I have given in my Pamphlet, three reasons in justification of what I said ; first that exceptions *must* be from the nature of the case, " for in *all* concrete matters," not only in precepts of obedience, rules are but general, and exceptions must occur. Then, in a later page, p. 334, I give actual instances, which have occurred in the history of Catholic teaching, of exceptions after large principles have been laid down. But my main reason lies in the absolute statements of theologians. I willingly endure to have about me a smack of Protestantism, which attaches to Cardinal Turrecremata in the 15th century, to Cardinals Jacobatius and Bellarmine in the 16th, to the Carmelites of Salamanca in the 17th, and to all theologians prior to them; and also to the whole Schola after them, such as to Fathers Corduba, Natalis Alexander, and Busenbaum, and so down to St. Alfonso Liguori, the latest Doctor of the Church, in the 18th, and to Cardinal Gousset and Archbishop Kenrick in the 19th.

On the subject of the supremacy of Conscience a correspondent has done me the favour of referring me to a passage in the life of the well-known M. Emery (Paris, 1862), Supérieur of St. Sulpice. It runs as follows :—

"La célébration du mariage de Napoléon avec l'Archiduchesse d'Autriche donna lieu à une autre difficulté sur la quelle M. Emery fut dans le cas de s'expliquer, non avec le gouvernement, mais avec quelques cardinaux qui désiraient connaître son sentiment. Il s'agissait de savoir si les cardinaux résident à Paris, au nombre de vingt-six, pouvaient en conscience assister à la cérémonie religieuse du mariage. Quelques jours avant cette cérémonie, M. Emery, consulté la-dessus par le cardinal della Somaglia, qui paraissait regarder cette assistance comme illicite, lui répondit que, *s'il était effectivement dans cette persuasion, il ne pourait en conscience assister à la cérémonie, parce qu'il n'est jamais*

permis d'agir contre sa conscience. Mais il ajouta que
cette assistance, au fond, ne lui paraissait pas illicite," &c.

It got about in consequence that he had denied that
any cardinal could with a safe conscience be present at
the religious ceremony. This led Cardinal Fesch to write
him a letter asking for an explanation, inasmuch as a
cardinal had distinctly stated "que M. Emery avait
confirmé ce cardinal dans son opinion, qu'il ne pouvait
pas, en conscience, assister au mariage de l'Empereur;"
whereas, Cardinal Fesch proceeds, "hier même, à trois
heures après midi, M. Emery, pour la seconde ou troi-
sième fois, m'avait protesté qui'l était d'une opinion
toute contraire, et qu'il pensait que les cardinaux
pouvaient assister à la cérémonie." In consequence he
asked for "une réponse catégorique" from M. Emery.

M. Emery in consequence wrote letters to both cardinals to show his consistency in the language he had
used in conversation with each of them, insisting for that
purpose on the distinction which has led to the introduction of his name and conduct into this place, viz.,
that every man must go by his own conscience, not by
that of another. He says to Cardinal Somaglia, "Vous
m'avez dit qu'après avoir fait les récherches les plus
exactes, vous étiez convaincu que *vous ne pouviez aller
au mariage sans blesser votre conscience.* J'ai dû vous
dire, et je vous ai dit, que, *dans cette supposition,* vous ne
deviez point y assister, parce que j'étais persuadé *comme
vous,* qu'on ne pouvait, qu'on ne devait jamais, agir contre
sa conscience, *même erronée.*" He adds, "Non que les
inconvénients soient une raison d'autoriser l'assistance
qui serait d'ailleurs illicite, mais ces inconvenients sont

une raison très-forte d'examiner le plus attentivement qu'il est possible, si réellement l'assistance est illicite, et si la conscience qu'on s'est formée à cette sujet n'est point une conscience erronée."—t. 2, pp. 249—254.

In the event Cardinal Somaglia kept to his view, contrary to M. Emery, and did not attend the marriage ceremony.

§ 6.

Supr., pp. 274, 275. Speaking of the proposition condemned in the Encyclical of 1864, to the effect that it is the right of any one to have liberty to give public utterance, in every possible shape, by every possible channel, without any let or hindrance from God or man, to all his notions whatever, I have said that " it seems a light epithet for the Pope to use, when he called such a doctrine of conscience a *deliramentum.* Presently I add, " Perhaps Mr. Gladstone will say, Why should the Pope take the trouble to condemn what is so wild ? but he does," &c.

On this Mr. Gladstone remarks, *Vat.*, p. 21, 22, " It appears to me that this is, to use a mild phrase, merely trifling with the subject. We are asked to believe that what the Pope intended to condemn was a state of things which never has existed in any country in the world. Now he says he is condemning one of the commonly prevailing errors of the time, familiarly known to the Bishops whom he addresses. What bishop knows of a State which by law allows a perfectly free course to blasphemy, filthiness, and sedition ?"

I do not find anything to show that the Pope is speaking of States, and not of writers; and, though I

do not pretend to know against what writers he is
speaking, yet there are writers who do maintain doctrines which carried out consistently would reach that
deliramentum which the Pope speaks of, if they have not
rather already reached it. We are a sober people; but
are not the doctrines of even so grave and patient a
thinker as the late Mr. J. S. Mill very much in that
direction? He says, "The appropriate region of human
liberty comprises first the inward domain of consciousness; demanding liberty of conscience in the most comprehensive sense, liberty of thought and feeling, absolute
freedom of opinion and sentiment on all subjects practical or speculative, scientific, moral, or theological. The
liberty of *expressing* and *publishing* opinion may *seem* to
fall under a different principle, since it belongs to that
part of the conduct of an individual which concerns other
people; but, being almost of as much importance as the
liberty of thought itself, and resting in great part on the
same reasons, *is practically inseparable from it,* &c. &c.
. . . No society in which these liberties are not on the
whole respected, is free, whatever may be its form of
government." (*On Liberty, Introd.*) Of course he does
not allow of a freedom to harm others, though we have
to consider well what he means by harming: but his is a
freedom which must meet with no "impediment from
our fellow-creatures, so long as what we do does not harm
them, even though they should think our conduct foolish,
perverse, or wrong." "The only freedom," he continues, "which deserves the name is that of pursuing
our own good in our own way, so long as we do not
attempt to deprive others of theirs, or impede their

efforts to obtain it. Each is the proper guardian of his own health, whether bodily, or mental and spiritual."

That is, no immoral doctrines, poems, novels, plays, conduct, acts, may be visited by the reprobation of public opinion ; nothing must be put down, I do not say by the laws, but even by society, by the press, by religious influence, merely on the ground of shocking the sense of decency and the modesty of a Christian community. Nay, the police must not visit Holywell Street, nor a licence be necessary for dancing-rooms : but the most revolting atrocities of heathen times and countries must for conscience-sake be allowed free exercise in our great cities. Averted looks indeed and silent disgust, or again rational expostulation, is admissible against them, but nothing of a more energetic character.

I do not impute this to Mr. Mill. He had too much English common sense to carry out his principles to these extreme but legitimate conclusions ; he strove to find means of limiting them by the introduction of other and antagonist principles ; but then that such a man held the theory of liberty which he has avowed, and that he has a great following, is a suggestion to us that the Holy See may have had abundant reason in the present state of the continent to anathematize a proposition, which to Mr. Gladstone seems so wild and unheard of.

§ 7.

Supr., pp. 277, 281. I have said that the Syllabus is to be received from the Pope with " profound submission." p. 277, and " by an act of obedience," p. 281 ; I add, "but not of faith," for it "has no dogmatic force." I maintain this still. I say, in spite of Professor Schulte, and the English Catholic writer to whom Mr. Gladstone refers, p. 32, I have as much right to maintain that the implicit condemnation with which it visits its eighty propositions is not *ex cathedra,* or an act of the Infallible Chair, as have those "gravest theologians," as Bishop Fessler speaks, who call its dogmatic force in question, *Fessler,* p. 91. I do not know what Fessler himself says of it more than that it is to be received with submission and obedience. I do not deny another's right to consider it in his private conscience an act of infallibility, or to say, in Mr. Gladstone's words, p. 35, that "utterances *ex cathedra* are not the only form in which Infallibility can speak;" I only say that I have a right to think otherwise. And when the Pope by letters approves of one writer who writes one way, and of another who writes in another, he makes neither opinion dogmatic, but both allowable. Mr. Gladstone speaks as if what the Pope says to Fr. Schrader undoes what he says to Bishop Fessler; why not say that his letter to Fessler neutralizes his letter to Schrader? I repeat, when I speak of minimizing, I am not turning the profession of it into a dogma; men, if they will, may maximize for me, provided they too keep from dogmatizing. This is my position all through these discussions, and must be kept in mind by any fair reasoner.

I grant the Pope has laid a great stress on the Syllabus; he is said in 1867 to have spoken of it as a "regula docendi;" I cannot tell whether *vivâ voce,* or in writing; any how this did not interfere with Fessler's "grave theologians" in 1871 considering the Pope was not in 1867 teaching dogmatically and infallibly. Moreover, how can a list of proscribed propositions be a "rule," except by turning to the Allocutions, &c., in which they are condemned? and in those Allocutions, when we turn to them, we find in what sense, and with what degree of force, severally. In itself the Syllabus can be no more than what the Pope calls it, a syllabus or collection of errors. Led by the references inserted in it to the Allocutions, &c., I have ventured to call it something more, viz., a list or index *raisonné;* an idea not attached to it by me first of all, for Père Daniel, in the October of that very year, 1867, tells us, in the *Etudes Religieuses,* "Au Syllabus lui-même il ne faut pas demander que le degré de clarté qui convient à une bonne table des matières," p. 514.

But, whether an index or not, and though it have a substantive character, it is at least clear that the only way in which it can be a "rule of teaching" is by its telling us what to avoid; and this consideration will explain what I mean by receiving it with "obedience," which to some persons is a difficult idea, when contrasted with accepting it with faith. I observe then that obedience is concerned with doing, but faith with affirming. Now, when we are told to avoid certain propositions, we are told primarily and directly not to do something; whereas, in order to affirm, we must have positive statements put before us. For instance, it is easy to understand, and in our teaching to avoid the proposition, "Wealth is the first of goods;" but who shall attempt to ascertain what the affirmative propositions are, one or more, which are necessarily involved in the prohibition of such a proposition, and which must be clearly set down before we can make an act of faith in them?

However, Mr. Gladstone argues, that, since the Pope's condemnation of the propositions of the Syllabus has, as I have allowed, a claim on the obedience of Catholics, that very fact tells in favour of the propositions condemned by him; he thinks I have here made a fatal admission. It is *enough*, he says, that the Syllabus "unquestionably demands obedience;" that is, enough, whether the propositions condemned in it deserve condemnation or not. Here are his very words: " What is *conclusive* . . . is this, that the obligation to *obey* it is asserted on all hands; . . . it is *therefore* absolutely superfluous to follow Dr. Newman through his references to the Briefs and Allocutions marginally noted," in order to ascertain their meaning and drift. . . . " I *abide* by my account of the *contents* of the Syllabus," p. 36. That is, the propositions may be as false as heathenism, but they have this redeeming virtue, that the Pope denounces them. His judgment of them may be as true as Scripture, but it carries this unpardonable sin with it, that it is given with a purpose, and not as a mere literary flourish. Therefore I will not inquire into the propositions at all; but my original conclusion shall be dogmatic and irreformable. Sit pro ratione voluntas.

Supra, p. 288, I have declined to discuss the difficulties which Mr. Gladstone raises upon our teaching respecting the marriage contract (on which I still think him either obscure or incorrect), because they do not fall within the scope to which I professed to confine my remarks; however, his fresh statements, as they are found, *Vat.*, p. 28, lead me to say as follows:—

The non-Roman marriages in England, he says, "do not at present fall under the foul epithets of Rome. But why? not because we marry . . . under the sanctions of religion, for our marriages are, in the eye of the Pope, purely civil marriages, but only for the technical . . . reason that the disciplinary decrees of Trent are not canonically in force in this country," &c.

Here Mr. Gladstone seems to consider that there are only two ways of marrying according to Catholic teaching; he omits a third, in which we consider the essence of the sacrament to lie. He speaks of civil marriage, and of marriage "under the sanctions of religion," by which phrase he seems to mean marriage with a rite and a minister. But it is also a *religious* marriage, if the parties, without a priest, by a mutual act of consent, as in the presence of God, marry themselves; and such a vow of each to other is, according to our theology, really the constituting act, the matter and form, the sacrament of marriage. That is, he omits the very contract which we specially call marriage. This being the case, it follows that every clause of the above passage is incorrect.

1. Mr. Gladstone says, that English non-Roman marriages are held valid at Rome, *not* because they are contracted "under the sanctions of religion." On the contrary, this is the very reason why they are held valid

there; viz., only because parties who have already received the Christian rite of baptism, proceed to give themselves to each other in the sight of God sacramentally, though they may not call it a sacrament.

2. Mr. Gladstone says, " our marriages are in the eye of the Pope *purely civil* marriages." Just the reverse, speaking, as he is, of Church of England marriages. They are considered, in the case of baptized persons, sacramental marriages.

3. Mr. Gladstone says, that they are received at Rome as valid, "*only for the technical*, &c., reason that the disciplinary decrees of Trent are not canonically in force in this country. There is nothing, unless it be motives of mere policy, to prevent the Pope from giving them [those decrees] force here, when he pleases. If, and when that is done, *every marriage thereafter concluded in the English* Church, will, according to his own words, be '*a filthy concubinage.*'" This is not so; I quote to the point two sufficient authorities, St. Alfonso Liguori and Archbishop Kenrick.

Speaking of the clandestinity of marriage (that is, when it is contracted without parish priest and witnesses,) as an impediment to its validity, St. Alfonso says, "As regards non-Catholics (infideles), or Catholics who live in non-Catholic districts, *or* where the Council of Trent has not been received . . . *such a marriage is valid.*"—tom. viii., p. 67, ed. 1845. Even then though the discipline of Trent *was* received in England, still it would not cease to be a Protestant country, and therefore marriages in Protestant churches would be valid.

B b

Archbishop Kenrick is still more explicit. He says,
"Constat Patres Tridentinos legem ita tulisse, ut hære-
ticorum cœtus jam ab Ecclesia divulsos non respiceret
. . . . Hoc igitur clandestinitatis impedimentum ad
hœreticos seorsim convenientes in locis ubi grassantur
hœreses, non est extendendum."—*Theol. Mor.*, t. 3,
p. 351.

Such being the Catholic rule as to recognition of Protestant marriages, the Pope could not, as Mr. Gladstone
thinks, any day invalidate English Protestant marriages
by introducing into England the discipline of Trent.
The only case, in which, consistently with the Council,
any opportunity might occur to the Pope, according to
his accusation, of playing fast and loose, is when there
was a doubt whether the number of Protestants in a
Catholic country was large enough to give them a clear
footing there, or when the Government refused to
recognize them. Whether such an opportunity has
practically occurred and has ever been acted on, I have
not the knowledge either to affirm or deny.

§ 8.

Supr., p. 302. "But if the fact be so that the Fathers
were not unanimous, is the definition valid? This
depends on the question whether unanimity, at least
moral, is or is not necessary for its validity." Vid. also
p. 303.

It should be borne in mind that these letters of mine
were not intended for publication, and are introduced
into my text as documents of 1870, with a view of
refuting the false reports of my bearing at that time

towards the Vatican Council and Definition. To alter their wording would have been to destroy their argumentative value. I said nothing to imply that on reflection I agreed to every proposition which I set down on my *primâ facie* view of the matter.

One passage of it, perhaps from my own fault, Mr. Gladstone has misunderstood. He quotes me, *Vat.*, p. 13, as holding that "a definition which the Pope approves, is not absolutely binding thereby, but requires a moral unanimity, and a subsequent reception by the Church." Nay, I considered that the Pope could define without either majority or minority; but that, if he chose to go by the method of a Council, in that case a moral unanimity was required of its Fathers. I say a few lines lower down, waiving the difficulty altogether, "Our merciful Lord would not care so little for His people . . . as to allow their visible head and such a large number of Bishops to lead them into error." Père Ramière, in his very kind review of me in the *Études Religieuses* for February, speaks of the notion of a moral unanimity as a piece of Gallicanism; but anyhow it has vanished altogether from theology now, since the Pope, if the Bishops in the Council, few or many, held back, might define a doctrine without them. A council of Bishops of the world around him, is only one of the various modes in which he exercises his infallibility. The seat of infallibility is in him, and they are adjuncts. The *Pastor Æternus* says, "Romani Pontifices, prout temporum et rerum conditio suadebat, *nunc* convocatis œcumenicis conciliis, *aut* rogatâ Ecclesiæ per orbem dispersæ sententiâ, *nunc* per synodos particulares, *nunc* aliis, quæ Divina suppeditabat Providentia, adhibitis auxiliis, ea tenenda definiverunt, quæ sacris Scripturis et Apostolicis Traditionibus consentanea, Deo adjutore, cognoverant."

Nor have I spoken of a subsequent reception by the Church as entering into the necessary conditions of a *de fide* decision. I said that by the " Securus judicat orbis terrarum" all acts of the rulers of the Church are ratified," p. 303. In this passage of my private letter I meant by " ratified" brought home to us as authentic. At this very moment it is certainly the handy, obvious, and serviceable argument for our accepting the Vatican definition of the Pope's Infallibility.

Supr., p. 306. I said in my first edition, at this page, that the definition at Ephesus seemed to be carried by 124 votes against 111 ; as this was professedly only an inference of my own, I have withdrawn it. Confining myself to the facts of the history, which are perplexed, I observe :—The Council was opened by St. Cyril on June 22 of the current year, without waiting for the Bishops representing the great Syrian patriarchate, who were a few days' journey from Ephesus, in spite of the protest on that account of sixty-eight of the Bishops already there. The numbers present at the opening are given in the Acts as about 150. The first Session in which Nestorius was condemned and a definition or exposition of faith made, was concluded before night. That exposition, as far as the Acts record, was contained in one of the letters of St. Cyril to Nestorius, which the Bishops in the Council one by one accepted as conformable to Apostolic teaching. Whether a further letter of St. Cyril's with his twelve anathematisms, which was also received by the Bishops, was actually accepted by them as their dogmatic utterance, is uncertain; though the Bishops distinctly tell the Pope and the Emperor that they have accepted it as well as the others, as being in accordance with the Catholic Creed. At the end of the acts of the first Session the signatures of about 200 Bishops are found, and writers of the day confirm this number, though there is nothing to show that the additional forty or fifty were added on the day on which the definition was passed, June 22, and it is more probable that they were added afterwards; *vid.* Tillemont, *Cyril*, note 34, and Fleury, *Hist.*, xxv. 42. And thus Tillemont, *ibid.*, thinks that the signatures in favour of Cyril altogether amounted to 220. The Legates of the Pope were not present; but they had arrived by July 10. The Syrian Bishops arrived on June 26th or 27th. As to Africa, then overrun by the Vandals, it was represented only by the deacon of the Bishop of Carthage, who sent him to make his apologies for Africa, to warn the Council against the Pelagians, and to testify the adherence of the African Churches to Apostolic doctrine. The countries which were represented at the Council, and took part in the definition were Egypt, Asia Minor, and Thrace, Greece, &c. The whole number of Bishops in Christendom at the time was about 1800; not 6000, as St. Dalmatius says at random. Gibbon says, "The Catholic Church was administered by the spiritual and legal jurisdiction of 1800 bishops, of whom 1000 were seated in the Greek, and 800 in the Latin provinces of the empire." He adds, "The numbers are not ascertained by any ancient writer or original catalogue; for the partial lists of the eastern churches are comparatively modern. The patient diligence of Charles à S. Paolo, of Luke Holstein, and of Bingham, has laboriously investigated all the episcopal sees of the Catholic Church."

To the same purport Fr. Ryder of this Oratory wrote, after my first edition, in answer to Fr. Botalla, S.J., as follows :—

"As regards the Council of Ephesus, there are few points on which learned men are less agreed than its precise numbers. The names given at the opening of the first Session (June 22, 431) in which Nestorius was condemned and St. Cyril approved, amounted to 159; standing aloof from those and protesting against this precipitation in not waiting for the Antiochenes, were sixty-eight. . . . Five days afterwards the Antiochenes with the Patriarch John at their head, about twenty-seven in number, arrived, and then and there anathematized St. Cyril and all his adherents, declaring null and void all they had done. This condemnation is signed by forty-three. The forty-three consists, besides the Antiochenes, of some who had signed the deposition of Nestorius and some of the sixty-eight protestors. The larger part of the sixty-eight, we may presume, went to swell St. Cyril's party, for we find 198 signatures to the deposition of Nestorius. Subsequently to this, in various official documents the majority refers to itself as 'about 200,' 'over 200'; but we have no signatures beyond the 198. On the other hand, we possess a document of the minority of July 17, containing fifty-three signatures. Afterwards the proportions of the schism were still more serious . . . John of Antioch's twenty-seven were delegates and representatives of the whole Antiochene Patriarchate, except Cyprus. Thus, on leaving Ephesus, John was able to hold a Council at Antioch, and condemn Cyril with far larger numbers than before. . . . They cannot be well set at less than 100. . . . [And elsewhere,] large portions of the Episcopate had no knowledge, or an utterly confused one, of what had been going on at Ephesus. St. Isidore, one of Cyril's own clergy, expostulates with him for his tyranny; and the works of Facundus and Liberatus show how deeply seated was the opposition of the African Church to the doctrine of Cyril."

§ 9.

Supra, pp. 320, &c. It has been objected to the explanation I have given from Fessler and others of the nature and range of the Pope's infallibility as now a dogma of the Church, that it was a lame and impotent conclusion of the Council, if so much effort was employed, as is involved in the convocation and sitting of an Ecumenical Council, in order to do so little. True, if it were called to do what it did and no more; but that such was its aim is a mere assumption. In the first place it can hardly be doubted that there were those in the Council who were desirous of a stronger definition; and the definition actually made, as being moderate, is so far the victory of those many bishops who considered any definition on the subject inopportune. And it was no slight fruit of their proceedings in the

Council, if a definition was to be, to have effected a moderate definition. But the true answer to the objection is that which is given by Bishop Ullathorne. The question of the Pope's infallibility was not one of the objects professed in convening the Council; and the Council is not yet ended.

He says in his "Expostulation Unravelled," "The Expostulation goes on to suggest that the Council was convened mainly with a view of defining the infallibility, and that the definition itself was brought about, chiefly for political objects, through the action of the Pontiff and a dominant party. A falser notion could not be entertained. I have the official catalogue before me of the *Schemata* prepared by the theologians for discussion in the Council. In them the infallibility is not even mentioned; for the greater part of them regard ecclesiastical discipline." P. 48, he adds, "Calamitous events suspended the Council."

Supr., p. 326, note. I have referred to Bishop Fessler's statement that only the last sentences of Boniface's *Unam Sanctam* are infallible. To this Mr. Gladstone replies, p. 45, that the word "Porro," introducing the final words to which the anathema is affixed, extends that anathema to the body of the Bull, which precedes the "Porro." But he does not seem to have observed, that there are two distinct heresies condemned in the Bull, and that the "Porro" is the connecting link between these two condemnations, that is, between the penultima and final sentences. The Pope first says, "Nisi duo, sicut Manichæus, fingat esse principia, *quod falsum et hæreticum judicamus* . . . porro, subesse Romano Pontifici, omni humanæ creaturæ declaramus, definimus, et pronunciamus omnino esse de necessitate salutis." That the Latin is deficient in classical terseness and perspicuity we may freely grant.

Supra, p. 327, I say, "We call 'infallibility' in the case of the Apostles, inspiration; in the case of the church, *assistentia.*"

On this Mr. Gladstone says, "On such a statement I have two remarks to make; first, we have this assurance on the strength only of *his own private judgment*, p. 102." How can he say so when, p. 328, I quote Father Perrone, saying, "*Never have Catholics* taught that the gift of infallibility is given by God to the Church after the manner of inspiration!"

Mr. Gladstone proceeds, "Secondly, that, if bidden by the self-assertion of the Pope, he will be required by his principles to retract it, and to assert, if occasion should arise, the contrary." I can only say to so hypothetical an argument what is laid down by Fessler and the Swiss bishops, that the Pope cannot, by virtue of his infallibility, reverse what has always been held; and that the "inspiration" of the church, in the sense in which the Apostles were inspired, is contrary to our received teaching. If Protestants are to speculate about our future, they should be impartial enough to recollect, that if, on the one hand, we believe that a Pope can add to our articles of faith, so, on the other, we hold also that a heretical Pope, *ipso facto*, ceases to be Pope by reason of his heresy, as I have said (*supr.*, p. 359).

Mr. Gladstone thus ends: "Thirdly, that he lives under a system of development, through which somebody's private opinion of to-day may become matter of faith for all the to-morrows of the future." I think he should give some proof of this; let us have one instance in which "somebody's private opinion" has become *de fide.* Instead of this, he goes on to assert (interrogatively) that Popes, *e.g.* Clement XI. and Gregory II., and the present Pope, have claimed the inspiration of the Apostles, and that Germans, Italians, French, have ascribed such a gift to him;—of course he means theologians, not mere courtiers, or sycophants, for the Pope cannot help having such, till human nature is changed. If Mr. Gladstone is merely haranguing as an Orator, I do not for an instant quarrel with him or attempt to encounter him; but if he is a controversialist, we have a right to look for arguments, not mere assertions.

THE END.

CARDINAL NEWMAN'S WORKS.

SERMONS.

	Cabinet Edition.	Popular Edition.
	s. d.	*s. d.*
PAROCHIAL AND PLAIN SERMONS. 8 vols. Crown 8vo, each	5 0	3 6
SELECTION, ADAPTED TO THE SEASONS OF THE ECCLESIASTICAL YEAR, from the ' Parochial and Plain Sermons'. Crown 8vo, ...	5 0	3 6
FIFTEEN SERMONS PREACHED BEFORE THE UNIVERSITY OF OXFORD, between A.D. 1826 and 1843. Crown 8vo,	5 0	3 6
SERMONS BEARING ON SUBJECTS OF THE DAY. Crown 8vo,	5 0	3 6
DISCOURSES ADDRESSED TO MIXED CONGREGATIONS AT THE ORATORY OF ST. PHILIP NERI, BIRMINGHAM. Crown 8vo, ...	6 0	3 6
SERMONS PREACHED ON VARIOUS OCCASIONS. (Before the Catholic University of Ireland ; St. Chad's, Birmingham ; The Oratory, Birmingham ; St. Mary's, Oscott, etc.) Crown 8vo,	6 0	3 6

TREATISES.

	Cabinet Edition.	Popular Edition.
LECTURES ON THE DOCTRINE OF JUSTIFICATION. Crown 8vo, ...	5 0	3 6
AN ESSAY ON THE DEVELOPMENT OF CHRISTIAN DOCTRINE. Crown 8vo, ...	6 0	3 6
THE IDEA OF A UNIVERSITY DEFINED AND ILLUSTRATED. Crown 8vo, ...	7 0	3 6
AN ESSAY IN AID OF A GRAMMAR OF ASSENT. Crown 8vo,	7 6	3 6

ESSAYS.

	Cabinet Edition.	Popular Edition.
ESSAYS ON BIBLICAL AND ON ECCLESIASTICAL MIRACLES. Crown 8vo, ...	6 0	3 6
DISCUSSIONS AND ARGUMENTS. 1. How to accomplish it. 2. The Antichrist of the Fathers. 3. Scripture and the Creed. 4. Tamworth Reading-Room. 5. Who's to blame? 6. An Argument for Christianity. Crown 8vo, ...	6 0	3 6
ESSAYS CRITICAL AND HISTORICAL. 2 vols. 1. Poetry. 2. Rationalism. 3. Apostolical Tradition. 4. De la Mennais. 5. Palmer on Faith and Unity. 6. St. Ignatius. 7. Prospects of the Anglican Church. 8. The Anglo-American Church. 9. Countess of Huntingdon. 10. Catholicity of the Anglican Church. 11. The Antichrist of Protestants. 12. Milman's Christianity. 13. Reformation of the Eleventh Century. 14. Private Judgment. 15. Davison. 16. Keble. Crown 8vo, ...	12 0	7 0

HISTORICAL.

Cabinet Popular
Edition. Edition.
s. d.   s. d.

HISTORICAL SKETCHES. 3 vols. 1. The Turks. 2. Cicero. 3.
Apollonius. 4. Primitive Christianity. 5. Church of the
Fathers. 6. St. Chrysostum. 7. Theodoret. 8. St. Benedict.
9. Benedictine Schools. 10. Universities. 11. Northmen and
Normans. 12. Medieval Oxford. 13. Convocation of Canter-
bury. Crown 8vo, ... each   6   0   3   6

THEOLOGICAL.

THE ARIANS OF THE FOURTH CENTURY. Crown 8vo, ...   6   0   3   6
SELECT TREATISES OF ST. ATHANASIUS IN CONTRO-
VERSY WITH THE ARIANS. Freely Translated. 2 vols.
Crown 8vo, ... 15   0   7   0
THEOLOGICAL TRACTS. 1. Dissertatiunculæ. 2. On the Text of
the Seven Epistles of St. Ignatius. 3. Doctrinal Causes of Arian-
ism. 4. Apollinarianism. 5. St. Cyril's Formula. 6. Ordo de
Tempore. 7. Douay Version of Scripture. Crown 8vo, ...   8   0   3   6

POLEMICAL.

THE VIA MEDIA OF THE ANGLICAN CHURCH. Illustrated
in Lectures, Letters, and Tracts written between 1830 and 1841.
With Notes. 2 vols. Vol. I. Prophetical Office of the Church.
Vol. II. Occasional Letters and Tracts. Crown 8vo, ... each   6   0   3   6
CERTAIN DIFFICULTIES FELT BY ANGLICANS IN
CATHOLIC TEACHING CONSIDERED. 2 vols.
    Vol I. Twelve Lectures addressed (in 1850) to the Anglican
    Party of 1833. Crown 8vo, ...   7   6   3   6
    Vol. II. Letters to Dr. Pusey concerning the Blessed Virgin
    and to the Duke of Norfolk in Defence of the Pope and
    Council, on the occasion of Mr. Gladstone's Expostulation
    of 1874. Crown 8vo, ...   5   6   3   6
LECTURES ON THE PRESENT POSITION OF CATHOLICS
IN ENGLAND (1851). Crown 8vo, ...   7   6   3   6
APOLOGIA PRO VITA SUA. Crown 8vo, ...   6   0   3   6

LITERARY.

VERSES ON VARIOUS OCCASIONS. Crown 8vo, ...   6   0   3   6
LOSS AND GAIN : the Story of a Convert. Crown 8vo, ...   6   0   3   6
CALLISTA : a Tale of the Third Century. Crown 8vo, ...   6   0   3   6
THE DREAM OF GERONTIUS. 16mo,   { Sewed,   0   6
                                 { Cloth,   1   0
LYRA APOSTOLICA. [Poems by J. W. BOWDEN, R. H. FROUDE, J.
KEBLE, J. H. NEWMAN, R. I. WILBERFORCE, and I. WILLIAMS;
and a New Preface by CARDINAL NEWMAN.] With red borders.
16mo, ...   2   6

DEVOTIONAL.

MEDITATIONS AND DEVOTIONS. Part I. Meditations for the
month of May. Novena of St. Philip. Part II. The Stations of
the Cross. Meditations and Intercessions for Good Friday.
Litanies, etc. Part III. Meditations on Christian Doctrine.
Conclusion. Oblong crown 8vo, ...   5   0

A
SELECT LIST OF WORKS
PUBLISHED BY
LONGMANS, GREEN, & CO.
LONDON, NEW YORK, AND BOMBAY.

MESSRS. LONGMANS, GREEN, & CO.

Issue the undermentioned Catalogues and Lists of their Publications, any of which may be had post free on application:—

1. MONTHLY LIST OF NEW BOOKS AND NEW EDITIONS.
2. QUARTERLY LIST OF ANNOUNCEMENTS AND NEW BOOKS.
3. NOTES ON BOOKS: BEING AN ANALYSIS OF THE WORKS PUBLISHED BY MESSRS. LONGMANS, GREEN & CO. DURING EACH QUARTER.
4. SCIENTIFIC AND TECHNICAL BOOKS.
5. MEDICAL AND SURGICAL BOOKS.
6. EDUCATIONAL AND SCHOOL BOOKS.
7. EDUCATIONAL BOOKS RECENTLY PUBLISHED.

8. BOOKS FOR ELEMENTARY SCHOOLS AND PUPIL TEACHERS.
9. BOOKS FOR SCHOOL PRIZES.
10. BOOKS FOR CHRISTMAS AND NEW YEAR PRESENTS.
11. THEOLOGICAL BOOKS (CHURCH OF ENGLAND).
12. THEOLOGICAL BOOKS (ROMAN CATHOLIC).
13. BOOKS IN GENERAL LITERATURE AND GENERAL THEOLOGY.

CARDINAL NEWMAN'S WORKS.

Parochial and Plain Sermons. Edited by REV. W. J. COPELAND, B.D., late Rector of Farnham, Essex. 8 vols. Sold separately. Crown 8vo. Cabinet Edition, 5s. each; Popular Edition, 3s. 6d. each.

CONTENTS OF VOL. I.:—Holiness necessary for Future Blessedness—The Immortality of the Soul—Knowledge of God's Will without Obedience—Secret Faults—Self-Denial the Test of Religious Earnestness—The Spiritual Mind—Sins of Ignorance and Weakness—God's Commandments not Grievous—The Religious Use of Excited Feelings—Profession without Practice—Profession without Hypocrisy—Profession without Ostentation—Promising without Doing—Religious Emotion—Religious Faith Rational—The Christian Mysteries—The Self-Wise Inquirer—Obedience the Remedy for Religious Perplexity—Times of Private Prayer—Forms of Private Prayer—The Resurrection of the Body—Witnesses of the Resurrection—Christian Reverence—The Religion of the Day—Scripture a Record of Human Sorrow—Christian Manhood.

CONTENTS OF VOL. II.:—The World's Benefactors—Faith without Sight—The Incarnation—Martyrdom—Love of Relations and Friends—The Mind of Little Children—Ceremonies of the Church—The Glory of the Christian Church—St. Paul's Conversion viewed in Reference to his Office—Secrecy and Suddenness of Divine Visitations—Divine Decrees—The Reverence Due to the Blessed Virgin Mary—Christ, a Quickening Spirit—Saving Knowledge—Self-Contemplation—Religious Cowardice—The Gospel Witnesses—Mysteries in Religion—The Indwelling Spirit—The Kingdom of the Saints—The Gospel, a Trust Committed to us—Tolerance of Religious Error—Rebuking Sin—The Christian Ministry—Human Responsibility—Guilelessness—The Danger of Riches—The Powers of Nature—The Danger of Accomplishments—Christian Zeal—Use of Saints' Days.

CARDINAL NEWMAN'S WORKS.

Parochial and Plain Sermons.—*Continued.*

CONTENTS OF VOL. III.:—Abraham and Lot—Wilfulness of Israel in Rejecting Samuel—Saul—Early Years of David—Jeroboam—Faith and Obedience—Christian Repentance—Contracted Views in Religion—A Particular Providence as revealed in the Gospel—Tears of Christ at the Grave of Lazarus—Bodily Suffering—The Humiliation of the Eternal Son—Jewish Zeal a Pattern to Christians—Submission to Church Authority—Contest between Truth and Falsehood in the Church—The Church Visible and Invisible—The Visible Church and Encouragement to Faith—The Gift of the Spirit—Regenerating Baptism—Infant Baptism—The Daily Service—The Good Part of Mary—Religious Worship a Remedy for Excitements—Intercession—The Intermediate State.

CONTENTS OF VOL IV.:—The Strictness of the Law of Christ—Obedience without Love, as instanced in the Character of Balaam—Moral Consequences of Single Sins—Acceptance of Religious Privileges Compulsory—Reliance on Religious Observances—The Individuality of the Soul—Chastisement amid Mercy—Peace and Joy amid Chastisement—The State of Grace—The Visible Church for the Sake of the Elect—The Communion of Saints—The Church a Home for the Lonely—The Invisible World—The Greatness and Littleness of Human Life—Moral Effects of Communion with God—Christ Hidden from the World—Christ Manifested in Remembrance—The Gainsaying of Korah—The Mysteriousness of our Present Being—The Ventures of Faith—Faith and Love—Watching—Keeping Fast and Festival.

CONTENTS OF VOL. V.:—Worship, a Preparation for Christ's Coming—Reverence, a Belief in God's Presence—Unreal Words—Shrinking from Christ's Coming—Equanimity—Remembrance of Past Mercies—The Mystery of Godliness—The State of Innocence—Christian Sympathy—Righteousness not of us, but in us—The Law of the Spirit—The New Works of the Gospel—The State of Salvation—Transgressions and Infirmities—Sins of Infirmity—Sincerity and Hypocrisy—The Testimony of Conscience—Many called, Few chosen—Present Blessings—Endurance, the Christian's Portion—Affliction, a School of Comfort—The Thought of God, the Stay of the Soul—Love, the One Thing Needful—The Power of the Will.

CONTENTS OF VOL. VI.:—Fasting, a Source of Trial—Life, the Season of Repentance—Apostolic Abstinence, a Pattern for Christians—Christ's Privations, a Meditation for Christians—Christ the Son of God made Man—The Incarnate Son, a Sufferer and Sacrifice—The Cross of Christ the Measure of the World—Difficulty of realising Sacred Privileges—The Gospel Sign Addressed to Faith—The Spiritual Presence of Christ in the Church—The Eucharistic Presence—Faith the Title for Justification—Judaism of the Present Day—The Fellowship of the Apostles—Rising with Christ—Warfare the Condition of Victory—Waiting for Christ—Subjection of the Reason and Feelings to the Revealed Word—The Gospel Palaces—The Visible Temple—Offerings for the Sanctuary—The Weapons of Saints—Faith Without Demonstration—The Mystery of the Holy Trinity—Peace in Believing.

CONTENTS OF VOL. VII.:—The Lapse of Time—Religion, a Weariness to the Natural Man—The World our Enemy—The Praise of Men—Temporal Advantages—The Season of Epiphany—The Duty of Self-Denial—The Yoke of Christ—Moses the Type of Christ—The Crucifixion—Attendance on Holy Communion—The Gospel Feast—Love of Religion, a new Nature—Religion Pleasant to the Religious—Mental Prayer—Infant Baptism—The Unity of the Church—Steadfastness in the Old Paths.

CONTENTS OF VOL. VIII.:—Reverence in Worship—Divine Calls—The Trial of Saul—The Call of David—Curiosity, a Temptation to Sin—Miracles no Remedy for Unbelief—Josiah, a Pattern for the Ignorant—Inward Witness to the Truth of the Gospel—Jeremiah, a Lesson for the Disappointed—Endurance of the World's Censure—Doing Glory to God in Pursuits of the World—Vanity of Human Glory—Truth Hidden when not Sought after—Obedience to God the Way to Faith in Christ—Sudden Conversions—The Shepherd of our Souls—Religious Joy—Ignorance of Evil.

Sermons Preached on Various Occasions. Crown 8vo. Cabinet
Edition, 6s.; Popular Edition, 3s. 6d.

CONTENTS:—Intellect the Instrument of Religious Training—The Religion of the Pharisee and the Religion of Mankind—Waiting for Christ—The Secret Power of Divine Grace—Dispositions for Faith—Omnipotence in Bonds—St. Paul's Characteristic Gift—St. Paul's Gift of Sympathy—Christ upon the Waters—The Second Spring—Order, the Witness and Instrument of Unity—The Mission of St. Philip Neri—The Tree beside the Waters—In the World but not of the World—The Pope and the Revolution.

CARDINAL NEWMAN'S WORKS.

Selection, Adapted to the Seasons of the Ecclesiastical Year, from the 'Parochial and Plain Sermons.' Edited by the REV. W. J. COPELAND, B.D. Crown 8vo. Cabinet Edition, 5s.; Popular Edition, 3s. 6d.

CONTENTS:—*Advent:* Self-Denial the Test of Religious Earnestness—Divine Calls—The Ventures of Faith—Watching. *Christmas Day:* Religious Joy. *New Year's Sunday:* The Lapse of Time. *Epiphany:* Remembrance of Past Mercies — Equanimity—The Immortality of the Soul — Christian Manhood — Sincerity and Hypocrisy — Christian Sympathy. *Septuagesima:* Present Blessings. *Sexagesima:* Endurance, the Christian's Portion. *Quinquagesima:* Love, the One Thing Needful. *Lent:* The Individuality of the Soul—Life, the Season of Repentance—Bodily Suffering—Tears of Christ at the Grave of Lazarus—Christ's Privations, a Meditation for Christians—The Cross of Christ the Measure of the ;World. *Good Friday:* The Crucifixion. *Easter Day:* Keeping Fast and Festval. *Easter Tide:* Witnesses of the Resurrection—A Particular Providence as revealed in the Gospel—Christ Manifested in Remembrance—The Invisible World—Waiting for Christ. *Ascension:* Warfare the Condition of Victory. *Sunday after Ascension:* Rising with Christ. *Whitsun Day:* The Weapons of Saints. *Trinity Sunday:* The Mysteriousness of our Present Being. *Sundays after Trinity:* Holiness Necessary for|Future Blessedness—The Religious Use of Excited Feelings—The Self-Wise Inquirer—Scripture a Record of Human Sorrow—The Danger of Riches—Obedience without Love, as instanced in the Character of Balaam—Moral Consequences of Single Sins—The Greatness and Littleness of Human Life—Moral Effects of Communion with God—The Thought of God the Stay of the Soul—The Power of the Will—The Gospel Palaces—Religion a Weariness to the Natural Man—The World our Enemy—The Praise of Men—Religion Pleasant to the Religious—Mental Prayer—Curiosity a Temptation to Sin—Miracles no Remedy for Unbelief—Jeremiah, a Lesson for the Disappointed—The Shepherd of our Souls—Doing Glory to God in Pursuits of the World.

Sermons Bearing upon Subjects of the Day. Edited by the REV. W. J. COPELAND, B.D., late Rector of Farnham, Essex. Crown 8vo. Cabinet Edition, 5s.; Popular Edition, 3s. 6d.

CONTENTS:—The Work of the Christian—Saintliness not Forfeited by the Penitent—Our Lord's Last Supper and His First—Dangers to the Penitent—The Three Offices of Christ—Faith and Experience—Faith unto the World—The Church and the World—Indulgence in Religious Privileges—Connection between Personal and Public Improvement—Christian Nobleness—Joshua a Type of Christ and His Followers—Elisha a Type of Christ and His Followers—The Christian Church a Continuation of the Jewish—The Principles of Contiuuity between the Jewish and Christian Churches—The Christian Church an Imperial Power—Sanctity the Token of the Christian Empire—Condition of the Members of the Christian Empire—The Apostolic Christian—Wisdom and Innocence—Invisible Presence of Christ—Outward and Inward Notes of the Church—Grounds for Steadfastness in our Religious Profession—Elijah the Prophet of the Latter Days—Feasting in Captivity—The Parting of Friends.

Fifteen Sermons Preached before the University of Oxford, between A.D. 1826 and 1843. Crown 8vo. Cabinet Edition, 5s.; Popular Edition, 3s. 6d.

CONTENTS:—The Philosophical Temper, first enjoined by the Gospel—The Influence of Natural and Revealed Religion respectively—Evangelical Sanctity the Perfection of Natural Virtue—The Usurpations of Reason—Personal Influence, the Means of Propagating the Truth—On Justice as a Principle of Divine Go, ernance—Contest between Faith and Sight—Human Responsibility, as independent of Circumstances—Wilfulness, the Sin of Saul—Faith and Reason, contrasted as Habits of Mind—The Nature of Faith in Relation to Reason—Love, the Safeguard of Faith against Superstition—Implicit and Explicit Reason—Wisdom, as contrasted with Faith and with Big)try—The Theory of Developments in Religious Doctrine.

CARDINAL NEWMAN'S WORKS.

Discourses Addressed to Mixed Congregations. Crown 8vo.
Cabinet Edition, 6s. ; Popular Edition, 3s. 6d.

CONTENTS :—The Salvation of the Hearer the Motive of the Preacher—Neglect of Divine Calls and Warnings—Men not Angels—The Priests of the Gospel—Purity and Love—Saintliness the Standard of Christian Principle—God's Will the End of Life—Perseverance in Grace—Nature and Grace—Illuminating Grace—Faith and Private Judgment—Faith and Doubt—Prospects of the Catholic Missioner—Mysteries of Nature and of Grace—The Mystery of Divine Condescension—The Infinitude of Divine Attributes—Mental Sufferings of our Lord in His Passion—The Glories of Mary for the Sake of Her Son—On the Fitness of the Glories of Mary.

Lectures on the Doctrine of Justification. Crown 8vo. Cabinet
Edition, 5s. ; Popular Edition, 3s. 6d.

CONTENTS :—Faith considered as the Instrumental Cause of Justification—Love considered as the Formal Cause of Justification—Primary Sense of the term 'Justification'—Secondary Senses of the term 'Justification'—Misuse of the term 'Just' or 'Righteous'—The Gift of Righteousness—The Characteristics of the Gift of Righteousness—Righteousness viewed as a Gift and as a Quality—Righteousness the Fruit of our Lord's Resurrection—The Office of Justifying Faith—The Nature of Justifying Faith—Faith viewed relatively to Rites and Works—On Preaching the Gospel—Appendix.

On the Development of Christian Doctrine. Crown 8vo. Cabinet
Edition, 6s. ; Popular Edition, 3s. 6d.

On the Idea of a University. Crown 8vo. Cabinet Edition, 7s. ;
Popular Edition, 3s. 6d.

An Essay in Aid of a Grammar of Assent. Crown 8vo. Cabinet
Edition, 7s. 6d. ; Popular Edition, 3s. 6d.

Two Essays on Miracles. 1. Of Scripture. 2. Of Ecclesiastical
History. Crown 8vo. Cabinet Edition, 6s. ; Popular Edition,
3s. 6d.

Discussions and Arguments. Crown 8vo. Cabinet Edition, 6s. ;
Popular Edition, 3s. 6d.

1. How to accomplish it. 2. The Antichrist of the Fathers. 3. Scripture and the Creed. 4. Tamworth Reading-room. 5. Who's to Blame ? 6. An Argument for Christianity.

Essays, Critical and Historical. 2 vols. Crown 8vo. Cabinet
Edition, 12s. ; Popular Edition, 7s.

1. Poetry. 2. Rationalism. 3. Apostolic Tradition. 4. De la Mennais. 5. Palmer on Faith and Unity. 6. St. Ignatius. 7. Prospects of the Anglican Church. 8. The Anglo-American Church. 9. Countess of Huntingdon. 10. Catholicity of the Anglican Church. 11. The Antichrist of Protestants. 12. Milman's Christianity. 13. Reformation of the XI. Century. 14. Private Judgment. 15. Davison. 16. Keble.

Apologia pro Vita Sua. Crown 8vo. Cabinet Edition, 6s. ; Popular
Edition, 3s. 6d.

Verses on Various Occasions. Crown 8vo. Cabinet Edition, 6s. ;
Popular Edition, 3s. 6d.

CARDINAL NEWMAN'S WORKS.

Historical Sketches. 3 vols. Crown 8vo. Cabinet Edition, 6s. each; Popular Edition, 3s. 6d.

1. The Turks. 2. Cicero. 3. Apollonius. 4. Primitive Christianity. 5. Church of the Fathers. 6. St. Chrysostom. 7. Theodoret. 8. St. Benedict. 9. Benedictine Schools. 10. Universities. 11. Northmen and Normans. 12. Mediæval Oxford. 13. Convocation of Canterbury.

The Arians of the Fourth Century. Crown 8vo. Cabinet Edition, 6s.; Popular Edition, 3s. 6d.

Select Treatises of St. Athanasius in Controversy with the Arians. Freely translated. 2 vols. Crown 8vo. Cabinet Edition, 15s.; Popular Edition, 7s.

Theological Tracts. Crown 8vo. Cabinet Edition, 8s.; Popular Edition, 3s. 6d.

1. Dissertatiunculæ. 2. On the Text of the Seven Epistles of St. Ignatius. 3. Doctrinal Causes of Arianism. 4. Apollinarianism. 5. St. Cyril's Formula. 6. Ordo de Tempore. 7. Douay Version of Scriptures.

The Via Media of the Anglican Church. 2 Vols. Crown 8vo. Cabinet Edition, 6s. each; Popular Edition, 3s. 6d. each.

Vol. I. Prophetical Office of the Church.

Vol. II. Occasional Letters and Tracts.

Certain Difficulties felt by Anglicans in Catholic Teaching Considered. 2 vols.

Vol. I. Twelve Lectures. Crown 8vo. Cabinet Edition, 7s. 6d.; Popular Edition, 3s. 6d.

Vol. II. Letters to Dr. Pusey concerning the Blessed Virgin, and to the Duke of Norfolk in defence of the Pope and Council. Crown 8vo. Cabinet Edition, 5s. 6d.; Popular Edition. 3s. 6d.

Present Position of Catholics in England. Crown 8vo. Cabinet Edition, 7s. 6d.; Popular Edition, 3s. 6d.

Loss and Gain. The Story of a Convert. Crown 8vo. Cabinet Edition, 6s.; Popular Edition, 3s. 6d.

Callista. A Tale of the Third Century. Crown 8vo. Cabinet Edition, 6s.; Popular Edition, 3s. 6d.

The Dream of Gerontius. 16mo, sewed, 6d.; cloth, 1s.

Meditations and Devotions. Part I. Meditations for the Month of May. Novena of St. Philip. Part II. The Stations of the Cross. Meditations and Intercessions for Good Friday. Litanies, etc. Part III. Meditations on Christian Doctrine. Conclusion. Oblong Crown 8vo. 5s. *net*.

CARDINAL NEWMAN'S WORKS.

COMPLETION OF THE POPULAR EDITION.

Parochial and Plain Sermons. 8 vols. Each	. .	3s. 6d.
Sermons preached on Various Occasions .	. .	3s. 6d.
Selection, from the Parochial and Plain Sermons	. .	3s. 6d.
Sermons bearing on Subjects of the Day .	. .	3s. 6d.
Sermons preached before the University of Oxford	. .	3s. 6d.
Discourses addressed to Mixed Congregations	. .	3s. 6d.
Lectures on the Doctrine of Justification .	. .	3s. 6d.
On the Development of Christian Doctrine .	. .	3s. 6d.
On the Idea of a University . .	. .	3s. 6d.
An Essay in Aid of a Grammar of Assent .	. .	3s. 6d.
Biblical and Ecclesiastical Miracles . .	. .	3s. 6d.
Discussions and Arguments on Various Subjects	. .	3s. 6d.
Essays, Critical and Historical. 2 vols. .	. .	7s. 0d.
Historical Sketches. 3 vols. Each . .	. .	3s. 6d.
The Arians of the Fourth Century . .	. .	3s. 6d.
The Via Media of the Anglican Church. 2 vols. Each	.	3s. 6d.
Difficulties felt by Anglicans considered. 2 vols. Each	.	3s. 6d.
Present Position of Catholics in England .	. .	3s. 6d.
Apologia pro Vita Sua . . .	. .	3s. 6d.
Theological Tracts . . .	. .	3s. 6d.
Select Treatises of St. Athanasius. 2 vols. .	. .	7s. 0d.
Verses on Various Occasions . .	. .	3s. 6d.
Loss and Gain	. .	3s. 6d.
Callista	. .	3s. 6d.

DOBRÉE.—Stories on the Rosary. By Louisa Emily Dobrée, Author of " Stories of the Seven Sacraments ". Part I. Crown 8vo. 1s. 6d.

FOUARD.—The Christ, The Son of God. A Life of Our Lord and Saviour Jesus Christ. By the Abbé Constant Fouard, Honorary Cathedral Canon, Professor of the Faculty of Theology at Rouen, etc., etc. Translated from the Fifth Edition with the Author's sanction. By George F. X. Griffith. With an Introduction by Cardinal Manning. Third Edition. With 3 Maps. 2 vols. Crown 8vo. 14s.

Saint Peter and the First Years of Christianity. By the Abbé Constant Fouard. Translated by George F. X. Griffith. Crown 8vo. 9s.

St. Paul and His Missions. By the Abbé Constant Fouard. Translated, with the Author's sanction and co-operation, by George F. X. Griffith. With 2 Maps. Crown 8vo. 9s.

CHRISTIAN BIOGRAPHIES:

Henri Dominique Lacordaire. A Biographical Sketch. By H. L. SIDNEY LEAR. With Frontispiece. Crown 8vo. 3s. 6d.

A Christian Painter of the Nineteenth Century; being the Life of Hippolyte Flandrin. By H. L. SIDNEY LEAR. Crown 8vo. 3s. 6d.

Bossuet and his Contemporaries. By H. L. SIDNEY LEAR. Crown 8vo. 3s. 6d.

Fénelon, Archbishop of Cambrai. A Biographical Sketch. By H. L. SIDNEX LEAR. Crown 8vo. 3s. 6d.

A Dominican Artist. A Sketch of the Life of the Rev. Père Besson, of the Order of St. Dominic. By H. L. SIDNEY LEAR. Crown 8vo. 3s. 6d.

The Life of Madame Louise de France, Daughter of Louis XV., also known as the Mother Thérèse de S. Augustin. By H. L. SIDNEY LEAR. Crown 8vo. 3s. 6d.

The Revival of Priestly Life in the Seventeenth Century in France. Charles de Condren—S. Philip Neri and Cardinal de Berulle—S. Vincent de Paul—S. Sulpice and Jean Jacques Olier. By H. L. SIDNEY LEAR. Crown 8vo. 3s. 6d.

Life of S. Francis de Sales, Bishop and Prince of Geneva. By H. L. SIDNEY LEAR. Crown 8vo. 3s. 6d.

Henri Perreyve. By A. GRATRY, PRÊTRE DE L'ORATOIRE, Professeur de Morale Evangélique à la Sorbonne, et Membre de l'Académie Française. Translated, by special permission, by H. L. SIDNEY LEAR. With Portrait. Crown 8vo. 3s. 6d.

DRANE—A Memoir of Mother Francis Raphael O.S.D. (Augusta Theodosia Drane), some time Prioress Provincial of the Congregation of Dominican Sisters of S. Catherine of Siena, Stone. With some of her Spiritual Notes and Letters. Edited by Rev. Father BERTRAND WILBERFORCE, O.P. With Portrait. Crown 8vo. 7s. 6d.

The History of St. Dominic, Founder of the Friar Preachers. By AUGUSTA THEODORA DRANE, author of "The History of St. Catherine of Siena and her Companions." With 32 Illustrations. 8vo. 15s.

FÉNELON.—Spiritual Letters to Men. By ARCHBISHOP FÉNELON. Translated by H. L. SIDNEY LEAR, author of "Life of Fénelon," "Life of S. Francis de Sales," etc. etc. 16mo. 2s. 6d.

Spiritual Letters to Women. By ARCHBISHOP FÉNELON. Translated by H. L. SIDNEY LEAR, author of "Life of Fenelon," "Life of S. Francis de Sales," etc. etc. 16mo. 2s. 6d.

GIBSON.—The Abbé de Lamennais and the Liberal Catholic Movement in France. By the Hon. W. Gibson. With Portrait. 8vo. 12s. 6d.

JAMESON—Works by Mrs. Jameson:

Sacred and Legendary Art. With 19 Etchings and 197 Woodcuts. 2 vols. Cloth, gilt top. 20s. *net.*

Legends of the Madonna: The Virgin Mary as Represented in Sacred and Legendary Art. With 27 Etchings and 165 Woodcuts. 1 vol. Cloth, gilt top. 10s. *net.*

Legends of the Monastic Orders. With 11 Etchings and 88 Woodcuts. 1 vol. Cloth, gilt top. 10s. *net.*

History of the Saviour, His Types and Precursors. Completed by Lady Eastlake. With 13 Etchings and 281 Woodcuts. 2 vols. Cloth, gilt top. 20s. *net.*

LYONS.—Christianity or Infallibility—Both or Neither. By the Rev. Daniel Lyons. Crown 8vo. 5s.

RIVINGTON.—The Primitive Church and the See of Peter. By the Rev. Luke Rivington, D.D. With an Introduction by the Cardinal Archbishop of Westminster. 8vo. 16s.

SODERINI.—Socialism and Catholicism. From the Italian of Count Edward Soderini. By Richard Jenery-Shee of the Inner Temple. With a Preface by Cardinal Vaughan. Cr. 8vo. 6s.

TYRRELL.—Nova et Vetera: Informal Meditations for Times of Spiritual Dryness. By George Tyrrell, S.J. Crown 8vo. 6s.

WISEMAN.—The Life and Times of Cardinal Wiseman. By Wilfrid Ward, Author of "William George Ward and the Catholic Revival". With 3 Portraits. 2 vols. Crown 8vo. 24s.

MANUALS OF CATHOLIC PHILOSOPHY.
(Stonyhurst Series.)
EDITED BY RICHARD F. CLARKE, S.J.

Logic. By Richard F. Clarke, S.J., D.D. Crown 8vo. 5s.

First Principles of Knowledge. By John Rickaby, S.J. Crown 8vo. 5s.

Moral Philosophy (Ethics and Natural Law). By Joseph Rickaby, S.J. Crown 8vo. 5s.

General Metaphysics. By John Rickaby, S.J. Crown 8vo. 5s.

Psychology. By Michael Maher, S.J. Crown 8vo. 6s. 6d.

Natural Theology. By Bernard Boedder, S.J. Crown 8vo. 6s. 6d.

Political Economy. By Charles S. Devas. Crown 8vo. 6s. 6d.

ENGLISH MANUALS OF CATHOLIC THEOLOGY.
Outlines of Dogmatic Theology. By Sylvester Joseph Hunter, of the Society of Jesus. Crown 8vo. 3 vols., 6s. 6d. each.

LONDON, NEW YORK, AND BOMBAY:
LONGMANS, GREEN, & CO.
5000/12/97

CPSIA information can be obtained
at www.ICGtesting.com
Printed in the USA
BVHW041539200319
543209BV00011B/73/P